MEDIATING AMERICA

Brian Shott

MEDIATING AMERICA

Black and Irish Press and the Struggle for Citizenship, 1870–1914

TEMPLE UNIVERSITY PRESS
Philadelphia • *Rome* • *Tokyo*

TEMPLE UNIVERSITY PRESS
Philadelphia, Pennsylvania 19122
tupress.temple.edu

Copyright © 2019 by Temple University—Of The Commonwealth System of Higher Education
All rights reserved
Published 2019

Library of Congress Cataloging-in-Publication Data

Names: Shott, Brian, 1968– author.
Title: Mediating America : Black and Irish press and the struggle for citizenship, 1870–1914 / Brian Shott.
Description: Philadelphia : Temple University Press, 2019. | Includes bibliographical references and index. |
Identifiers: LCCN 2018022172 (print) | LCCN 2018032063 (ebook) | ISBN 9781439915592 (E-Book) | ISBN 9781439915578 (hardback) | ISBN 9781439915585 (paper)
Subjects: LCSH: Newspaper editors—United States—Biography. | African American press—History—19th century. | Irish-American newspapers—History—19th century. | Minorities—Press coverage—United States—History—19th century. | Journalism—Social aspects—United States—History—19th century. | United States—Race relations—History—19th century. | Citizenship—United States—History—19th century. | BISAC: HISTORY / United States / 19th Century. | SOCIAL SCIENCE / Media Studies.
Classification: LCC PN4871 (ebook) | LCC PN4871 .S555 2019 (print) | DDC 070.0922 [B]—dc23
LC record available at https://lccn.loc.gov/2018022172

To Wendy

CONTENTS

Acknowledgments ix

Introduction: Battling for Belonging When Print Was King 1

Part I. The Irish American Press: Exiled Editors Forging New Borders of Belonging 15

1 Patrick Ford and the Writing of Irish America 21

2 Father Peter Yorke: A Publisher-Priest in the Fault Lines of American Identity 56

Part II. The African American Press: Flexibility in the Fight for Freedom 87

3 Forty Acres and a Carabao: T. Thomas Fortune, Newspapers, and the Pacific's Unstable Color Lines, 1902–1903 93

4 J. Samuel Stemons's One-Man Press: The Act of Newspapering in Black Philadelphia, 1906–1907 130

Conclusion: Wired for Connection—and Conflict 159

Notes 171

Bibliography 209

Index 225

ACKNOWLEDGMENTS

Completion of this book would not have been possible without help from many outstanding individuals, some of whom are mentioned here. When, at the age of forty, I decided I would return to academia for an advanced degree, it was difficult to find professors from my alma mater, Wesleyan University, willing or able to write a recommendation for me. Richard Ohmann was a wonderful exception, though he will surely find lacking the discussion of American print capitalism herein. I thank Richard for his kindness and his incredible scholarship. At the University of California at Santa Cruz, my dissertation advisor, David Brundage, provided consistent and continued academic expertise, friendship, and moral support, for which I am grateful. Catherine Jones was like a second advisor, lending her own impressive knowledge and friendship. Martin Berger's patience and close reading of a dissertation chapter on images in the black and Irish press was invaluable. Walks around campus talking technology with Minghui Hu were memorable, fun, and important.

A number of other professors at UC Santa Cruz helped train me in the practice of history writing and research, including Matt O'Hara, Dana Frank, Marilyn Westerkamp, Marc Cioc, Matthew Lasar, Greg O'Malley, Eric Porter, Bruce Thompson, and Jonathan Beecher.

My cohort at UCSC—most notably Benjamin Pietrenka, Dustin Wright, Meg Gudgeirsson, and Nickolas Conrad—made it all worthwhile, as did the graduate students ahead of us, including Jeremy Tai, Amanda Shuman, Martin Rizzo, Noel Smyth, Elyse Banks, and many more.

Librarians and archivists at Bancroft Library, the Historical Society of Pennsylvania, the Tamiment Library at New York University, the Gleeson Library/Geschke Center, the Library of Congress, the National Library of the Philippines, and the Ateneo de Manila University Library were hugely helpful. Guy Emerson Mount shared with me his important research on T. Thomas Fortune, and Bonnie M. Miller generously discussed her work on images in the black press. Benjamin Johnson at the *Journal of the Gilded Age and Progressive Era* helped focus my writing on Fortune's Pacific quest. Discussions with David Prior as the book was nearing its completion helped me think further about Reconstruction and empire. Joshua Brown and Charles Postel also gave great advice and encouragement.

Journalism historians linked to two conferences were supportive as I presented aspects of my work there, including David Sachsman at the Symposium on the 19th Century Press, the Civil War, and Free Expression, and David Abrahamson and David R. Davies with the American Journalism Historians Association.

Though they were not directly involved in this book, I would be remiss to neglect the strong influence of journalists and intellectuals at New America Media in San Francisco, which closed its doors as I was completing the manuscript. Sandy Close, Franz Schurmann, Andrew Lam, Sandip Roy, Hilary Abramson, Mary Jo McConahay, and many others shaped my thinking and writing and introduced me to the fascinating world of ethnic media, which no doubt influenced my choice of dissertation topic as I pursued my Ph.D.

In Singapore, I'm very grateful to two history professors, Ian Gordon at the National University of Singapore and Justin Clark at Nanyang Technological University, and to R. Ramachandran for their welcoming support as I completed the manuscript far from home.

I'm grateful to my parents, Diane and Roger, and my brother, Eric. Their financial support and respect for intellectual endeavors made it possible for me to pursue an advanced degree in a field not currently known for its job opportunities.

Temple University Press was a pleasure to work with. Aaron Javsicas always believed in the project and sent the manuscript to two superb anonymous readers. Marinanicole Miller helped whip into shape the images printed in this book, and Dave Wilson skillfully shepherded the project along. At Newgen, project manager and editor Rebecca Logan and eagle-eyed copy editor Kathleen Deselle saved me from embarrassment innumerable times and ended once and for all my unhealthy love affair with the comma.

Jim and Diana Rockett graciously provided a research home away from home in Manila. Finally, immense gratitude goes to my lovely wife, Wendy Rockett, for her editing expertise, her patience, and her drive to make me give the Philippines the respect and attention it deserves.

MEDIATING AMERICA

INTRODUCTION

Battling for Belonging When Print Was King

Saturday was publication day aboard the British convict ship *Hougoumont*. Cutting through the waves on a 14,000-mile journey from England to Australia in 1867, the three-masted vessel held 280 prisoners. Among them were sixty-two Fenians—a secret society of Irish nationalists dedicated to the violent overthrow of British rule in Ireland—who each week eagerly awaited the next issue of the *Wild Goose*, a handwritten and decorated newspaper produced onboard by several of their group. The Fenians read the paper aloud to each other. "Amid the dim glare of the lamp, the men at night would group strangely on extemporized seats," wrote John Boyle O'Reilly, assistant editor of the journal. "The yellow light fell down on the dark forms, throwing a ghastly glare on the pale faces."[1] O'Reilly would later escape from Australia and travel to Boston, where until his death in 1890 he edited the *Pilot*, one of the most important Irish American newspapers of the nineteenth century.

The zeal with which a group of Irish prisoners labored to produce a tiny, onboard journal may seem strange today, when media forms include radio, television, and the near-instantaneous communication of internet and wireless devices. Some scholars refer to the time between the creation of the printing press in the fifteenth century and the dawn of television in the 1940s as the era of the printed word; in the nineteenth century in particular, rising literacy rates and new printing technologies produced an explosion of reading material.[2] The printing of periodicals, handbills, and other materials was a common occupation in the 1800s, and many well-known figures from American history began their writing lives at newspapers—as printer's devils, reporters, editors, or publishers. In the nineteenth century, for example, abolitionist William Lloyd Garrison pushed for the emancipation of slaves through his weekly, the *Liberator* (1831–1865). Radical economist Henry George, advocate of a tax on land and author of the best-selling *Progress and Poverty*, spent his early working years typesetting, writing, and editing at a variety of papers, eventually founding the *San Francisco Daily Evening Post*. Former slave Frederick Douglass, inspired by Garrison's newspaper, founded the *North Star* in 1847. Philosopher John Dewey and influential early sociologist Robert E. Park hoped to spread their ideas in a newspaper called "Thought News"; Park, in fact, was a journalist for various newspapers from 1887 to 1898.[3] Walt Whitman, Mark Twain, Theodore Dreiser, and many other American poets and novelists began their writing careers at newspapers.[4] Print, in short, was king, and the newspaper medium in particular served as both training ground and sounding board for a wide variety of Americans who hoped to spread their vision for social and political life.

Especially vigorous in the nineteenth century were newspapers, mainly weeklies, created by and for those who, like Douglass and O'Reilly, fell outside of majority, native-born American norms or Anglo-Saxon, Protestant heritage. African Americans and European immigrants vigorously embraced the newsweekly as a forum to move public opinion, cohere group identity, and secure a spot for themselves as full citizens of the United States. Black and ethnic media—defined here as presses produced primarily by and for African Americans or American immigrant groups—educated their readerships in the ways of the mainstream population even as they might aggressively push for change. African Americans founded *Freedom's Journal*, the first black periodical, in 1827, and by 1890 more than 600 black papers had been started. Many failed, but more than 150 were operating in 1900, asserting citizenship rights long deferred.[5] Ethnic or immigrant media likewise pushed for group rights while also linking new Americans to the Old Country. Irish nationalists in particular used the newspaper medium to push for Irish independence from Great Britain and to defend Catholicism—and worked to make such struggles seem part of the American grain. Foreign news was frequently covered in black and ethnic presses; editors were keenly aware of how racial and religious fissures in American identity could shift during the years of U.S. expansion abroad. The newspaper, in short, was key in the black and Irish struggle for full American belonging.

This book explores African American and Irish American newspaper editors in the late nineteenth and early twentieth centuries and how they understood and advocated for perceived group interests through their weekly presses. Black and Irish journalists saw themselves, through their newspapers, as able to form, organize, and channel political groups, including far-flung diaspora; communicate solutions to national tensions related to race, labor, and civil rights; and preserve, craft, and calibrate race nationalisms—and even recover and reinvigorate racial identity. As such, I explore newspapers as more than just bully pulpits used to spread particular viewpoints or as forums for debating the issues of the day. Editors strove to make the newspaper itself a site for the construction of ethnic, racial, or religious identity, through columns that tried to revive lost languages, for example, or via illustrations and photographs designed to meld American and Old World iconography or to counter racist imagery. And unlike many studies of black or ethnic media, I pay particular attention to the materiality of these presses in an attempt to tease out, where possible, how the newspaper medium itself—through illustrations, cartoons, and halftone photographs; as a site of labor and profit; via advertisements and page layout; and by way of journalism's evolving conventions and technology—shaped and constrained editors' struggles around American citizenship during a tumultuous time of racial unrest, economic turmoil, and imperial expansion.

Media influence on racial and ethnic identity should not be taken for granted. Can the press really create identities, or does it merely respond to, or at most magnify or modify, group and individual self-conceptions that stem from other sources? Especially since Benedict Anderson's *Imagined Communities*, many scholars seem confident that print media is historically and intimately tied to notions of nationhood and race.[6] Jeremy Popkin writes convincingly of the explosion of print media in Revolutionary France, which "altered the basic framework for daily life for much of the population and created new frameworks for social interaction."[7] In fact, Popkin stresses the speed with which media can prompt new forms of identity. Print media, Popkin agrees, performs the roles described in Anderson's "imagined community," as well as James W. Carey's ritual view of communication, whereby newspapers are seen not simply as transmitters of information but as dramatic portrayers and maintainers of life's overall form, order, and tone.[8] But these two theorists stress gradual processes of identity formation. According to Popkin, print media in the French Revolution "directs attention to sudden processes of identity *transformation*," not just maintenance; media can "restructure identity and redefine community boundaries" with surprising speed.[9]

The effect of the medium on the message is a complicated affair and often remains elusive in this study. Where it cannot be determined, attention to what race activists *hoped* their presses could achieve and what they thought newspaper technologies might do can shed new light on late nineteenth-century struggles for American citizenship. "What preacher ever reached as many minds as the newspaper can reach?" asked the editor of a Catholic weekly in Portland, Oregon, in the 1870s. "The preacher's word, when once spoken, dies with the echo of his voice; but the printed word remains and men may read it again and again."[10]

Citizenship in this book refers to more than formal legal rights or responsibilities and encompasses the broader acceptance of a particular group as part of the American fabric. The end of the Civil War put notions of citizenship in flux; Reconstruction amendments to the Constitution were hotly debated over several years, bringing into focus a multiplicity of races—American Indians and Chinese immigrants in addition to freedmen—in conjunction with ideas of "heathen" religious status. Scholars have long studied the relationship between newspapers and nationalism; most prominently, Anderson posited that it was through print capitalism—the circulation of books, newspapers, and other print media in the vernacular language—that communities in the Americas and Europe first imagined themselves as nation-states.[11] But concepts of nationhood and belonging are not set in stone. They are continually contested, particularly in heterogeneous nations such as the United States, which became home to millions of descendants of African slaves and experienced multiple waves of immigration after its founding. If newspapers helped people imagine nationhood itself—a "deep, horizontal comradeship," according to Anderson[12]—such media also surely played a role in expanding or, conversely, policing notions of citizenship within the nation. Black and Irish newspaper editors sensed this and fought fiercely through their newspapers for inclusion in citizenship's shifting "borders of belonging."[13]

What does it mean, particularly for the study of campaigns for social justice and political rights in the United States, that so many U.S. activists and intellectuals—"race men" in the parlance of the time—started at and in many cases remained intimately connected to newspapers during their battles over American belonging? Did newspaper entrepreneurialism strengthen and broaden or stifle and narrow activists' intellectual work? Did weekly race papers encourage cross-racial solidarities or inhibit them? Does the highly personal infighting among rival editors within a racial group point to healthy political debate, or did sitting at the helm of these very personal presses present a kind of moral hazard—of ambition, say, or flattery?

To shed light on these and other difficult questions, this book considers four editors in depth: two African Americans, T. Thomas Fortune and James Samuel Stemons, and two Irish Americans, the Reverend Peter C. Yorke and Patrick Ford.[14] Ford is a well-known figure in Irish American history. Publishing the storied *Irish World and American Industrial Liberator* helped him become a major player in Irish nationalism and (for a time) labor activism in America. There is still much to be done with Ford and his newspaper, as I hope to demonstrate. Father Yorke was famous more regionally, as a San Francisco labor leader and preeminent Irish American advocate; beyond academic circles his virulent anti-Chinese sentiments and white Christian nationalism may be less known. Fortune is a giant in African American journalism history, but his fascinating trip to Hawaii and the Philippines as an agent of the U.S. government has remained largely unexamined for several decades. Stemons and the rich personal letters he left behind are slowly becoming known to historians; I believe I am the first to detail his efforts to transform one Philadelphia newspaper and found another.

Each editor receives his own chapter. Part I considers the Irish editors, Ford and Yorke; Part II explores African American journalists Fortune and Stemons. Brief introductions to the Irish American and African American press occur before each section. Though I examine the words and newspapers of several other black and Irish American editors throughout, a close, largely biographical approach toward these four journalists enables me to tease out how newspapering may have affected their activism. Directing a newspaper in the "age of personal journalism" made these editors public figures and public intellectuals with influence in debates around group empowerment.[15] For African American editors in particular, pressures were acute; individual success or failure in the marketplace might be seen as reflecting on the race as a whole. And the newspaper medium introduced its own rules and priorities, including aesthetic genres in visual elements on the page—cartoons, illustrations, and advertisements—that might undermine, not simply augment, editors' agendas. Funding a newspaper might require support from an outside party, as when Ford's *Irish World* received Republican Party patronage or when James Samuel Stemons operated under church sponsorship. When subscription fees or advertising revenues could not make a newspaper profitable, some editors found financial gain through public speaking engagements. Other activist-editors presented economic, not just ideological, competition, and seeing one's name in print—call it the moral hazards of celebrity culture—always threatened to turn tactical disagreements into ego trips. Following each editor closely through time surfaces these pressures and potentials. Ultimately, these race activists' thinking, I believe, cannot be separated from their newspapering—the newspaper form and practice influenced what, when, how, and to whom they communicated their beliefs.

Now is an auspicious moment to look again at African American and Irish American newspapers and journalists. Many major studies of black and ethnic media are several decades old. As late as 1987, Sally M. Miller could write that the only major work on ethnic media was Robert E. Park's *The Immigrant Press and Its Control*, published in 1922.[16] Though scholarship on the African American press as a whole is more current, the sole biography of T. Thomas Fortune, perhaps the top black journalist of his time, is more than forty-five years old.[17] A frequently cited study of the Irish American press dates from 1976, and the most thorough examination of Patrick Ford, for whom a biography does not yet exist, remains James Rodechko's 1968 Ph.D. dissertation.[18]

Yet since the 1970s, several academic fields have changed dramatically, and new fields and subfields relevant to this study have emerged. (More primary source material, too, has been digitized, aiding researchers in accessing far-flung newspaper archives and tracing particular issues in the press through searchable databases.) In immigration studies, Oscar Handlin's metaphor of "uprooted" immigrant groups, backward-looking and conservative, has given way to scholarship that stresses a less primordial and more dynamic conception of group culture and boundaries.[19] I posit that this ongoing "invention of ethnicity" happened frequently through the newspapers of the ethnic press.[20] In the related field of "whiteness" scholarship, Matthew Frye Jacobson and other historians have traced the evolution of the late nineteenth-century's "probationary white groups"—Celts, Slavs, Hebrews, Iberics—into twentieth-century Caucasians; David R. Roediger has approached the same questions from labor history, examining white racism and the formation of working-class politics. Whiteness scholarship has been repeatedly debated and refined. Following Eric L. Goldstein, this book does not reveal the Irish "becoming" white so much as negotiating and successfully enhancing their whiteness within a field of competing identities.[21] Newspapers and other periodicals, I assert, were key to this negotiation.

The blossoming of the field of religious history in recent years helps me trace religion as a key component in these activists' struggles for American belonging. One recent historian, looking primarily at conflict between Catholics and Protestants, claimed that in the nineteenth century, religion's role was as central as that of race or ethnicity in the construction of group and national identity.[22] Joshua Paddison argues that race and religion were, in fact, "mutually constitutive" of citizenship during Reconstruction, especially in the American West.[23] Each historian sheds light especially on the Irish American journalists profiled in this study. Catholicism was both an important wellspring and precarious fault line of Irish American identity, yet Patrick Ford strove for a racially egalitarian vision of American citizenship, while Father Yorke advocated economic justice through a religio-racial vision of Christian white male supremacy. And as we shall see, publisher-priests like Yorke brought the priesthood further into the public realm and into tension with Rome, which kept a watchful eye on Irish American newspapers in the late 1800s.

Empire and its intersection with race and nation, particularly the Philippine-American War and the first years of U.S. rule in Spain's former colony, is another common theme in most of the following chapters. Wars of empire highlighted and heightened struggles over American belonging, offering the race men of the black and Irish press new possibilities for group advancement, even as imperialism raised the specter of Anglo-Saxon backlash and retrenchment. In the country at large, white nationalist fantasies could be mustered to either push forward or hinder the hand of U.S. imperialism; black and Irish editors had to navigate these tricky currents.[24] The U.S. effort to end Spanish control of Cuba was supported by most of the black and Irish press, which was eager to join the fight and prove American belonging. Irish American editors even labeled the Spanish army "Iberian Orangemen," despite their misgivings about anti-Catholic rhetoric in the U.S. buildup to war.[25] But after U.S. troops stayed on in Cuba and Americans, not Cuban rebels, dictated the terms of victory over Spain, the Philippine-American War across the Pacific became much more contentious. African Americans debated through their presses the role of black soldiers in the Philippine-American War and the race's proper relationship to Filipinos, with some editors putting racial affinities over national ones. Historians have linked U.S. imperial projects and their justifications abroad to educational and vocational uplift programs—and coercive segregation and disenfranchisement—for African Americans and American Indians at home, a phenomenon some call "Jim Crow colonialism."[26] As we shall see, T. Thomas Fortune preached Booker T. Washington's Tuskegee uplift pedagogies as he traveled to Hawaii and the Philippines, even as he simultaneously tried to turn white civilizationist rhetoric against itself. The Irish, meanwhile, feared that in the Philippines the United States was imitating English imperial brutality. Empire rattled old racial conceptions and introduced new narratives and histories that Americans could embrace or reject. It thus complicates linear histories of national identity and immigrant assimilation.[27]

One way to focus on these activists' strategies and their newspaper presses' materiality is to pay special attention to visual culture. Where possible, I draw on images from the editors' own newspapers, but many come from other black or Irish weeklies, mainstream periodicals, or circulated advertising cards. Racial images in these other print culture formats were frequently reprinted in newspapers. All the race activists herein kept watch on how their groups were depicted in these forums, each knowing intuitively that filler cartoons and other illustrations were more than an irritant or insult to their group—they threatened to fix African Americans or the Irish in the national imagination as second-class citizens.[28] I analyze these images as more than symbolic representations of racial ideas developed elsewhere—perhaps in the minds of race scientists or novelists or union leaders—and then translated visually into sketches or cartoons. Instead, I see such imagery as constitutive of the nation's conversation about race, class, religion, and citizenship from the start—a force that, in conjunction with other cultural forms, helped to create and promote both exclusionary and inclusionary racial viewpoints. The very words "cliché" and "stereotype," in fact, originally referred to the printing plates of stock images that "cut agencies" provided to the periodical press.[29] And even when commentators in the pages that follow appear to be referring to actual human beings and not caricatures, they often classified black and ethnic Americans through a typology that so closely matched the visual elements of nineteenth-century periodicals that one easily detects this discriminatory visual field in the background, its power to shape thinking about race, and the interpenetration of race science, stage shows, and illustrated racial humor in periodicals.

A focus on images also helps highlight the differing trajectories of Irish Americans and African Americans. African Americans struggled against racist aesthetic genres throughout the nineteenth and twentieth centuries. One black cartoonist examined herein produced images in minstrel form, making his editor uneasy. But his characters might still critique white power—to some extent, the genre proved a "pliable sign" for African Americans who worked within it.[30] By contrast, Irish Americans, who like African Americans protested vehemently against racial ridicule in print and on stage,[31] found that by the end of the century they might laugh along with non-Irish Americans at softened depictions of comic Irish characters, images that had largely lost their derogatory, simian features. Advertisers even tried to link the vigor and righteousness of the Irish fight against discrimination to their own products but took a different tact with black caricatures.

Empire, too, introduced new visual tropes. The African American leader Booker T. Washington worked closely with T. Thomas Fortune during Fortune's Pacific journey, and as Fortune prepared to travel from Honolulu to Manila, Washington told a Brooklyn audience that presently, "the Filipino seems to be undergoing the interesting experience of being carefully examined." If his hair was deemed long enough and his nose and feet small enough, Washington said, the Filipino would be "designated and treated as a white man." (If not, the Tuskegee leader seemed to hint, the Filipino just might become to African Americans an ally along the color line.)[32] Much of this bodily examination, Washington and other black activists knew, would be done by illustrators in mainstream periodicals. African Americans in America's new territories responded to these potentials, using photography, for example, to depict the Philippines as fertile ground for black dignity and advancement.

There are several reasons to examine black and Irish editors together, as opposed to other groups who also faced discrimination during the Gilded Age and Progressive Era. Certainly, other marginalized late nineteenth-century U.S. groups used their newspapers, particularly the powerful German-language press and perhaps the smaller but influential Yiddish press in New York, to fight stridently for their own visions of American belonging and societal change.³³ But because most Americans could not read these papers, focusing on English-language media enables me to gauge, when appropriate, black and Irish journalists' effect on broader public policy debates. Furthermore, examining two groups with divergent outcomes through the turn of the twentieth century helps contrast the relative importance of each group's racial, class, and religious differences to their American citizenship. In the late nineteenth century, the Irish still faced discrimination, particularly a nativist backlash against Catholicism, as a Church empowered by Irish immigration flexed its muscle and worried Protestants. But the overall trajectory of Irish America was positive; increasing numbers of Irish moved up the economic ladder, albeit more slowly than some immigrant groups. For the Irish, conceptions of race by skin tone began to displace or at least encompass racial conceptions more closely tied to nationality—the Celtic race "became white" (or perhaps better, enhanced its whiteness). African Americans, by contrast, saw in the nineteenth century's second half the end of government commitment to their welfare, with the withdrawal of federal troops from the South in 1877, resulting in disenfranchisement, lynchings, and the onset of Jim Crow toward the end of the century—a period one historian has called the "nadir" of black history.³⁴ Black, Irish, and mainstream newspapers alike reported on the so-called Negro Problem—a vaguely and variously defined, typically paternalistic construction by whites that often imagined black racial pathology and asked how to or even whether to more completely integrate blacks into mainstream American life. And as with debates over Irish nationalism, intellectual debate might be hard to distinguish from economic competition as race men offered their own solutions in their own newspapers.³⁵

Following African American and Irish American journalists and their newspapers also reveals important cross-racial commentary as the two groups, often in competition for low-wage work, gauged one another. Many scholarly studies portray the Irish in America as the enforcers—through their powerful urban political machines, representation on city police forces, and dominance of labor unions—of a virulent white supremacy. More recent whiteness scholarship, though it recognizes the prohibitionary nature of ethnic Americans' citizenship, typically has the Irish and other immigrant groups emerging victorious, and still racist, in their quest for full American belonging. Most recently, however, some scholars have emphasized the solidarity that many Irish and Irish American nationalists expressed toward nonwhite victims of British imperialism during the nineteenth century and sometimes toward oppressed groups at home.³⁶ Ford in particular pushed such racial egalitarianism through the internationally circulated *Irish World*, calling African Americans "brothers," sympathizing with Native Americans, and denoting South Asians "brown Irishmen."³⁷ T. Thomas Fortune looked with envy on Irish organizing efforts and hoped to model a black civil rights organization on the Land League, an Irish nationalist group.[38] From Frederick Douglass's trip to Ireland in 1840, where he met with and was compared to the famed Irish nationalist Daniel O'Connell, to black nationalist Marcus Garvey's Harlem-based Liberty Hall in the 1920s, which he named after the Dublin headquarters of Irish labor union members and revolutionaries, African Americans and Irish Americans demonstrated a "persistent if elusive affinity" for one another and for each group's freedom struggle.[39] Black and Irish newspapers were often the site for expressions of both affinity and resentment between the two groups, and the interplay between black and Irish nationalisms, religious concerns, responses to empire, and visual elements within these presses lends greater insight into the building of competing, racialized discourses of citizenship in the late nineteenth century.

My study begins with Irish American journalist Patrick Ford, whose prominence among Irish nationalists worldwide, combined with the long run of the *Irish World*, reveals the whole sweep of late nineteenth-century Irish American history and introduces many of the main themes of this book: editors' stands on ethnic nationalisms; the complex interplay between race, labor, religion, and empire in the construction of citizenship; and a close textual look at newspaper elements. The powerful *World*, with its respectable circulation of more than a hundred thousand by 1900, was viewed with admiration and envy by many black and ethnic Americans and even, to an extent, feared by its enemies in Great Britain and the United States. With Ford the newspaper weekly itself became a locus for the excavation, maintenance, and construction of Irish American history, language, and identity. Social movements discussed within a newspaper frame were lent legitimacy and magnified; Ford's newspaper could help reveal a movement to itself as members read about the fund-raising efforts and spirited resistance of like-minded souls across the nation and across the Atlantic. Ford, who started in journalism as a printer's devil for famed abolitionist William Lloyd Garrison, mostly maintained his racial egalitarianism throughout his life. But running a successful weekly could mean giving space to diverse voices, and Ford lost some control of his egalitarian message as his top columnist backpedaled on African American rights.

Remaining with the Irish but shifting to the West Coast, Chapter 2's exploration of Father Peter C. Yorke and his newspaper-based activism further elucidates the importance of race, labor, and religion to Irish American identity and examines more closely the Irish American encounter with Asia as a key element of race and citizenship in the late nineteenth century. Editing a newspaper and publishing his own writings in other San Francisco newspapers enabled Yorke to lend moral suasion to labor struggles and calibrate Catholic doctrine in support of both workers' rights and notions of Western and Caucasian civilizational superiority in the face of Chinese labor competition. Simultaneously, it brought him into conflict with the Catholic Church as increasing channels of print communication blurred lines of Church authority. Making arguments from Catholic perspectives could also foment backlash and incite anti-Catholic anger from the populace at large in an age when urban reform efforts often had a Protestant, anti-immigrant cast. Despite these hazards, Yorke and other Irish American newspaper editors exercised considerable clout and, in a campaign to defend a perceived threat to Catholicism in the Philippines, wound up influencing U.S. educational policy in the islands. The American priesthood itself, I argue, was changed in part by lay and clerical Catholic editors and their newspapers, which brought priests more fully into the public arena. Scholars who have judged Catholic thought as intellectually dormant during these years must not neglect Yorke's and other Irish American newspaper editors' creative use of religious doctrine as they confronted issues of the day.

The next two chapters focus on African American editors. Empire remains prominent in the frame in Chapter 3 as I follow one of the most famous black editors of the time, T. Thomas Fortune, on his state-sponsored journey to Hawaii and the Philippines. In late 1902 mental and physical exhaustion, financial distress, and the feeling that he deserved a political appointment—combined with aspirations to serve as a broker for the export of African American labor abroad—led Fortune to secure a government appointment to investigate trade and labor conditions on the outposts of U.S. empire. Though Fortune was away from his own storied paper, the *New York Age*, the chapter examines local ethnic newspaper reaction to his visit and continues to explore newspapering as a material and ideological practice, for Fortune employed the tools of his publishing trade, including photography, polling, and even poetry during his travels. In Hawaii Fortune publicly allied himself with island business interests and a missionary educational tradition connected to Booker T. Washington. He was treated respectfully by the sons and daughters of abolitionists—and by a planter oligarchy eager to end federal exclusion of Chinese so as to obtain cheap field labor—but his hopes for African American emigration were vigorously opposed by most papers connected to this planter establishment. Hawaii's robust in-language indigenous and ethnic newspapers, meanwhile, had their own views on black labor in the islands. In Manila a fiercely independent, entrepreneurial, and militaristic U.S. press, itself at odds with many of the goals of the U.S. commission government in the Philippines, attacked Fortune and his plan. Fortune attempted to survey public opinion on black immigration to the Philippines by circulating a questionnaire and, on a trek through northern Luzon, used a camera and a portable painted background to craft a portrait of himself as an intrepid African American explorer and cast the Philippines as a possible home for millions of African Americans. Recent scholarship has emphasized both Washington's and Fortune's complicity with Western imperial projects; this chapter posits that both men also saw empire and African American participation in it as a force that could destabilize racial regimes. Fortune in particular saw newspapers as a key instigator of new political and racial alignments.

Chapter 4 explores the work of a black journalist, mostly unknown to scholars, who hoped to establish himself as an expert on race relations. Though the print editions of James Samuel Stemons's newspapers are lost to history, the voluminous notes he left behind on the nuts and bolts of publishing a small weekly in early twentieth-century Philadelphia provide invaluable glimpses into a black weekly's newsroom, if not quite its balance books. Extensive letters between Stemons and his sister reveal much of the business side of running a weekly African American press as well as the print economy of other formats, including pamphlet publishing. They portray an economically challenging but, for Stemons and other reformers, enticing arena whereby publishing—essentially self-publishing—could lead to name recognition and entry into debate over the so-called Negro Problem, including potentially lucrative speaking engagements. Historians in their investigations have tended to examine newspapers with extensive runs to track changes in opinion or emphasis on particular topics through time; less studied are the many hundreds of newspapers, including black weeklies, that lasted just months or even weeks. These intensely personal and competitive ventures influenced public debate even as their operation helped shape the politics of the time; Stemons seemed to have had both a political critique and, in modern parlance, one eye toward his Stemons "brand." Stemons in particular and perhaps Father Yorke show how figures currently unknown to most historians participated in vibrant, diverse forums whose intellectual output has, with the passage of time, come to be associated with only a handful of top black and Irish leaders.

The central figures in this study move through many relevant historiographies, and as such this book builds on and offers critiques of several of them: journalism history, Irish American history, African American history, and broader histories of the nineteenth and late nineteenth century. Much work on Gilded Age journalism has focused on the rise and prominence of the large metropolitan dailies and their jingoistic fervor for war at century's end; mainstream weekly newspapers as well as immigrant newsweeklies have often been overlooked. Yet the power and reach of the newsweekly endured well into the twentieth century. Frank Luther Mott places the high point of weekly newspapers in 1914–1915 and notes that weeklies in rural areas held their own for some time against dailies after the latter started free rural delivery.[40] With respect to the more metropolitan immigrant press, older scholarship that stressed the process of assimilation naturally saw ethnic media as having largely completed its task of helping newcomers adjust to American society by 1900 or so. But black and Irish weeklies as sites for the creation of race and ethnicity continued, as did their clout. As Chapter 3 demonstrates, the "race papers" of two groups affected U.S. policy in the Philippines: the Irish pushed for and won the appointment of Catholics to educational bodies in the islands, and the white soldier press harassed U.S. commissioners by opposing U.S. plans to Filipinize governance there.

The chapters that follow also complicate the notion of print culture as a unifying force in American nationhood. As has been noted, scholars posit newspapers as key sites of nationalism. More popularly, media is regarded as a fourth estate keeping watch over the nation's democratic institutions. In a different vein, and building on Trish Loughran's important reassessment of Anderson, I find newspapers as sites of discord and division as well as unity.[41] The newspapers in this study—white or "mainstream," African American, or Irish alike—could be sites for the promotion of racio-religious nationalisms that clashed with the country's civic nationalism, its ideology of universal human equality and governance by democratic consent.[42] The twenty-first-century rise of internet-based race nationalisms, especially those delivered within journalistic frames and with a Christian cast, make the examination of the deep roots of such publishing important.

Religion in this book comes up time and again as a fault line for American belonging, with importance for the construction of race in the late nineteenth century. Following recent scholars who see Reconstruction as a multiregional and multiracial process that reimagined citizenship's boundaries, I find the West Coast's Chinese question integral to discussions of race and inextricably bound up in questions of religion. The rhetoric in Father Yorke's speech to the California Chinese Exclusion Convention in 1901 is not so different from similar anti-Chinese speeches during Reconstruction and shows the Irish shoring up their own fault lines in citizenship by creating a broader-based Christianity and European cultural heritage. But scholars who seek to make multiracial California and the West a key part of the decades-long debate over American citizenship after the Civil War might productively broaden their horizons to encompass direct U.S. encounters with Asia at the turn of the century. Chapter 3 shows that African American hopes for opportunity abroad intersected with American imperialism in tense, complex, and surprising ways. Fortune's state-sponsored visit to American possessions in the Pacific surfaces the (somewhat) egalitarian racial views of Hawaiian missionary culture; virulent, Southern-style white nationalist presses abroad that resisted more paternalistic relations with Filipinos; a split among the black press over national or cross-racial affinities with Filipinos; racist beliefs among "people of color" groups in the region, promulgated from their own newsweeklies; and, combined with Stemons's intimations of publishers freezing out black authors in 1907, disturbing hints in the early twentieth century of a wish on the part of U.S. political and cultural leaders to be done with the Negro Problem once and for all—perhaps with a Philippines solution.[43] Empire was in deep communication with race, religion, and domestic politics at century's end.

Finally, this book both supports and troubles recent scholarship on the Progressive Era. Much in the pages that follow confirms the negative aspects of many Progressives uncovered by historians, including the anti-Catholic and anti-immigrant biases in their urban reform efforts and their support of segregation and abandonment of African American rights. But Ford, Fortune, Stemons, and Yorke were reformers themselves, black and Irish muckrakers who, like Progressives, used fact-based rhetoric and publishing in their efforts to remake America. Where to draw the boundaries of Progressivism has always challenged historians of the era. Perhaps more exploration of the "unexpected places" of black and Irish writing and activism—like that handwritten, ship-based Fenian journal or a black newspaper lasting weeks, not years—can better uncover and describe the period's passion for reform.[44]

The activist-editors herein never seemed to tire of print periodicals. After all, newspapers could pull old institutions, such as the Catholic Church, in new directions, and a vibrant ethnic press united around an issue could effect policy change at even the highest levels of government. Yet the strife produced by individually empowered activists directing their own sounding boards could strain and break coalitions, too. And newspaper weeklies might promote illusions of power, a mirage of influence over a virtual or at least fleeting public sphere; Stemons's newspapers, for example, lasted as long as his investors thought there was any chance of profit and no longer. Activist-editors fought against destructive racial ideologies but found whole discourses, whether of race and labor or education and uplift, and entire aesthetic sensibilities, such as minstrelsy, difficult to write or draw or photograph around.

No simple historical lines can be drawn from our own twenty-first-century world to the lives of Ford, Yorke, Fortune, and Stemons. Yet something of the vibrancy and vulnerability, brilliance and amateurism, earnestness and arrogance of these four newspapermen's enterprises recalls today's online media, risen from the ashes of the large, commercial dailies that grew to dominate the twentieth century. The United States will succeed or fail in defining itself, in creating inclusive or exclusive American identities, through conversations mediated by modern communication technologies. To suggest that we have gone back to blogging collapses important distinctions between our time and the long nineteenth century. But I do hope some wisdom about the promises and perils of very personal media may be gleaned from this study.

I

THE IRISH AMERICAN PRESS

Exiled Editors Forging New Borders
of Belonging

B Y THE TIME Patrick Ford and the Reverend Peter C. Yorke began their publishing ventures in the United States, Irish American newspapers had been in existence for many decades. The *Shamrock*, or *Hibernian Chronicle*, was perhaps the first, in 1810. Based in New York City, the *Shamrock* gleaned dispatches from Irish newspapers in Dublin, Cork, and Belfast. It collapsed around 1824; its successor appears to have been the New York–based *Truth Teller*.[1] Scholars of the Irish in America seem to disagree on the extent to which this early stage of pre-famine journalism was Catholic in nature, nationalist, or a combination of the two; William Leonard Joyce sees these first presses as successfully balancing affinity for Irish independence with their Catholic sympathies. Yet this early newspaper scene still saw bitter wars of words and libel suits among editors, and some censured or suspended Catholic priests took up newspapering, such as the Reverend Thomas C. Levins with his *Green Lantern*. Readership remained small; circulation for the *Truth Teller*, the largest during this time, peaked at around three thousand and was mainly regional.[2]

The Irish American weekly truly burgeoned in the 1840s, powered mainly by two factors: an influx of Irish Catholic readers fleeing famine in Ireland and the simultaneous arrival of exiles from the Young Ireland movement, who brought their militant nationalisms and, oftentimes, anti-Church politics with them. Young Ireland started as the radical wing of Daniel O'Connell's Loyal National Repeal Association (LNRA), which sought to end the Act of Union that placed Ireland constitutionally within the United Kingdom (those in favor of such a move were dubbed Repealers). Young Ireland coalesced in 1842 around a political weekly that the activists named the *Nation*. Soon the rebels became frustrated with O'Connellism's goals (repeal the act but remain federated somehow to Great Britain) and tactics (moral force persuasion and legal maneuvers). The militant *Nation* rapidly became successful; its head editor, Charles Gavan Duffy, claimed that the first issue sold out in just hours and that vendors smashed the newspaper's office window to snare more copies. Irish American editors in New York and Boston watched closely and quickly set up exchange agreements with the *Nation* and other Irish papers across the Atlantic. Irish American publishers sought Irish news and cultural authenticity; Young Ireland sought allies and financial support from Irish America. A complete split from the LNRA in 1845, British arrests of Young Irelander John Mitchel on treason charges, and a haphazard armed rebellion in 1848 in County Tipperary that was quickly suppressed by the British led several Young Irelanders to flee to America. One, Thomas D'Arcy McGee, escaped dressed as a priest.[3]

McGee, in fact, set up the first self-proclaimed Irish nationalist newspaper in the United States in 1848, which he named the *Nation*, after the Dublin paper. Only twenty-three at the time and blaming the Church for the failure of the 1848 revolt, McGee set about clashing with Bishop John Hughes in New York. But Hughes fought back against McGee in another paper, the *Freeman's Journal*, and called on all dioceses, parishes, and churches to reject the *Nation*, which folded less than two years after opening its doors. McGee started another paper, the *American Celt*, and embarked on an increasingly conservative political odyssey in which his sympathies for the pope increased as his Irish nationalism waned. McGee wound up in Canada, advocated a strong alliance with Great Britain, and was assassinated by Fenians in 1865.

Mitchel escaped from prison in Australia and reached U.S. shores in 1853. A supporter of slavery, he would edit a Confederate newspaper during the Civil War and later a more moderate Irish nationalist paper, the *Irish Citizen* (New York). Mitchel's full-hearted support for human bondage was unusual among Irish American editors, but the issue created immense tension for Irish nationalists in America. Most in the Irish American press rejected O'Connell's embrace of abolitionism, choosing to remain quiet on slavery for fear of being seen as ungrateful to their new American home.

Around midcentury, the largest circulating newspaper was Patrick Lynch's *Irish-American*. Lynch, a veteran Repealer, tried perhaps more than any other nineteenth-century editor to embrace both Catholicism and Irish nationalism and smooth over tensions between the two. After his death in 1857, his son Patrick Meehan would edit the paper until 1906 and clash with

Patrick Ford over the Skirmishing Fund—monies raised in America for Irish armed conflict with Great Britain.[4]

Midcentury was also the time of famine in Ireland, which boosted Irish emigration to the United States, though those rates were high throughout much of the nineteenth century. Between the end of the American War of Independence in 1783 and the economic panic of 1819, close to 200,000 Irish immigrated to the United States, forming the nation's largest immigrant group in those years.[5] A majority of these earlier immigrants were Protestant. In the next thirty years preceding the Great Famine in 1845, up to one million more Irish reached North America to form a third of all U.S. immigrants. Most of these were Irish Catholic. Population growth in Ireland, agricultural depression, and the pressures of mechanization on Irish textile industries drove many Irish abroad. The partial failure of Ireland's potato crop in 1845 and its complete failure in the winter of 1846–1847 caused more than a million Irish to die from starvation and disease and further stoked the exodus from Ireland. Numbers of emigrants to the United States per year peaked at 221,000 in 1850; between the start of the famine and 1890, three million Irish crossed the Atlantic to the United States.[6]

The famine boosted Irish nationalism, as many Irish charged England with orchestrating it, while the migration it inspired simultaneously gave Irish American newspapers a readership. The movement for Irish independence had been set back following the collapse of the American Repeal movement just a few years earlier. O'Connell, the Irish activist leading the charge to grant Ireland legislative independence from England by repealing the Act of Union, had strained relations with Irish nationalists in America by linking the Irish cause to the abolition of slavery. Those ties broke completely with his "American Eagle" speech, when, in the midst of a virtual standoff between England and the United States over U.S. annexation of the Oregon territory, O'Connell essentially chose sides with England (if it would only repeal the Act of Union).[7]

A rural and mostly Catholic population encountered discrimination in America; the native Protestant population believed the Irish to be clannish, violent, prone to drunkenness, and, largely due to their Catholicism, incapable of the independent thought necessary for democracy. Anti-Catholic organizing and rioting was perhaps worst at midcentury, with riots in Philadelphia, New York, and other cities; violent conflicts over schooling; and the rise of organized nativism, including the Know-Nothing Party in the 1850s.

Often, "Irish" and "Catholic" were one in the same; Irish newspapers were written for Catholics, and newspapers that stressed Catholicism were filled with Irish culture and politics. Editors themselves expressed confusion about where the lines were drawn, and, as will be seen, Yorke, when he was forced from the *Monitor* (an official Church organ) and founded the *Leader*, tried to capitalize on his multiple identities as an ordained priest at an independent newspaper.

Ford would come onto the scene in the late nineteenth century as Irish immigration continued and the Irish increasingly formed a powerful segment of the U.S. labor movement. Though Irish nationalism in America would wane by the turn of the century (before exploding again during and after World War I) and the most virulent anti-Catholic agitation had also declined since midcentury, flare-ups of nativism continued as American Protective Association (APA) ministers flexed their muscles on the West Coast and anti-Catholic images and publications achieved mass circulation. The Spanish-American and Philippine-American Wars, too, exposed fissures in American identity and politics to which Irish editors felt compelled to respond. The Boston *Pilot* and Ford's *Irish World* were the most powerful Irish American newspapers in the late nineteenth century; each could be staunchly anti-imperialist and racially egalitarian, oftentimes promoting a vision of a multiethnic, multiracial America. "The American is neither Anglo-Saxon nor Celt, nor German, nor French, nor anything else individually," claimed the *Pilot*'s James Jeffrey Roche, who saw the nation's strength in its diversity.[8] It would be Ford, however, who most tried to combine Irish pride and nationalism with radical social change.

One well-cited review of the Irish American press sees Catholicism and Irish nationalism as two "strategies" editors used to advocate for American belonging while simultaneously promoting a unique Irish identity: "The story of the relations between these two strategies is the story of the nineteenth-century Irish American press."[9] This is one useful approach to the Irish press, but it may tend to cast Catholicism as the spoiler of stances for radical social change when in fact, as we shall see, different editors molded either strategy to suit a wide ideological range of campaigns. It also neglects the racial journey of the Irish and the charged relationship between religion, race, and citizenship in the late nineteenth century. More recently, Cian T. McMahon has suggested that the Irish weekly, through its far-flung distribution, helped grow a "borderless Irish reading public" and fostered an "Irish global nationalism" that posited Celts everywhere as natural republicans capable of forging solidarities with victims of oppression worldwide even as they expanded the parameters of citizenship at home.[10] Father Yorke and other Irish American editors on the West Coast may complicate this notion, for many Irish imagined a different kind of transnational community: one united by white working-class identity and fortified by its white Christian heritage.

1

PATRICK FORD AND THE WRITING OF IRISH AMERICA

The storm-bell of the Irish World *boomed across the Atlantic with a very audible note of alarm indeed, that was heard in every mountain-glen in Ireland. There was scarcely a cabin in the West to which some relative in America did not despatch [sic] a weekly copy of the* Irish World. . . . *It was as if some vast Irish-American invasion was sweeping the country with new and irresistible principles of Liberty and Democracy.*
—William O'Brien, *Recollections* (1905)

In appearance and manner, the editor of the Irish World *is quite the opposite of the man you would figure to yourself after reading his dynamite appeals and exordiums in his own journal. Quiet and unobtrusive alike in look and speech, he is as mild a mannered man as ever scuttled a ship.*
—Henri Le Caron [Thomas Beach], *Twenty-Five Years in the Secret Service* (1893)

Patrick Ford made his reasons for publishing the *Irish World* clear from its 1870 start. In the newspaper's first several years, Ford printed a 1,300-word mission statement on page 4, the editorial page—a kind of preamble to the paper. Though Ford's political views would evolve over the years, much of the spirit of the statement accurately reflects the *World*'s outlook, emphasis, and priorities over all four decades of Ford's guidance of the paper.

The Irish, according to Ford, were a people, and a global one. Under the words "Read—Reflect—Act," the mission statement first linked the newspaper to individual Irishmen and those Irish to others worldwide. "Every journal worthy of an existence should have an aim. . . . More, every man, whose life is not a lie, has an aim." What is true of individuals "is true likewise of peoples. . . . All Irishmen, and all Irishmen's sons, the world over, are part of one mighty whole." Constant "forces of attraction" drew the race "instinctively together, and knit them into an integral body."[1]

Religion, Ford wrote, was one unifier of the Irish. They were a "providential people," guided by God's right hand "through the ages, a cloud by day, and a pillar of fire by night." And the Irish were united by a common mission, which was also the mission of the *Irish World*: first, "to achieve, in this our day, self-government for Ireland"; second, "to bear aloft . . . the standard of the Cross" into "every nook and corner of this land"; and third, to "hold the state true to the principles . . . of the Declaration of Independence" and to "confront the pretensions of Anglo-Saxon ascendancy," which violated the Constitution and the role played by "our predecessors in the Revolution" who "won with the sword our right to citizenship." The *World* would fight "a floating prejudice in this country, imported from England, that the Irish are an inferior race," which had particularly had an impact on the young, who had become "weak-kneed." The Irish are "not on this soil as intruders. All races meet here on equal footing; and no race can, with any legitimate pretensions, monopolize for itself the name American."[2]

The *Irish World*, Ford wrote, would engage in much educational work, for "an imperfect knowledge of ourselves and of our early history in this country," forgetfulness of a "sense of self-respect which all people should retain," had enabled "vainglorious and supercilious upstarts of other nationalities to ride rough-shod over us." Ford described the paper as "a Vehicle of News" and listed its weekly sections, which included biographical sketches of Irish poets and other historical figures "full of fire, spirit, and patriotism"; news from "32 counties of Ireland," which Ford claimed was the most of any newspaper; personals; a correspondence section; and a "weekly calendar of important historical events."[3]

All this would help the Irish "assert themselves. Let them walk before the world such as they are—such as nature and grace have made them." Anyone who agreed with these principles, Ford added, should "signify his assent by sending in his name and subscription, and getting his neighbor to do the same." Ford ended with a final pitch, inviting "all who *think* with us, and share in our faith, to *act* with us also, and grow their faith by their works"—in other words, subscribe, at $2.50 for a full year.[4]

For Ford, the newspaper itself was to be a touchstone of Irish American identity. But the components of Irish American identity that Ford described in his mission statement or would go on to embrace in the coming years—Catholicism, transatlantic and worldwide solidarities, labor rights, and "race"—would prove difficult to, in his words, "knit . . . into an integral body."[5]

Patrick Ford was born in Galway, Ireland, in 1837, the son of Edward and Ann Ford. The family immigrated to the United States in 1845 when Ford was a young boy. Obituaries of his parents in the *Irish World* in 1870 and

1880 claimed they were compelled to leave Ireland because of the potato famine. Ford said he had few memories of Ireland and considered himself shaped by America and the city of Boston, where the family settled.

When he was fifteen, Ford worked as a printer's devil for famed abolitionist William Lloyd Garrison's *Liberator*. He would cite, as an early formative moment, watching federal troops escort fugitive slave Anthony Burns through the streets of Boston to be shipped back to the South. Burns had escaped from slavery and stowed away aboard a ship to Boston in March 1854. His Virginia owner soon learned of his whereabouts, and Burns was arrested that year by a deputy marshal and imprisoned in the federal courthouse. Despite a vigorous legal defense, attempts by supporters to purchase him from his owner, and a biracial mob of abolitionists who rushed the courthouse in an attempt to free him, federal troops, state militia, and local police marched Burns past crowds of angry Bostonians to the wharf, where he was placed on board a ship bound for the South. Ford had witnessed one of several seminal events of the 1850s that increased sectional tensions and drove the nation to war. "We went to bed one night old fashioned, Compromise Union Whigs," wrote one wealthy Boston merchant, "and waked up stark mad Abolitionists."[6]

Ford (see Figure 1.1) edited an antislavery newspaper in Boston briefly, enlisted with the Ninth Massachusetts Volunteers, and fought in the battle

Figure 1.1 Patrick Ford, editor of the *Irish World and American Industrial Liberator*. Photographic print, 1900. (Courtesy of the Library of Congress.)

of Fredericksburg in 1862. Following the Civil War, he edited a Reconstruction newspaper in South Carolina before moving to New York in 1870, where he founded the *Irish World*. Ford controlled the newspaper every year until his death in 1913 except for a brief ownership dispute with John T. Hoag in 1883. The paper remained a Ford family operation well into the twentieth century; it ceased publication in 1951.[7] (Historians often describe either the *Irish World* or the Boston *Pilot* as the leading Irish American newspaper of the time; circulation figures suggest that Ford's paper overtook the *Pilot* by the turn of the century, which may explain the discrepancy.)[8]

Most historians describe Ford as, for a time, a "radical" advocate of Irish independence from Great Britain and of the rights of the industrial worker in the United States. They trace a growing conservatism in Ford's positions as he became dismayed by labor violence and adopted more moderate positions consistent with the Catholic Church and the nation at large. Detailed examination of the *Irish World* suggests that this view is largely correct, particularly if advocacy of militant, organized struggle against capitalist control is one's primary test for radicalism. Ford's severance from the economist Henry George, advocate of a single tax on land to fight economic inequalities, was bitter and final, and by the end of his life he would denounce socialism and militant trade unionism. (Ford would also end up entertaining anti-Semitic notions of Jewish financial conspiracy.)

By some measures, however, Ford's trajectory from start to finish is more ambiguous and suggests space for different or additional analyses of him, his newspaper, and the complexities of Irish American identity. Ford's fierce anti-imperialism remained a constant in the *Irish World* and involved repeated, passionate calls for solidarity with (typically nonwhite) victims of colonialism around the globe. Simultaneously, to complicate the picture, Ford's leading columnist, an Irish American Protestant minister and professor, would in the late 1890s turn his back on full African American citizenship rights and call the Fifteenth Amendment a "mistake." And, importantly, elements of a more conservative Catholic outlook were present in the *Irish World* from the start; Ford's long-running "Temperance" column is one case in point.

This chapter attempts to bring new light to Ford and his newspaper through attention to the newspaper medium itself and how it both enabled and constrained Ford's efforts to calibrate various aspects of Irish American identity. Through various sections of his paper and via the legitimacy that a news medium lent to the actions of a network of Irish activists at home and abroad, Ford advocated for what he felt was best for the "Irish race." If stretching Irish sympathies around the globe threatened to dilute a vigorous Irish American identity based largely on Ireland's quest for independence, perhaps a Gaelic-language column could refocus the Irish on their roots. Conversely, if Catholic German Americans were pushing for German-language priests and dioceses—a plan Ford perceived as threatening Catholicism and perhaps Irish ascendency in Catholic America—Ford might defend the dominance of the English language in America. Separate races and cultures across the globe should unite against empire based on their common human rights—but once U.S. expansion was a fait accompli, defending Catholicism might also mean promoting it as a better civilizer of the so-called savages than Protestantism. In the *Irish World*, the benchmarks of Irish American identity orbited around each other in constant, sometimes conflicting interplay.

The Irish Image

From the first issues of the *Irish World* and into the 1900s, Ford attacked stereotypes that "libeled" Irish dignity "on the stage, in the pulpit, and through the press," as he wrote in 1871. Ford called *Harpers Weekly*, the widely circulated cultural and political magazine that printed the satirical cartoons of Thomas Nast, the skewerer of Tammany Hall, "the pictorial organ of Anglo-Saxon 'civilization,'" and denounced its "vile caricatures of the Irish."[9]

Ford was criticizing an entire genre of art within the covers of magazines and newspapers in the nineteenth century that Roger Fischer calls filler cartoons: black-and-white drawings that "exploited stereotypes and situations that comprised the pro forma running gags of the era," including "decadent society fops" desperately miming London fashion; "college louts" competing on Ivy League gridirons; "wily farmers fleecing vacationing city tenderfoots"; and most of all, ethnic immigrants, American Indians, and African Americans, cast as hopeless cases for assimilation.[10] Interestingly, Fischer finds that in *Puck* and *Judge*, popular illustrated weeklies in the late nineteenth century from which newspapers frequently borrowed illustrations, these filler cartoons often sharply contradicted the messages of the large, colorized illustrations on the cover. *Puck* often portrayed the foolishness of anti-Semitism in its cover art, for example, while inside the magazine filler cartoons might depict Jews as greedy Shylocks. The ethnic joke existed in a kind of free-floating way within and across a variety of media, drawing the ire of race men like Ford.

The Mick Moloney Collection at New York University contains hundreds of Irish American postcards, greeting cards, trading cards, and ephemera and provides an excellent resource to study images of the Irish that so incensed Irish editors like Ford. Many ethnic gags on the cards are reprints from *Puck* or *Judge*. Others are trading cards with Irish American figures on the front and advertisements on the back that may or may not possess an obvious connection to the front image. Though we will return to images Ford himself printed in the *Irish World*, a close look at the Moloney collection reveals a gradual visual shift in Irish caricature from negative, stereotypical images earlier in the nineteenth century to more positive portrayals in the twentieth.[11]

"Paternal Authority" is a trading card released by the Arbuckle Bros. Coffee Co., most likely in 1888 or 1889, in a series of one hundred satirical cards that reprinted cartoons originally published in *Puck*, *Judge*, and *Texas Siftings* in 1887 and 1888 (see Figure 1.2).[12] It is No. 20 in the series, identifiable by the number on the lower-left corner of the back of the card. The father is drawn in the simian style first used by British cartoonists and popularized in the United States largely by Thomas Nast. L. Perry Curtis, Jr., author of perhaps the most extensive study of the Irish image in British and American publications, places the most notable rise of the Irish simian image in the 1860s in Great Britain, when a convergence of Fenian violence and scientific speculation about humanity's primate origins compelled privileged British and Scottish classes to half-seriously posit Irish Celts as a kind of "missing link" between animal savagery and civilization.[13] The ad copy on the back of this card makes no reference to the front-side cartoon.

Another card in the collection, "Pat's Prevention," in which a foolish Irish wagoner pulls the tail of his charging horse to keep it from running right through the harness, follows a similar pattern. A list of the product's supposed virtues printed on the reverse side—"strength, purity, and deliciousness"—is not directly related to the derogatory ethnic gag on the front. Here the corporation may simply hope to profit from the popularity of ethnic jokes and their circulation.

Figure 1.2 "Paternal Authority," an advertising card for Arbuckle's Ariosa Coffee, ca. 1888. (Courtesy of the Mick Moloney Irish-American Music and Popular Culture Irish Americana Collection, Tamiment Library and Robert F. Wagner Labor Archives, New York University.)

In "A New Vehicle," an ad card for Dr. Joseph Haas's Hog and Poultry Remedy, which most likely comes from the late 1890s, Pat's appearance retains some monkey-like features, but his contraption, though jury-rigged, has a certain ingenious quality, and the tone of the text on the back of the card is not mocking (Figures 1.3 and 1.4). In "Bound for Donnybrook Fair," an ad card for Pond's Extract from 1892, the Irishman, bound for the fair

Figures 1.3 and 1.4 "A New Vehicle," an undated advertising card most likely from the 1890s. (Courtesy of the Mick Moloney Irish-American Music and Popular Culture Irish Americana Collection, Tamiment Library and Robert F. Wagner Labor Archives, New York University.)

with a container of the product, also shows somewhat milder stereotypical features. The sales pitch on the reverse side is straightforward, listing all the ailments that Pond's soothes.

Ford was a key figure in the fight against the ridicule of the Irish; he described the stereotypical stage Irishman as "a drunken 'loafer,' who will not work, spends half or all of his wife's earnings, and beats her into the bargain." By 1904 Ford was still sensitive to associations between apes and Irish, reporting on efforts of Irish activists to rename "Miss Dooley," a gorilla at a New York City zoo.[14] Due in part to these newspaper campaigns by Ford, Yorke, and other activist-editors, the Irish image was improving—and advertisers took note.

In addition to "Donnybrook Fair," other cards in the collection show a transitional style between advertising via racist gag versus ethnic pride. In fact, a card advertising soap produced by the R. W. Bell Manufacturing Company hints at anti-Irish discrimination (see Figures 1.5 and 1.6). It de-

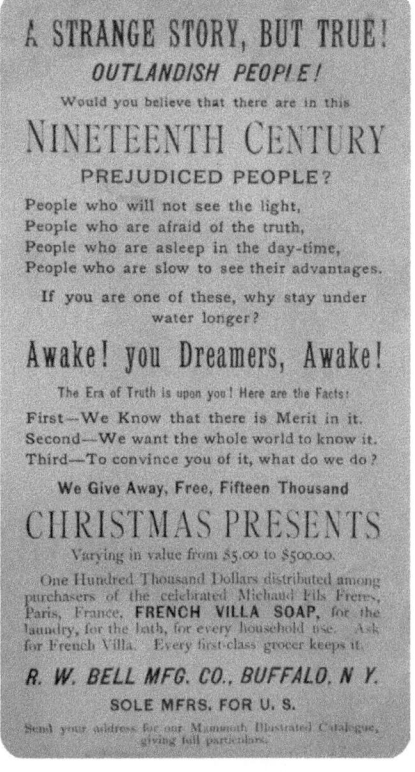

Figures 1.5 and 1.6 An Irish hod carrier in an undated advertising card most likely from the 1890s. (Courtesy of the Mick Moloney Irish-American Music and Popular Culture Irish Americana Collection, Tamiment Library and Robert F. Wagner Labor Archives, New York University.)

picts a self-contained, if somewhat stereotypical Irish worker (he retains the broad upper lip) and asks in its ad copy, "Would you believe that there are in this nineteenth century prejudiced people?" The suggestion is that this prejudice is against the "truth" of the company's superior soap; between the lines it is suggested that the Irish, too, are maligned.[15]

In an advertising card in the collection for Schultz's Irish Soap, prejudice is more explicitly linked to the Irish. Text on the card's back suggests a battle for legitimacy on the part of the product that evokes a gallant story of the Irish experience:

> The history of Irish Soap is brief; yet suggestive, as it teaches how true merit wins against all opposition. First, then, it was born in obscurity; abused, buffeted and ridiculed through its early infancy; denounced, libeled and slandered throughout its youth and up till today. But in the face of all this, Irish Soap grew and prospered. . . . [T]his success was not attained by heavy advertising, but by its own merits, almost unaided. Its many friends have been gained and retained by its own intrinsic worth.

Here, the very struggle of the Irish against negative stereotypes itself shows Irish strength of character, something the manufacturers hope will be transferred to their product.

Susan L. Mizruchi has observed that Americans have often assumed that "social mobility required giving up ethnic attachments."[16] Contemporary historians are better versed in how the creation of accepted American ethnicities often involved stressing cultural differences as well as similarities to mainstream U.S. society.[17] Yet historical writing on advertising often focuses exclusively on advertisers' use of negative racial stereotypes. In addition to demeaning portrayals of black and ethnic Americans, in the latter half of the nineteenth century, Mizruchi writes, "there was in fact much productive fusion of ethnic identities and economic aspirations." Though capitalist aspirations could produce degrading stereotypes, "American capitalist energies also sponsored nuanced and creative conceptions of cultural difference." Mizruchi tracks the interplay of the rapid growth of U.S. corporate capitalism in the late nineteenth century with the era's explosive rates of immigration to America and concludes that both forces produced the world's first "multicultural, modern capitalist society."[18]

Perhaps no card in the collection demonstrates the shift from images of Irish mishap to Irish success—and the continued importance of hierarchies in the era's race science—than a leather postcard depicting a Native American and an Irishman sent by U.S. mail to an address in Brownsville, Pennsylvania, in April 1908 (see Figure 1.7). "The Indian with his pipe of peace

Figure 1.7 Leather postcard, April 1908. (Courtesy of the Mick Moloney Irish-American Music and Popular Culture Irish Americana Collection, Tamiment Library and Robert F. Wagner Labor Archives, New York University.)

has slowly passed away," the card reads. "But the Irishman with his piece of pipe has come prepared to stay." Irish success could be contrasted to supposed losers and perceived unassimilables of American society.

By 1911, when cigarette company Royal Bengals began producing its "Heroes of History" trading cards, Irish Americans were well on the way toward respectability in mainstream society. Irish heroes in the series include Irish nationalist patriots Charles Stewart Parnell and Daniel O'Connell and sports figures Tom Collins and George Gardiner; reverse sides are both biographical and list athletic feats and statistics, much like modern baseball cards. Here, Irishness is about moral and physical strength and perseverance. By 1900 approximately one-third of Major League Baseball players were of Irish origin.[19] Beyond sport, Joshua Brown suggests that Irish American participation in the labor movements of the 1880s helped dispel imagined racial characteristics and led to more realistic portrayals, for "signs of difference now settled on the new wave of immigrants from Italy and Eastern Europe," with physiognomic codes now more commonly applied to Italians and Polish, for example.[20] This has implications for the black image in the white mind. T. Thomas Fortune's encounter with the Hawaiian planter press in Chapter 3 shows the strong links between race making and labor needs; James Samuel Stemons, too, understood the importance of African American inclusion in unionized factory labor. African Americans' exclusion from labor unions and their segregation into different sporting leagues may have helped to freeze their "signs of difference" in circulated images of the time.

That the cards were designed for collecting recalls the "dances between people and things" and the meanings produced therein in Robin Bernstein's *Racial Innocence*.[21] Bernstein's "scripted things"—dolls, for example, or playing cards for the game "Uncle Tom and Little Eva"—issue a "culturally specific invitation" to their holders to perform actions and meanings.[22] In this vein, if postcards with Irish in-jokes tended to stop once they reached their particular destination, Irish trading cards had a life of longer movement. Such cards might circulate beyond an initial economic transaction, where one consumer received the card along with his or her purchase of a pack of cigarettes. The cards' own nomenclature offers an implicit suggestion: find other sympathetic collectors and trade one card for another. In Bernstein's formulation, the cards themselves might be said to "script" the circulation of Irish pride.

Ford would keep his attention on Irish portrayals in mainstream venues for his entire life. Irish of all political stripes and economic classes could unite behind campaigns to rid the stage of the insulting Irish brute or clueless Irish maid. Ford would use his own illustrators to depict more positive portrayals of the Irish or their allies in the *Irish World*, as shown in a later section. In the early stages of the *World*, however, Ford waded into much more contentious waters—that of labor radicalism and social reform, which brought him into conflict with other Irish American nationalists and their own newspaper presses.

A Transatlantic Land and Labor Movement

In the 1870s and through much of the 1880s, Ford sought to combine Irish nationalism with radical domestic social reform. To understand this time period, Kevin Kenny writes, "it is necessary to think of the American Irish in a trans-national setting, a single, complex and diverse Irish culture that existed simultaneously on both sides of the Atlantic Ocean."[23] Ford and his newspaper stood at this nexus; the *Irish World*'s masthead, with its twin globes and juxtaposed scenes of Irish countryside and metropolitan America, depicts these transatlantic ties. But other Irish American activists had their own ideas of who the Irish were and what they stood for—and many of them had their own newspapers.

Three major and competing strains of Irish American nationalism existed in the late 1870s. The revolutionary Fenians, who had launched several abortive raids on Canada shortly after the Civil War in an attempt to hurt Great Britain, had by the late 1870s become overshadowed by the secretive Clan na Gael, founded in New York City and led by John Devoy, strong-willed editor of the *Irish Nation* (1881–1885) and the *Gaelic-American* (1903–1928). (A leader of the Fenians, New York–based Jeremiah O'Donovan Rossa, was himself the editor of a newspaper, the *United Irishman*.)[24] In 1877 the Clan bound itself to the Irish Republican Brotherhood in Dublin. A more popular but far less militant strain than these "physical force" nationalists was the constitutionalism of Charles Stewart Parnell (1846–1891) and his mass Catholic movement for home rule, which sought constitutional autonomy rather than complete independence for Ireland.[25] Finally, there were the radical social reformers, chief among them Michael Davitt in Ireland, who would visit New York in 1878 on a successful fund-raising tour, and Patrick Ford in New York.[26] These activists combined concerns with land ownership and labor rights in both America and Ireland with their quest for Ireland's independence.

In the first two or three years of the *World*, Ford did not seem particularly focused on labor or on social issues aside from negative stage and pen portrayals of the Irish. After the depression of 1873 and into the 1880s, however, Ford's sympathy for the working class comes through strongly in the *World*. He was particularly concerned that repression in 1877 against the Molly Maguires—a secretive group of coal miners in Pennsylvania's Schuylkill region who fought violently against mine owners—would fall on Irish Americans as a whole. A Pinkerton detective had tied the group to the Ancient Order of Hibernians, an Irish American fraternal and aid organization. When eleven men, allegedly members of the group, were hanged on June 21, 1877, Ford doubted they received a fair trial or even whether the Molly Maguires existed at all. If the men were indeed guilty, Ford asked, what caused them to commit the crimes? "The grinding tyranny of the coal ring!" he answered. "Drive a rat into a corner and he will fight back."[27] As tough times for workers continued and massive strikes by railroad workers in 1877 rocked the nation, Ford became increasingly concerned with the lives of workers. He denounced an economic order of railroad barons, "coal rings," and other business interests that tyrannized laborers.[28] In rejecting a militia law in Illinois that he said forbade workingmen in Chicago from marching with muskets, he went as far as to hint at armed resistance: "There might arise circumstances in which the ballot-box would need support of the cartridge box."[29]

In the final weeks of December 1878, Ford added "and American Industrial Liberator" to his newspaper's masthead. In an article titled "The Irish World's Sub-Head," Ford reprinted the "outline" of a conversation he had with a friend who wished the *World* had a name that sounded "more American." When Ford objected, "Is not the Irish World a good enough American paper?" the friend insisted that it was one of the best American papers in the country but that too many were missing its excellent coverage of "the Money Question and the Labor Question" because they thought the *World* must deal only with "Ireland and sad Irish news." Ford claimed that "many others have spoken and written to the same effect" and agreed to add the subhead. "How do you like it, reader? How does our subhead satisfy you?"[30]

It would take the continued threat of famine to solidify the different strains of Irish nationalism into what was dubbed the New Departure. Two successive crop failures in Ireland in 1879 threatened another great famine and increased agitation among farmers for decreases in rents, and Davitt's organizing led to the Land League, which the constitutionalist Parnell headed and which demanded a halt to evictions and "the land for the people"—the institution of laws to enable Irish tenants to fairly purchase the land they worked. Parnell's 1879–1880 trip to the United States to raise funds for the Land League was a huge success—he gathered $300,000—and Ford "found himself at the vanguard of a radical movement headed by Michael Davitt on one side of the ocean and the trade union movement of New York City on the other."[31] In January 1881, Ford declared, "Every wage slave in America—every workingman—has a direct and vital interest at stake in this movement. Liberate the soil and you liberate the loom and the forge. Destroy the occupation of the landlord in Ireland and you sound the doom of the factory lord of America.... The cause of the poor tenant in Donegal is the cause of the factory slave in Fall River."[32] Such rhetoric and Ford's and Davitt's friendship with radical economist Henry George and adoption of a plan to eliminate private land ownership in Ireland brought backlash, however, from conservative clergy, who objected to what sounded like socialism, and from Devoy and other Irish nationalists, who feared that the primacy of Irish independence was being sacrificed on idealistic altars of social revolution. Conservatives cut Ford out of the loop, attempting to channel all Land League funds directly to counties in Ireland. Ford formed his own group and raised $350,000 for the league, but the New Departure was all but over by 1882.[33]

Gauging Ford's Support

Kenny, in a discussion of the challenges posed to scholars when speculating on the sensibilities of historical groups such as the Irish, cautions historians to resist taking the views of elite nationalists and their publications as a stand-in for those of their whole group, especially the poor and minimally literate. "Themes of banishment, exile, and regeneration can certainly be found in the Irish American ethnic press and in popular literature and culture," Kenny writes, but "projecting onto the mass of ordinary migrants such a conception, especially a transnational identification with Irish settlers elsewhere," may be a mistake.[34] Ford's fund-raising efforts, through campaigns in the newspaper, may provide one way of gauging among ordinary Irish Americans the depth and scope of identification with Ford's solidarities and viewpoints.

Ford's ability to raise significant funds for physical force nationalism in Ireland in the mid-1870s and, during the New Departure, for the Land Leagues in the late 1870s and early 1880s, demonstrates that many ordinary Irish Americans did indeed identify with Ford's transatlantic sympathies and political views. In 1876 Ford headed the Skirmishing Fund, which would raise money for armed conflict, including dynamite bombings of British targets.[35] The *World* frequently pitched readers to send in money and regularly listed recent contributors. A Skirmishing Fund column in March 1877 is typical, listing donations from groups called the Trans-Atlantic Club and the Skirmishing Sons of Liberty, from the Wisconsin towns of Trimbelle and Ellesworth, respectively. "We have not forgotten the artificial famine of '48, or the men judicially murdered," wrote Bernard Casey of Trimbelle. "[Fifteen dollars] to aid in demolishing the broken arch of London bridge," wrote Michael O'Shea of McAlister, Indiana. Most listed donations were three dollars or less, often just one dollar.[36] Eric Foner has examined Ford's Land League lists in the *Irish World* and determined that here, too, working-class support was widespread for Ford's fund-raising.[37]

Ford in the 1890s and Beyond

In broad outline, historians agree on the factors influencing Ford's move away from militant support for labor and land reform in the 1880s. After the Haymarket Affair in 1886, when a dynamite bomb thrown by someone in the crowd during a labor protest killed several police and reinvigorated a nativist backlash, Irish Americans risked being associated with anarchists and a "foreign element." Ford began to disfavor labor strikes and physical force nationalism in favor of parliamentary tactics.[38] Henry George's criticisms of the Catholic Church and his failure to support the tariff also dismayed Ford.

The extremely challenging economics of running a newspaper—a common complaint of almost all the editors mentioned in this book—could constrain race men in their activism. The same medium that amplified Ford's voice could also soften it; financial worries may have forced Ford to moderate his politics and search for patrons. Though the lack of personal papers for Ford makes it difficult to get behind the scenes at the *Irish World*, some insights can be gleaned from existing sources. The 1880s were a particularly rough time for Ford. John Devoy harangued him to repay a $12,000 loan attained years earlier from the Skirmishing Fund. Ford lost control of the paper briefly in 1883, and other investors claimed that they lost money and that Ford used fund-raising campaigns for Ireland fraudulently to support his newspaper. Patrick Meehan made such charges in his newspaper, the *Irish-American*; Ford denied it in editorials in his *Irish World*. The claims may have had some truth; James Rodechko reports that when Ford acted as a distributing agency for Henry George's *Progress and Poverty*, George received several complaints that Ford was mishandling money from sale of the book.[39] Ford neither ran many advertisements in the *World* nor used a family publishing company to print anything but the *World*. With his early circulation figures below fifty thousand in most of the 1870s, financial strain might be expected.[40]

Ford's solution was Republican Party patronage, starting in 1884. He was not alone among New York Irish nationalists. The Republican and Democratic Parties were in "unstable equilibrium" in the early 1880s, and Irish nationalists and reformers saw an opportunity to gain Republican patronage and influence in return for pulling enough Irish away from their longtime party, the Democrats, to allow Republican presidential candidate James G. Blaine to defeat Grover Cleveland in national elections. Ford, Devoy, and other Irish American nationalists aligned with the Republicans. Competing Irish American papers claimed Ford received anywhere from $24,000 to $50,000 from the party during and after the election. Cleveland won the election anyway, but many observers at the time thought the strategy would have worked had it not been for the remarks of a Presbyterian clergyman, the Reverend Samuel Burchard, who, with Blaine present, described the Democrats as the party of "rum, Romanism, and rebellion," a slight against the Irish that checked their move to the opposite party.[41]

It is also likely—but harder to trace—that Ford's positions relate in part to how he perceived the *Irish World*'s subscriber base. A strong labor position in the paper's early years would have matched New York City's Irish demographics. Though conditions after the 1846 famine improved in Ireland, most emigrants arrived in the city looking for unskilled, menial labor.[42] The majority of Irish drove horses, unloaded ships on the docks, hauled bricks (or hods) on constructions sites, served patrons in bars and restaurants, or cleaned houses and took care of children. Could such a group provide a significant portion of Ford's readership? It seems possible. By 1900, 95 percent of emigrants leaving Ireland were literate.[43] Furthermore, Ford surely observed New York's German American community and its response to labor unrest around the time he started the *World*. German piano makers joined a movement for an eight-hour workday in the spring of 1872; William Steinway responded by forming an employers' association and used the conservative *New Yorker Staats-Zeitung* to portray the workers as militant communists promoting class war. The *Staats-Zeitung* became the voice of New York's German middle and upper classes, but another paper, the *New Yorker Volkszeitung*, achieved success as the voice of New York's socialist movement. Its first editor had, like Ford, run an abolitionist press in the Civil War.[44]

At first glance, changing demographics suggest that there was no need for Ford to tone down his support for labor; by 1900 about 65 percent of New York's Irish were still unskilled or semiskilled workers. Yet the Irish were making economic progress, and an increasing number of foremen, engineers, firemen, conductors, carpenters, and electricians could be seen on the streets, railways, and worksites of the city. The Irish were drawn to journalism and other professions; in the 1890s the number of Irish white-collar professionals more than doubled, from 4.3 percent to 10.3 percent.[45] The Irish were becoming better integrated into American life, marked by their presence in show business and sports and the move of upper-working-class and lower-middle-class Irish from Brooklyn to Manhattan and the Bronx. Ford added a women's section to the paper in the 1890s, reduced the size of the labor section (which disappeared entirely in the early 1900s), and increased coverage of Church news. (Ford read Pope Leo XIII's 1891 encyclical *Rerum Novarum* with a different emphasis than Father Peter Yorke; he acknowledged the pope's support for labor unions but stressed that the gospel held the key to harmony between workers and bosses.)[46]

Whatever the combination of events, opportunities, and preexisting tendencies that contributed to Ford's movement away from advocacy of wide-ranging economic and social reform, the *Irish World* moved into the 1890s with no shortage of vitality and causes to rally behind. New causes meant new connections and sometimes new columns. The Irish world of the newspaper's title was still a global one, with affinities toward others who fought empire's treachery, wherever they might be. And an outward thrust of Irish identification might be balanced by a look to the past, a grounding in Irish history and language that could ensure that the tribe knew its roots.

A Gaelic Revival

Preservation of the Irish language seems a natural strategy for coalescing and promoting Irish American identity, especially for a community that many historians describe as viewing itself, at least until the twentieth century, as "exiled" in America.[47] Yet Ford expressed initial skepticism about initiatives to revive Gaelic, the Celtic language of Ireland and Scotland. Perhaps Ford sensed that promoting an aspect of an immigrant community's uniqueness risked marginalizing that community, the way that Catholicism estranged the Irish from mainstream American acceptance. Nevertheless, a Gaelic column became a long-running section of the *World* sometime after 1896.

In pre-famine Ireland (before 1845), about half the population could speak Irish; by the turn of the century that number was reduced to roughly 14 percent, with less than 1 percent claiming to speak only Irish. International economies of scale and their impact on traditional production—a shift away from tillage farming and an influx of factory-made goods—hit Irish-speaking districts such as Connacht and Munster particularly hard (nearly 70 percent of Irish immigrants in America at the turn of the century came from these two provinces, which together constituted only 42 percent of the Irish population). Ironically, the rapid loss of native Irish speakers from Ireland did not necessarily mean a concomitant increase in the United States; frequently, adults in Ireland were so adamant that their children learn English to increase their prospects for successful emigration that they refused to speak to them in their native tongue.[48]

Gaelic societies appeared in the United States decades before the Gaelic revival emerged in Ireland in 1893.[49] Letter writers to the *Irish World* debated the importance of maintaining the language in the United States. Ford himself doubted that many Irish Americans would learn Gaelic but supported its acquisition as a point of pride and self-esteem to help counter Anglo-Saxon claims of Irish cultural inferiority.[50] Notices in the *Irish World* for Gaelic study groups suggest that these societies were in large part social gatherings, isolated from each other and focused on entertainment along with language acquisition and practice.[51]

It was not until the late 1890s that Ford devoted an entire column to the language: "Our Gaelic World" and "Gaelic Notes." By this time the Gaelic revival had begun in Ireland. In these later years, the revival was linked to statehood for Ireland. "History shows that the revival of the language of a people precedes any permanent national re-awakening," claimed an announcement in the *Irish World* heralding a Gaelic League fund-raising drive in America. "No country altogether losing its language can hope to preserve its historic individuality.... [T]he future of the language is the future of the race."[52]

The Irish language was frequently linked to race in the *Irish World* and other publications. An article by the Reverend Thomas J. Shahan of the Catholic University of America described Gaelic as a kind of essence that held secrets of the race's history and character. "The Gaelic tongue is the oldest in Europe," he wrote in the *World*. It "contains the answers to a hundred perplexing problems," including the "origin of the nations of Europe" and the "nature of ancient law and institutions in the common Oriental land from whence we have all come." Gaelic, like its relative Sanskrit, Shahan wrote, was one of "the oldest forms of that mysterious Aryan speech which we once had in common." (By "Aryan," Shahan refers to speakers of the Indo-European language, not a racial group.) Shahan made it clear that he did not expect Gaelic to become widely used in America, only Ireland, and that the broader battle was to infuse English, which through "God's provenance" was "destined to be sovereign over more millions," with Gaelic's vitality. He was also concerned that other peoples were the experts in the Irish language, not the Irish themselves. The best Irish dictionary, Shahan lamented, was produced by a German; the best Gaelic journal was written in French—all "foreigners," Shahan wrote, "who are not of our blood and who cannot feel as we do upon this subject."[53]

Úna Ní Bhroiméil describes an Irish American dependence on a "transmuted ethnicity" rather than one received through a "daily ethnic way of life," which in turn may have ideologized language maintenance and attached it to other Irish American nationalisms.[54]

Cahenslyism and German American Catholics

Yet language use, because it draws boundaries and can exclude, by its nature divides as well as unites. Ford and other Catholic Irish American editors feared for the unity of their Church—and likely feared the power of German America—when Peter Paul Cahensly, an activist German merchant and immigrant to Minnesota, began pushing for German-speaking parishes and priests in the late 1880s. Cahensly and other German Catholics claimed that German immigrants were losing their Catholic faith and their children losing their language because of a lack of German-speaking priests, bishops, and teachers in the United States. At an 1888 meeting of German Catholic societies in Minnesota, Archbishop John Ireland, long favored by Ford, cracked down. Ireland announced that he was in no way against the continued use of German but advocated a home-based, not school-based, bilingualism: "Yes, speak the German language and teach it to your children. But . . . see that your children learn well, and speak well, the English language. . . . Through an exaggerated love of old habits and of Trans-Atlantic lands are you to forget the present and the future and reduce to social inferiority your sons and daughters?" By educating German children in schools in which German was predominant, German Americans would "push back [their] children in the race of life; keep them out of the higher professions, close to them legislative halls, narrow down their business prospects, for the sake of a land they have never seen and will never see." Ireland feared for Church unity—"confusion and chaos would reign"—if "all our separate nationalities had their separate clerical unions, and their separate conventions."[55]

Cahensly and other German Catholics kept up the pressure, petitioning the Holy See for national parishes presided over by priests of the same nationality and for in-language parish schools. They claimed that Ireland's plan for some state support for parish schools in St. Paul (the "Faribault Plan") was in fact an "Irish Plan" to eliminate the teaching of German and the German-language teaching of all subjects in German American parochial schools.[56]

The strength of the German American press is evident in the dispute over Cahenslyism. German-language newspapers, according to Ireland, were using the term "Americanization" as a disparagement. Some Catholic Germans, Ireland wrote, "hate America, and they hate me for being an American. It is difficult for one who does not follow the German Catholic newspapers to realize how fearfully foreign and un-American the leaders of Catholic thought among the Germans have been and are."[57]

In the 1890s, Ford ran several glowing portraits of Archbishop Ireland and hailed his defeat of Cahenslyism, which Ford described as a movement "favor[ing] the dissolving into distinct and separate branches the organization of the Church in America rather than to work in harmony with the spirit of American institutions for its unification and cosmopolitan harmony."[58] Here, Ford stressed American unity:

> The United States is not, and has not been for a century, a group of European colonies. It is a Nation, with a national spirit, national institutions, national unity, and a national population. Colonial disintegration is contrary to its instinct... so thoroughly is this American spirit of unity and nationality infused into the hearts of American Catholics that they would regard any seeming departure from that patriotic instinct as a grave and unfortunate calamity.[59]

The importance of language retention to the unity and self-worth of a people or "race" clearly garnered less sympathy among the English-speaking, Catholic hierarchy–dominating Irish if the strength of the (largely Irish) Catholic Church in America seemed in jeopardy.[60]

The Biases of Communication

Ford's attempt to balance forces of Irish American uniqueness, such as language, with a broad-based American nationalism may be reflected in the newspaper medium itself, which Canadian political economist and communications theorist Harold Innis thought of as a medium "biased" toward space: a communications technology that, through its ease of dissemination but relative lack of durability, facilitated communication over distance. Innis contrasted such media with others biased toward time, which tended to be durable and immobile, such as script in clay tablets or on stone monuments.[61] According to Paul Heyer's reading of Innis's work, time-biased media tend to "favor" an emphasis on custom, genealogical continuity, and the sacred; this "impedes individualism as a dynamic for innovation, but permits it to flourish in terms of expressive communication." Orality, therefore, had a time bias, and although Innis thought that Western society was far too space-biased, he also recognized the hierarchical, custom-bound nature of oral societies.[62]

Though such constructions have struck many academics as simplistic, deterministic, or contradictory, recent scholarship recognizes more complexity in Innis's work and to some extent that of his colleague Marshall McLuhan.[63] Menahem Blondheim, for example, defends Innis as not contradictory and not a technological determinist. He responds to Innis's apparent contradiction with the oral medium—Innis saw it as time-biased, but spoken words seem the least durable of all media—by showing how the effervescence of oral communication biases forms of preservation that stress the internalization, repetition, and transmission of the message: "Precisely the limitations on the durability of oral knowledge bind and bias an oral society to its past."[64] Blondheim interprets Innis as saying that "if a socio-political system is shaped to be effective in its control over, say, space, its problem becomes time; it is threatened by discontinuity through time." By contrast, time-biased systems with time-binding media in place may focus on expanding the reach of their communications through space. A bias generates "a counter-bias as a corrective, in the cause of equilibrium."[65]

From this perspective, many of the *Irish World*'s initiatives make sense. The dislocations of the Irish might require knitting together through both time and space. The masthead, naturally, suggests the newspaper's attempt to connect Ireland and the United States through space. Ford's transnational (space-biased) identifications with victims of empire are "balanced" by time-biased, custom-bound considerations: calendars tied to Irish history, an Irish-language column with some Irish script. The phenomenon of time and space biases is reflected in the Church's approach to media (studied more in-depth in Chapter 2); while the Church was excited about the Catholic press and its ability to spread the faith, it feared an empowered, individualistic priesthood, loss of continuity with dogma, and weakened hierarchical control.

"News" from Ireland

The news format itself allowed Ford throughout his tenure at the *World* to lend a certain fact-based authenticity to his interests and viewpoints. Through the framework of newspaper sections, including letters to the editor, calendars of Irish history, and news dispatches from other U.S. states and from Ireland, Ford was able to give favored activist movements and political perspectives a certain currency.

In an "Irish World Calendar" column, days of the week would be matched with the same month and numerical day from particular years past to bring the reader short descriptions of British outrages, Irish patriot actions, or world events. An entry for January 13 might include "Slavery Abolished in Mexico, 1825" and "O'Connell's First Speech against the Union, 1800."[66] Ford's "Answers to Correspondents" column allowed him to stress Irish American political positions and pride. To Terrence Walsh of Montreal, Ford replied, "We have no disposition to question your sincerity. Many others, too, think with you, that the moral-suasion policy is best for Ireland, and that that country might get along very well under 'liberal English laws.' We are not of such. We are thoroughly satisfied that no 'laws' made in London can ever suit the Irish nation." And to Mary in Boston, "It is quite allowable for your mistress to dictate to you in household affairs; but she has no right to throw obstacles in the way of your attending your religious duties."[67] Naturally, Ford was inclined to select letters that engaged his special concerns for Irish America.

"News from Ireland" often corresponded to particular movements Ford was engaged with at the time. In July 1890, a letter from John MacPhilpin, editor of the *Tuam News* (County Galway) on the "Irish Type Fund" was printed on the front page in a column format. MacPhilpin wrote that the Irish language was making progress in national schools and thanked specific contributors to a Gaelic column in the *News* that would soon be printed in Irish characters. "English letters and English accent, however grand they may appear to some, are, to say the least, quite un-Keltic, and therefore most unfit to display the natural grace and energy of the Irish language," MacPhilpin wrote.[68] A few months later, the Irish news section of the *Irish World*, now called "Tidings from the Old Country—Recent Happenings in the Various Towns and Countries throughout Ireland," printed a news item about efforts by the same editor (now spelled "McPhilpin") to get the Tuam town commissioners to print advertisements of the board in both English and Irish. Even without reference to the activist tone of the item—"No wonder the Irish language is dying out. This is a public example of how it is treated in private"—it seems clear that the unsigned listing was submitted by McPhilpin himself.[69] This does not disqualify it as "news" but demonstrates how the journalistic medium and its airs of neutrality and simple observation could impart a broader-based nature to what might have been, in fact, a small network or movement of like-minded Irish nationalists.

An objection could be raised that readers of newspapers in the nineteenth century did not possess any expectation of objectivity in the first place. The contemporary notion of objective news—and the concept itself has been under fire for a few decades, as philosophers and cultural theorists have emphasized the impossibility of perspectives uncolored by subjectivity—took time to develop in U.S. newspapers. But scholarship suggests that journalism in the late nineteenth century was expected to conform to relatively similar notions of fairness. Most journalism scholars agree that most

U.S. newspapers began to shed their strict political party orientation in the 1830s; the penny press might pride itself on its nonpartisan reporting. Other facets of more modern notions of "objective" journalism came into place during the nineteenth century; one scholar cites "balance" along with the inverted pyramid structure and "facticity"; another "impartiality."[70]

Ford appeared to regard the *Irish World* itself as a kind of diplomat of Irish America. In 1890 Ford realized than many of the Ireland-based papers in his newspaper exchange had not been receiving the *Irish World* for four or five years. He found through investigation that British officials had seized the *World*. Ford wrote that he was reluctant to contact the U.S. government about the matter for fear of appearing to use the issue to publicize his paper. Yet this was not a simple business matter but "a matter of law and of justice, involving the rights of a great nation." Ford implied that his newspaper's unimpeded circulation was an international issue—that the *World* was in a sense an organ of the United States.[71]

Ford and the Church

Ford described his break with Henry George as based around religion, and he would increase his coverage of religion into the 1890s. An important study of the late nineteenth-century Irish in Worcester, Massachusetts, describes the community's turn toward a more rigorous Catholicism, one that mirrored Protestant values of self-discipline and self-improvement and quelled much conflict between the two Christian faiths. (In this view, later, turn-of-the-century economic depression and a new influx of immigrants from Southern Europe then broke this uneasy truce between Protestantism and Catholicism.)[72] During this upswing of religious observance, Ford continued to write favorably about America's more liberal Catholic leaders. The *World* profiled Thomas Hecker's St. Paul parish in June 1895, noting positively Father Hecker's "innovation," "love of experiment and enterprise," and "Yankee touch" as well as his emphasis on publishing books and newspapers to spread the faith.[73] But Hecker and other American Catholics would come under increasing scrutiny from Rome, in large part because of their publishing efforts.

Also in 1895, the pope would release his encyclical *Longinqua* to the bishops and archbishops of the United States. The pope wrote in much the same vein regarding the press as he would four years later in *Testem Benevolentiae Nostrae*, the 1899 papal encyclical addressed to James Cardinal Gibbons of Baltimore that sought to rein in "Americanism," the more liberal American Catholicism that stressed individuality and press freedoms. In *Longinqua*, the pope was optimistic about the press's ability to do good and concerned about its potential for evil. He admonished Catholic writers "who waste their strength by discord" and who criticized the Church. "The bishops," he wrote, "placed in the lofty position of authority, are to be obeyed, and suitable honor befitting the magnitude and sanctity of their office should be paid them."[74]

Ford's response to *Longinqua* demonstrates the tricky position Irish American editors were in with respect to the Church. One section of the encyclical in particular concerned Ford. The pope had written that although he celebrated the "equity" of law in the United States, which had helped the Church to grow, "it would be very erroneous to draw the conclusion that in America is to be sought the type of the most desirable status of the Church, or that it would be universally lawful or expedient for State and Church to be, as in America, dissevered and divorced." In fact, the Church would grow stronger still in the United States, the pope wrote, if, "in addition to liberty, she enjoyed the favor of the laws and the patronage of the public authority."[75]

Ford, writing in the *World*, feared that "anti-Catholic bigots" would read these words from the pope and conclude that the pontiff was conspiring "to establish a union between Church and State" in the United States.[76] "While there is no possibility of such a union in this country," Ford wrote, "there is no doubt that if Catholic teachings molded our legislation great benefits would accrue to the country."[77] The pope's words were ambiguous enough to require clarification from Catholic Irish American editors, who, when writing about the pope, had to tread a careful line, preempting nativist arguments while taking care not to cross the pontiff. A week before, when printing for his readers the entire encyclical on the front page of the *World*, Ford also printed a speech by Francesco Satolli, an apostolic delegate to the United States. Satolli, speaking at the Gridiron Club in Washington, D.C., praised the press as a kind of fourth estate that kept government in check, hailed journalists as engaged in "high and noble work," and even called the press "a kind of social priesthood."[78] High-ranking Catholics in the United States and the Vatican did, it would seem, remain optimistic about the power of Irish newspapers to spread the one true faith. (Unlike Father Yorke, Patrick Ford seems to have not written in his newspaper about *Testem Benevolentiae Nostrae*.) But the Church would have more trouble with Father Peter Yorke (see Chapter 2), whose outspokenness in his newspaper ventures troubled the Catholic hierarchy in San Francisco.

Ford and Race

At first glance, Ford appears to remain staunch in his espousal of racial egalitarianism throughout his tenure at the *Irish World*—a marked contrast to Father Yorke and other Irish Americans on the West Coast and in many ways a departure from the history of Irish Americans and race in the United

States. Scholars have long examined Irish American and African American relations, finding both cooperation and conflict. However much scholars debate how "white" the Irish were considered, or sought to be, most conclude that the Irish distanced themselves from African Americans throughout the nineteenth century to ease acceptance into mainstream society. Whether the transatlantic Irish movement to repeal the parliamentary union between Ireland and Great Britain fizzled as a result of Daniel O'Connell's repeated calls for abolition or broke apart only after his fiery 1945 speech in which he allied Ireland and Great Britain against the "American eagle,"[79] an attempt to "construct an Irish identity that required opposition to slavery and other forms of oppression as one of its essential components" had failed at midcentury.[80] Vicious Irish-led antidraft and anti-black riots in New York City in 1863 and Irish American political machines and their control of civil service positions such as fire and police enhanced Irish America's position as a key enforcer of a white racial order. Some scholars believe Irish cultural traits that helped make them targets of British oppression worked in their favor across the Atlantic:

> The very qualities of the "mob" that led to [the Irish] being despised and discriminated against—their clannishness and their readiness for violence, their loyalty and organizational capacities—were nonetheless the very ones that enabled them to play a foundational role in both the construction of America, and in its policing. . . . Considered "not yet ready" for citizenship in Britain, in the United States they exercised their organizational strength to contain, on behalf of a white racial state, a Black population regarded as *never to be ready* even after their formal emancipation.[81]

Obviously, such broad overviews miss important alliances and affinities between the Irish and nonwhite races. Throughout the 1890s, Ford would still mention with reverence the legacy of his former mentor, William Lloyd Garrison, and give much coverage to Garrison's namesake son, who also spoke for racial justice and anti-imperialism.[82] "Leaving out the Indians, the veritable Americans . . . there are the Anglo-Americans, the Franco-Americans, the Irish-Americans, the Spanish-Americans, the German-Americans, and the African-Americans," Ford wrote in the summer of 1871.[83] The newspaper's editorials typically condemned lynching without hesitation, particularly in the 1890s.[84] The *Irish World* even once hinted that Southern governors who failed to provide protection to African Americans fleeing lynch gangs—notably Governor Benjamin Tillman of South Carolina, who had sent John Peterson, a black man who fled to the statehouse for protection, back to his hometown to face the mob—might be made accessories to murder.[85] Ford called lynching "terrorism" and wrote that if "every man who takes part in lynching were regarded and treated as a murderer it would be a good beginning" in the fight against mob rule.[86]

Ford tried to address Chinese exclusion without the rampant racism expressed by many West Coast Irish. He explained that his support for Chinese exclusion was "not because of the color of the Chinaman's skin, nor because of his language, or his religion," but because the Chinese were brought into the country "virtually as bond slaves" by large, moneyed interests. Racial hostility to the Chinese, he insisted, was "unchristian, undemocratic, and uncivilized."[87]

Imperial moves at the turn of the century brought a new emphasis on race and religion, as the Irish suspected something particularly Protestant about American uplift efforts abroad.[88] Historian Stuart Anderson sees the late 1890s through the early 1900s as a period when "American Anglophobia" and British condescension toward the United States gave way to friendlier relations, powered by the doctrine of Anglo-Saxonism. Many scholars, leaders, and commentators of the time held that the civilization of the English-speaking nations was the most advanced, "largely due to the innate racial superiority of the people who were descended from the ancient Anglo-Saxon invaders of Britain." The superior characteristics of the "Anglo-Saxon race" were both biologically and culturally determined and included "industry, intelligence, adventurousness, and a talent for self-government."[89]

Ford and others in the Irish American press attacked these notions with a passion. "'Anglo-Saxon,' Humbug," read a typical headline in the *Irish World*. "The Hyphenated Term 'Anglo-Saxon' Has no Proper Application to American People or to Anything American." Those who used the term "deliberately invite a division among 70,000,000 of Americans on racial lines.... German-Americans have already formed a national organization for the purpose of teaching a necessary lesson to the Anglomaniacs. Irish-Americans ought not be behind our German-American friends in this good work."[90] Under the headline, "Wanted—a Definition," the *World* laughed off an attempt by a Protestant minister who suggested that "Anglo-Saxon" referred to anyone who used the English language. The "8 million negroes of the South ... our colored brethren" would be surprised to learn "that the 'Anglo-Saxon' blanket can be so stretched as to cover them too."[91]

Ford's fight against imperialism and Anglo-Saxon notions of American racial identity brought in many nonwhite peoples as potential allies. The *Irish World* scoffed at any association between British rule and liberty: "There are no good spots in England's treatment of conquered peoples—it is blood-red and unmerciful throughout Ireland, America, India and South Africa."[92] In an editorial sarcastically titled "'Civilizing' the Filipinos," Ford wrote, "If your skin is not white and you do not belong to the 'Anglo-Saxon race' you are entitled to no consideration."[93] When during the Philippine-American War much of the U.S. press did an about-face on Filipino leader Emilio Aguinaldo—describing him as dignified and intelligent when he was fighting the Spanish and treacherous and weak when war broke out between Filipino rebels and U.S. troops—Ford remained positive toward him throughout the war and its aftermath.

New scholarship stresses transnational, multiracial identities stemming from Irish nationalists' battles against imperialism. Cian McMahon is careful to list anti-black and anti-Amerindian Irish Americans such as John Mitchel and Thomas Francis Meagher alongside racial egalitarians such as Ford, John Boyle O'Reilly, and James A. McMaster. He notes that, "sticking up for the Maori carried few political liabilities for people living thousands of miles away." But to McMahon it is important that the Irish, particularly the Young Irelanders of the mid-nineteenth century, "situated their Celtic identity in a transnational context."[94] The Irish may indeed have helped to expand modern parameters of citizenship and identity, as McMahon contends. But Chapter 2's focus on Father Peter Yorke shows that, on the West Coast of North America, some working-class Irish were key participants in the creation of transnational identities exclusive to white people.

Furthermore, in addition to the Irish encounter with Asians and the labor competition that inspired transnational white working-class nationalisms, in the domestic fight against the notion of America as an Anglo-Saxon nation, race pluralism might also stop at white ethnic borders. "We repudiate any suggestion that American civilization or progress is materially indebted to any supposed Anglo-Saxon element in our composition," said a former president of the American-Irish Historical Society, as reported in the *World*. "On the contrary, we assert that all European nationalities have contributed to our advancement and magnificent citizenship."[95] Ford's editorials often included "African-Americans" or "Afro-Americans" in this American family, but reports he reprinted from other presses frequently did not.

The *Irish World* and British and American Imperialism

Examination of the Irish American press's response to the South African (or Boer) War and the Philippine-American War reveals political, racial, and religious tensions in American citizenship; we return to the Philippines in Chapter 2 to examine the Irish American press's power to shape educational policy there. Ireland's impassioned fight against British rule meant Irish American editors often expressed sympathy and sometimes outright solidarity with indigenous populations suffering the depredations of British or other European imperial aggression worldwide. When Great Britain declared war on Paul Kruger's Transvaal Republic in October 1899, ostensibly to protect British settlers, the Irish press issued a call to arms to defend the Dutch Boer in southern Africa. "Freedom's Fight Begun in Africa," the *Irish World* announced at the start of the war.[96] Starting in late 1899, Ford reprinted for several months at the top of the *World's* editorial page (under the headline "Ho for the Transvaal!") a list of ports and steamers that Irish American volunteers could use to travel across the Atlantic to southern Africa to join the fight.[97] Seeing parallels to Irish history, Ford and other Irish American editors admired the rural existence of the Boer and juxtaposed that life against "capitalist" aggression.[98] When a British general suggested that England was fighting the Boers to protect not only British settlers but also the Boers themselves (from black revolt), the *Irish World* responded in disbelief: "Those who have read the history of the English in Ireland need no prompters to tell them what all this British fear of a black outbreak against the Boers means! We have of the numberless Mullaghmasts [a sixteenth-century massacre of Irish clan leaders by a British army] to which Irish chieftains were invited," only "to be murdered, while their pious British conferees were saying grace!"[99]

But Ford and others in the Irish press were also quick to draw parallels between U.S. history and the Boers' struggle. The *Kentucky Irish American* compared the Boers to patriots in the American Revolution in an extended analogy. The South African War was "beginning to assume the features of the American Revolution in its second year," with both the Boers and the American patriots of the past harrying British troops, "defeating or eluding pursuers, disappearing and then bobbing up always stronger."[100] By comparing the Boers to both Irish rebels and American patriots, Irish American editors laid claim to a key aspect of U.S. identity: the right to self-government. Irish Americans, united as a group around this principle, expressed essential American principles when they threw their support behind the Boers as well as when they advocated Irish independence. Irish newspapers, with their frequent columns praising the independence heroes of the past, provided a space to make Old World nationalisms empower New World identities.[101]

Ford employed illustrations in the *World* to drive home these points. Boer fighters, his newspaper asserted, were "like our Minute Men of '76" (Figure 1.8). Frequently drawn with beards, guns, and formal attire, they tend to resemble the *Irish World*'s many illustrated profiles of Irish nationalists of old. One illustration in particular combines elements of American and Irish history and mythology: a portrait of South African Republic leader Paul Kruger, his profile stamped onto a coin, evoking the origins of republicanism (Figure 1.9). Small drawings in the corners depict scenes of life in the Transvaal; many illustrations in the *Irish World* stress the working of the land by the Dutch Boer, aligning with America's veneration of the yeoman

Figure 1.8 Illustration depicting Dutch Boer fighters, from *Irish World*, April 12, 1902.

Figure 1.9 Illustration of South African Republic leader Paul Kruger, from *Irish World*, December 9, 1899.

farmer. Even the depiction of Johannesburg, though not especially detailed, could pass for parts of Dublin, with its tall stone buildings and wide streets.

The images show Ford's ability through his newspaper to assign the iconography of democracy across disparate cultures—Irish, Dutch Boer, ancient Rome—to claim solidarities against common enemies and emphasize Irish American belonging. Yet the absence of Africans, in both text and image, in Irish American coverage of the South African War suggests whiteness is an important bridge or principle of inclusion across these differences. In the South African War, Irish American editors' commitment to indigenous peoples worldwide faltered. When a British general suggested that England was fighting the Boers in part to protect the Boers from black revolt, the *Irish World* was right to respond cynically. But the *World*'s take on race relations in southern Africa was itself highly dubious. "There will be no black uprising," the paper wrote, "although we see no reason why the Boers . . . should not invite the black man, who in five cases out of six trust the Boer rather than the British, to fall in and do his portion of the fighting."[102] Other Irish American newspapers portrayed southern Africa's indigenous population as more akin to enemy than ally. Rather than examine Boers' brutality toward black Africans, Irish journalists sometimes stressed longtime British collusion with nonwhite "savages." The *Pilot* wrote that British colonial secretary Joseph Chamberlain "threatens to arm and enlist the African savages against the Boers" and that British politician A. J. Balfour "goes him one better by suggesting the use of barbarous Sikhs and Ghoorkas from India for the same purpose."[103] Irish nationalist and feminist Maud Gonne, on a U.S. speaking tour, claimed that the English had armed black Africans, "and these savages had outrage [sic] Boer women."[104] The anti-British element of Irish American identity raised the Boer to the status of near-saint and trumped other possible alignments.

U.S. imperial moves at the turn of the century did not, initially, draw such heated criticism from the Irish American press. In April 1898, the United States declared war on Spain, ostensibly to help Cubans in their uprising against the Spanish, after the suspicious sinking of the U.S.S. *Maine* in Havana's harbor and much agitation for war among the public and press. The next month, across the world, U.S. admiral George Dewey destroyed the Spanish fleet in Manila Bay and prepared to attack Manila. President William McKinley claimed that, in response to this rash move, he was forced to find the Philippines on a map and later prayed to God for guidance on what to do with the new possessions. McKinley's solution was "benevolent assimilation," which he described as official U.S. policy toward the Philippines in December 1898, after the Treaty of Paris earlier that year ended the Spanish-American War (the United States would pay Spain $20 million for the possession of Guam, Puerto Rico, and the Philippines). McKinley took pains to instruct military officers to "win the confidence, respect and affection" of Filipinos by "assuring them in every possible way that full measure of individual rights and liberties which is the heritage of free peoples." This would "prov[e] to them that the mission of the United States is one of benevolent assimilation, substituting the mild sway of justice and right for arbitrary rule."[105] Cartoonists responded with images of Uncle Sam or McKinley as schoolmasters, adoptive parents, or disciplinarians bringing new, wayward children—Hawaii, Puerto Rico, and the Philippines—into the American fold.[106] As explored further in Chapters 2 and 3, Irish Americans and African Americans would have much at stake in U.S. efforts to school Filipinos.

The Irish American press, overall, viewed Cuba as a righteous fight, identifying Cuban rebels as freedom fighters like the Irish. The *Catholic Citizen* was an exception, sympathizing with the rebels but recoiling at the anti-Catholic rhetoric in relation to Spain that the war produced domestically. James Jeffrey Roche of the Boston *Pilot* was among the most ardent supporters of the war in Cuba—until Spanish forces were defeated and it looked as if U.S. troops might be staying for good. Ford's *Irish World* was lukewarm, developing an "Ireland First" take on the war.[107]

Across the Pacific, Filipinos revolting against Spanish rule were allies with the United States for a time. After Spanish surrender, however, a tense standoff between U.S. troops and Filipino rebels outside Manila exploded into fighting on February 4, 1899, and the United States began battling Filipino revolutionaries on the archipelago in a brutal war that would kill 4,165 U.S. troops and as many as 20,000 Filipino combatants and 750,000 civilians.[108] (President Theodore Roosevelt would declare fighting over on July 4, 1902, though armed resistance to the United States would continue until 1913, particularly on southern islands.) The Irish press by now was, overall, strongly against annexation, sometimes siding directly with Filipinos and fearing that the United States was being tricked by Great Britain into a confrontational quagmire with China in the Pacific.

As the confrontation escalated, discussion in the Irish American press quickly turned to the preservation of the Philippines' Catholic character and institutions. U.S. censorship of news in the Philippines could not prevent the leakage of reports of U.S. Army desecration of the islands' Catholic churches. "Outraging a People's Religion," the *Irish World* screamed in September 1899, with the subhead, "United States Army Officers, Graduates of West Point, Ruthlessly Trample upon Sacred Things."[109] The article describes a church altar turned into a makeshift telegraph station. Ford ran an illustration along with the article, assuring readers that it closely matched the photo from which it was drawn.

Though Ford remained against U.S. occupation of the Philippines—unlike, for example, liberal archbishop John Ireland, who worked with American authorities to smooth the withdrawal of Spanish clergy from the island[110]—anti-imperialist sentiments in the *Irish World* coexisted with pro-Catholic viewpoints that might lend support to imperial projects. When Philippine rebel leader Emilio Aguinaldo was captured and armed resistance died down significantly, debate in the Irish American press shifted to how the U.S. should administer these lands, and here many Irish American editors asserted that the nation could learn much from Catholic nations and their experience of colonialism. When some Protestant missionaries sneered at what they called the dark legacy of Spanish colonization in Latin America and the Philippines, Irish American editors turned this on its head, claiming that America had much to learn from Catholicism when it came to administering foreign peoples. "Can the Indian Be Civilized?" one heading in the *World* asked. "Catholicity Is the Only Agency Capable of Solving the Indian Problem." The article, by "Father de Smet," is typical of many in the *Irish World* and the Irish American press. It defended the humanity of the indigenous, especially against the depredations of Protestant explorers and missionaries, but did so within the racialized discourse of savagery and civilization of the time. Father de Smet praised Christopher Columbus as a "missionary bearer of peace and truth" and the Catholic church as a force that "cured [Amerindians in South America] of their natural indolence and depraved habits."[111] Ford's own editorials tended to be significantly less derogatory in their description of the indigenous, who still, however, might need civilizing. In the Philippines, Ford wrote, the Catholic Church had "succeeded so well that the natives are thoroughly civilized instead of being wiped off the face of the earth" as in Hawaii, because of Protestant missionaries.[112] As long as American nativists threatened to regard Catholics as less than fully American, Catholicism needed shoring up, and thus Ford and other Irish American editors were pulled into defending the Church's past. Inevitably, that meant at least some embrace of a racialized, civilizing mission. A sustained, searching, and intellectually consistent critique of imperialism—consistent across geography and time—seemed impossible for Ford and other Catholic editors.

Domestically, Ford and some other Irish American editors continued to defend African Americans and denounce lynching. In the late 1890s and early 1900s, lynching was increasingly spoken about in the *World* in terms of its violation of moral law.[113] But Ford went farther, drawing connections between lynching and imperialism. He found it "more than a coincidence that lynchings have become more frequent than ever since the inauguration of the policy of imperialism, which inspires a feeling of contempt for that sort of human equality proclaimed by the Declaration of Independence."[114] In Boston the *Pilot*'s editor James Jeffrey Roche echoed Ford's analysis. Two of the nation's largest Irish American papers were loudly antiracist and anti-imperialist and could draw connections between the two.

Another headline asked, "Reaping What We Sowed—Does American Lawlessness and Barbarity Abroad Not Increase American Lawlessness and Barbarity at Home?"[115] When Sam Hose was lynched near Atlanta, Georgia, in April 1899—a barbaric murder that, as Chapter 3 shows, Filipino rebels tried to use to spark defections of black U.S. troops—Ford included an angry subheading in an article on Hose: "And We Are Carrying Civilization to the People of the Philippines."[116] But the *Irish World*'s commitment to full African American citizenship would falter in the early twentieth century, not directly through Ford, but through one of his most prolific columnists, Robert Ellis Thompson.

Thompson and Reconstruction's "Mistake"

Rodechko suggests that Patrick Ford held the *Irish World* firmly under his control: "When writers failed to express the changing attitudes of the paper, they were replaced by men more in sympathy with Ford's opinions."[117] It seems more likely that the *Irish World*'s growth and the addition of columnists meant that Ford lost some editorial command; columnists do not tend to stay at newspapers long if their leashes are too short. Some wiggle room surely existed at the *World*; Ford and Henry George always disagreed about the tariff, for example, and Thompson and Ford split briefly in the 1912 presidential election (Ford supported Roosevelt; Thompson went with Taft).[118] Thompson was born in Ireland in 1844, came to the United States at age thirteen, and graduated from the University of Pennsylvania in 1865, becoming an instructor there in 1868.[119] Despite his Ulster origins, he supported Irish nationalism. Thompson began writing for Ford in 1884 when he was a Presbyterian minister and professor of sociology and quickly became Ford's leading columnist, penning columns for more than twenty-five years.[120]

On the subject of empire, Thompson, like Ford, combined his faith with a staunch anti-imperialist stance. He announced in a column in early 1900, "The nation is the creation of the will of God, an empire the creation of the will of man seeking to destroy the work of God." Thompson felt that "in the fight against the evil tendencies President McKinley has introduced into our Government," those who stood against wars of empire might call themselves something other than "Anti-Imperialist." Instead of stressing "negation," Thompson wrote, why not stress positive truths and beliefs? "We stand for the rights of nations, which have been bestowed upon them by the Almighty God, and against wicked denial of those rights by any and every power on earth." The nation is the "great instrument of human advance," improving on the imperfect, tribal organization of "Family and Magistrate" that preceded it. Empire destroys this divine plan of nationhood; the Irish "know what harm have been done to the Irish mind and spirit by the alien rule of England... and they are desirous to save the Filipinos, the Boers, the Poles, the French Canadians and every other people from the same evils."[121]

When he turned his attention to the American South and lynch mobs, Thompson saw the lawlessness there as an outgrowth of the "perversion" of human relationships wreaked by slavery. Yet more trouble arose during Reconstruction, according to Thompson, for social equality for black Americans was "a blunder," and political equality was of "no use" to them. Legal equality, however, by which Thompson seemed to mean the right to a fair trial, was "indispensable" and something that the government must assure to African Americans if Southern states would not. Thompson went as far as to call for changing the Fifteenth Amendment so as not to "force the ballot into the negro's hand" but to "throw round every man, white and black, citizen and alien, the protection of just law justly enforced."[122] Thompson would compromise full African American citizenship for a more limited conception of rights in order to maintain order in the South.

Five years later, Thompson again expressed outrage at lynching but repeated his stance against black suffrage. In an article in the *Irish World* titled "Our Brother in Black," Thompson took to task Charles Darwin, Herbert Spencer, Thomas Carlyle, and Republican imperialists for lessening notions of "natural rights" and promoting instead a philosophy of might makes right, which hurt African Americans more than perhaps any other people in the world. After all, Thompson wrote, if America had "gone into the business" of "putting down and keeping down the Filipinos," why worry about a few lynch mobs "not more lawless than major Quinn and his fellows in Luzon?" But Thompson agreed that African Americans had shown cultural and moral "deterioration" since slavery, because of their separation from white society; they voted in lockstep for the Republican Party, "like a certain class of Irishman who must vote the Republican ticket forever."[123] The next year in another column, Thompson suggested that Southerners might end lynching if the Fourteenth and Fifteenth Amendments were repealed.[124]

Thompson repeated this theme in greater detail in his book *The Hand of God in American History*, published in 1902. In a quick recounting of U.S. history that periodically paused to note divine reward and retribution in the American past, Thompson addressed Reconstruction's failure. In Thompson's view, in the face of Southerners' attempts to reestablish something akin to slavery in the South, the Republican Party had lost Lincoln's faith that the war was God's plan and had pushed too hard and fast to secure African American voting rights and, by extension, their party's political standing, which was on shaky ground after the president's assassination. Lincoln, according to Thompson, would have proceeded more gradually and with more religious faith.[125]

Thompson's columns gave the impression that the *Irish World* was backsliding on support for African American rights. Through Thompson and his prominently displayed writing, the *World* had at least in part adopted a hierarchical and racialized vision of democracy that put African Americans at the bottom, in need of, or perhaps incapable of, further civilizing. Thompson's writings, at least to some degree, made the newspaper's decades-long campaign against "Anglo-Saxonism" less an expansion of American pluralism and more the securing of whiteness, of race-based privileges.[126]

Immigrant Nationalism and the American Fabric

A rich scholarship and active debate continues on the relationship between Irish nationalism—the assumption that the Irish are a nation that must gain independence from Britain—and broader themes in U.S. history, including race relations, class conflict, assimilation, and the creation of ethnicity.[127] Historian Thomas N. Brown would describe Ford's intellectual and political legacy in this way: Irish American nationalism was a response to the pressures put on immigrant Irish, including nativism; though its rhetoric could be radical, nationalism's aims were ultimately conservative. Irish Americans sought respectability, and as more and more transformed themselves into "lace-curtain" Irish, their radicalism waned.[128] Eric Foner has modified this view, positing that Irish American nationalism and Land League activism did indeed help the Irish assimilate into America—but not solely as respectable members of the middle class. Instead, through their identification with abolitionists such as Wendell Phillips and radical economists like Henry George, many Irish Americans like Ford sought to "transform their society even as they became a more integral part of it."[129] These views are not incompatible, of course; the Irish in America may have invigorated a labor movement and, through attention to British and U.S. imperial efforts and their victims across the globe, broadened conceptions of citizenship even as the Irish themselves moved toward more normative American viewpoints. Perhaps Ford's experience with Robert Ellis Thompson moves the scales back toward assimilation and consent, at least with respect to African Americans' loss of rights in the decades-long American toleration of Jim Crow, a kind of codified, regional apartheid. One factor in the waning of the more racially egalitarian views of some Irish nationalists could be their encounter with Protestant reformers and Progressives like Thompson, who seem to have used segregation as a kind of "shield" between groups to halt social discord that threatened their overall projects of reform.[130]

Ford's Irish nationalism was entwined with imagining an Irish American community and to some extent even inventing that ethnicity. "Much of what seems the venerable survival of ancient customs turns out to have been shaped or even created wholesale by nineteenth-century nationalists intent on establishing a pedigree for a certain cultural group," writes historian of technology David E. Nye, mentioning Scottish tartans, which did not represent clans until the 1800s. Central to this process, Nye says, are communication technologies: "Newly invented traditions are almost always disseminated and discussed through the media."[131] So many of the debates of Irish nationalists, the most prominent of whom often produced their own newspapers, had at their heart the maintenance and shaping of Irish American identity. Through the newspaper medium, however, they had to constantly calibrate their own notions of what was best for the Irish with the economics and social and ethical expectations of newspaper publishing. Subscribers and patrons had to be sought. Columnists could not, ultimately, be told what to write, and changing conditions in America brought new debates over what to maintain, heighten, contain, or leave behind from Irish culture. Ford and other publishers were negotiating, not controlling, Irish identity in America.

2

FATHER PETER YORKE

A Publisher-Priest in the Fault Lines of American Identity

The American people reads. Perhaps its reading is not deep, but it is wide; moreover, it is impartial. . . . Every fad, every humbug, every political measure, every social dream has its expounders, has its readers—why not the old Church that gave printing to the world? We hardly realize what a powerful engine the printing press is.
—Peter C. Yorke, *The Ghosts of Bigotry* (1894)

The priests of all future dispensations shall be members of the press.
—John Boyle O'Reilly, address to the Boston Press Club, November 8, 1879[1]

The Reverend Peter C. Yorke (Figure 2.1) left behind a huge amount of written material, from instruction manuals on Catholic education to fiery editorials in support of workers' right to strike to reprinted speeches advocating the expulsion of Chinese immigrants. A bold defender of the Church, Yorke carefully read papal encyclicals and translated them into marching orders for organized labor. Yet through the newspaper medium in particular, Yorke became a public figure in new ways, far beyond what he would have experienced as a more typical parish priest. He entered into political debates and issued immediate rejoinders against his adversaries. His criticism of state-sponsored education, which he felt was anti-Catholic, and his endorsement of some politicians over others led to his appointment to the board of regents of the University of California. His outspoken nature and public presence in San Francisco turned the city's Catholic hierarchy against him, but when pushed out of the editorship of the city's official Catholic Church publication, the *Monitor*, he started his own newspaper, the *Leader*, which was popularly accepted as the last word on Irish Catholic opinion in the city.[2] Yet in reading Yorke's writings, one is transported to a time when the Irish still felt embattled in their struggle for American belonging, fearing anti-Catholic bias, Progressive educational and urban reform, and the loss of decent wages for low-skilled work.

Figure 2.1 The Reverend Peter C. Yorke, early twentieth century. Photographic print. (Courtesy of Gleeson Library/Geschke Center, University of San Francisco.)

As with Patrick Ford, religion, not just race and class, was an important arena in Yorke's Irish advocacy. With Yorke, however, the intersection between race and religion was more pronounced. Much twentieth-century historiography avoided or neglected consideration of religion's powerful place in American life. This has changed rapidly over the last few decades.[3] Most recently, several new studies, many of them based on the U.S. West, place religion in alliance with race and class in the production of American citizenship.[4] In the West, particularly on the West Coast, one group of racial "others" that was used to help create a unifying whiteness was Asians, most prominently "heathen" Chinese. Notions of racial and religious superiority combined to produce a normative whiteness that could encompass, unite, and help make claims for full social and political rights for a diverse group of immigrants of European origin. Father Yorke participated passionately in the production of a white working-class identity, skillfully using the print medium to advocate for Irish Americans in San Francisco and sometimes using Asians as a foil for white labor solidarity and Irish American belonging.

Yorke's biographers tended to ignore his racism toward Chinese and Japanese and his bigoted but more paternalistic views of African Americans until the 1970s. Historian James Walsh discusses those views in some detail, using them to strike back at hagiographic depictions of Yorke and to cast him instead as an "ethnic militant" not above demagoguery in the operation of his own personal press. Walsh views Yorke's late-1890s campaign against the anti-Catholic APA as largely a media-created furor that the priest used to promote himself as an ethnic leader in a city not particularly known for hostility toward Catholics.[5]

Walsh's work corrects the idealized image of Yorke as a morally unimpeachable protector San Francisco's downtrodden. Yet he casts Yorke as part of a "relatively uncommitted intellectually and close-minded" Catholic leadership, his legacy itself "highly consistent with the intellectual history of American Catholicism."[6] Walsh faults Yorke for assuming that "Catholic doctrine, as he understood it, contained within its principles the solutions to all problems."[7] Historians will continue to debate the relative vigor of Catholic intellectual contribution in nineteenth- and early twentieth-century America.[8] But, for example, Yorke's discomfort with the educational agenda proposed by the largely Protestant reform movement around the turn of the century shows, in a long view of educational debates about standardization, pre-professionalism, and the role of the humanities, some prescience. His critiques of Progressive thought show a creativity that, while informed by his faith, do not adhere strictly to or flow automatically from Catholic doctrine. He took Pope Leo XIII's encyclical *Rerum Novarum*, for example, as a green light for vigorous labor activism and adapted it to his purposes. And while Walsh is surely right about Yorke's penchant for exaggeration and even demagoguery, Yorke's and other Irish Catholic editors' use of weekly presses to secure political change is impressive. Much history writing on journalism of the late nineteenth century focuses on the jingoistic, mainstream yellow press; the era can be misread as one in which industrialization and the birth of mass culture and consumption pushes out smaller newspaper weeklies. Yorke's experience, however, shows, no retreat into ethnic or religious ghettoization but rather an outward push that demonstrates that late nineteenth-century Irish media in combination had enough clout to change, for instance, U.S. educational policy in the Philippines. Yorke used the *Monitor* and the *Leader* to bring personal, Irish, and Catholic perspectives into public debate. Yorke and other Irish Catholic editors' embrace of the printed word in turn affected the priesthood and possibly even changed the faith itself.

An Early Battle against Anti-Catholic Bigotry

Peter Yorke was born on August 13, 1864, in Galway, an important commercial center in the west of Ireland. At age eleven he stopped his secular education and began to study for the priesthood in Tuam, in County Galway.

In 1882, at age eighteen, he entered the national seminary, St. Patrick's College in Maynooth, where he studied philosophy, theology, scripture, and Church history. He left for the United States in 1886 to complete his studies at St. Mary's Seminary in Baltimore. He was ordained there in December 1887 and assigned to the Archdiocese of San Francisco, arriving in early 1888. However, San Francisco's Archbishop Patrick W. Riordan soon sent him back to the East Coast for graduate studies in theology at the newly opened Catholic University of America in Washington, D.C. Yorke returned to San Francisco in 1891, became chancellor of the archdiocese in 1894, and served in a variety of parish positions in the Bay Area until his death on April 5, 1925.[9]

Yorke's first public battle, against local Protestant ministers associated with the APA, reveals a Roman Catholic priest using print journalism to counter anti-Catholic bigotry and assert Irish American citizenship. The APA began in Clinton, Iowa, in 1887 with Henry Bowers, who claimed a coalition of Roman Catholics had conspired to defeat him in the town's mayoral election. The APA sought to remove Catholics from political office and denounced Catholic institutions, especially Catholic schools. Often the organization portrayed itself as the protector of female innocence, allegedly in danger of corruption by Catholic priests or in Catholic group homes for girls and women convicted of crimes.[10] By the mid-1890s, the APA had at least half a million members in the Northeast, Midwest, and on the Pacific Coast.[11]

A school textbook published in 1894 sparked the APA fight in San Francisco. Archbishop Riordan deemed *Outlines of Medieval and Modern History*, adopted for use in city grade schools, to be anti-Catholic. Riordan tried to get the city's board of education to withdraw the book, and the APA responded with a flood of editorials in local papers decrying the influence of "Rome's Red Hand" on city schools. Riordan appointed Yorke editor-in-chief of the *Monitor*, by then the official newspaper of the Archdiocese of San Francisco, in the fall of 1894 and tasked him with defeating the APA.[12]

Yorke took up the charge, responding with biting editorials, demands that his adversaries reveal their sources for their supposed Catholic conspiracies, and lengthy theological debates. He went even further, having *Monitor* reporters clandestinely join local APA lodges. He then printed in the *Monitor* the APA's confidential lodge oath, lists of APA officers and members, and names of businessmen whom the APA was boycotting for their refusal to join the organization. He challenged the *San Francisco Chronicle*, which had printed numerous anti-Catholic sermons from APA-associated ministers, to publish his own lectures; when they refused he used the *Examiner*. When the *Examiner* tired of the controversy, declaring it would no longer print letters from either side, Yorke switched to the *Call*. When the

Examiner's readership then declined, the paper reversed its decision and printed a special supplement containing all the controversial lectures and debate and let Yorke respond in print to the latest APA lectures, often in the same issue.[13] Across the country in New York, Patrick Ford's *Irish World* noticed Father Yorke, naming the *Monitor* in 1895 "one of the principal and best-managed Catholic journals in America."[14]

How serious a threat to San Francisco's Catholics was the APA? Historian Joseph S. Brusher calls the APA a "lunatic fringe" denounced by respectable Protestants, including Reverends Washington Gladden, Lyman Abbot, and Elbert Hubbard.[15] The APA traded in conspiracy theories, circulating a bogus encyclical from Pope Leo XIII in which the pontiff called on Catholics to "exterminate all heretics found in the jurisdiction of the United States of America."[16] Walsh sees San Francisco as "unfertile ground indeed" for nativism; in 1900 a full third of the population was foreign-born, with the Irish, numbering about ninety-five thousand, making up the second-largest ethnic group after Germans.[17] Walsh estimates that Protestants could have been outnumbered in San Francisco by more than five to one. Thus, Yorke's beating back of the APA in San Francisco appears to be not much more than a media-created sensation.

In this book, however, the power of smaller late nineteenth-century presses to shape public opinion and effect policy is precisely the point and may be relatively unexplored compared to studies of the larger newspaper dailies. Historian Justin Nordstrom believes anti-Catholic print publications in the early twentieth century remain understudied and significant sources of anti-Catholic and, importantly, Progressive attitudes and thought. One nativist paper, the *Menace*, published in Aurora, Missouri, achieved a circulation of more than 1.5 million by 1915, dwarfing even the largest big-city newspapers of its time.[18] Yorke may have honestly feared a resurgence of anti-Catholic nativism similar to that of the mid-1800s, when Catholics and Protestants battled over the funding of public education. Anti-Catholicism, at least nationally, was still alive well into the twentieth century.

In any case, Father Yorke became famous for pushing back the APA in San Francisco; Cronin cites the end of the APA battle in the city as March 1896, when the last Protestant minister to oppose Yorke, Charles W. Wendte, withdrew from the controversy after he and Yorke had quarreled in a twenty-nine-letter debate that was printed in local newspapers. Across the country, Patrick Ford printed a letter in the *World* from "an old New Yorker, now resident in San Francisco," who proclaimed Yorke "another Father Burke" because of his APA victory. Thomas Nicolas Burke was admired by the Irish for his battles against British historian James Froude and his harsh justifications of British rule in Ireland. Irish American opposition to Froude's U.S. lecture tour in 1872 forced the historian to abandon it and return early to

England. Regardless of the level of threat, Yorke appeared to have vanquished a formidable foe.

At the close of the APA fight, Yorke published a series of lectures titled "The Ghosts of Bigotry," which provides an early hint of how he would use Catholic doctrine to suit his purposes and the tensions present between his public persona, his publishing, and his role as a Catholic priest. In "Ghosts," Yorke announced a "Catholic Truth Society" to explain the faith and combat lies about it. Yet he found it necessary to justify at some length how an empowered laity, promoting these Catholic truths, would not in fact conflict with the Church hierarchy. In Catholic theology, Yorke wrote, the task of preaching the gospel was given to the apostles and their successors, the bishops and the pope.[19] These figures decided who may preach the gospel, "but this oversight does not mean that there is not on each of us the obligation of making our religion known . . . on the laity, too, rests the duty of giving a reason for the faith that is in them." When the archbishop of the diocese organizes the laity into these truth societies, Yorke wrote, "there is no break with the traditions of the Church, nothing opposed to Catholic habits of thought."[20] To Yorke, Catholics had a responsibility to publish.

Labor, the Press, and the Pope: Yorke and *Rerum Novarum*

Though Yorke's position as a parish priest made his forays into public life tricky, his Catholicism could empower his reform efforts, not simply inhibit them. In fact, Pope Leo XIII's encyclical *"Rerum Novarum*: Rights and Duties of Capital and Labor," issued from Rome in May 1891, was reportedly the instigation and frame for Yorke's labor activism in the 1901 Teamsters' strike in San Francisco. The encyclical is a remarkable document of its time and is worth exploring briefly.[21]

The pope's support for labor and, importantly, labor unions, was clear and strong in *Rerum*. So was the Church's disdain for socialism. The pope began by sketching the era's trying times. Revolution was in the air:

> That the spirit of revolutionary change, which has long been disturbing the nations of the world, should have passed beyond the sphere of politics and made its influence felt in the cognate sphere of practical economics is not surprising. The elements of the conflict now raging are unmistakable, in the vast expansion of industrial pursuits and the marvellous discoveries of science; in the changed relations between masters and workmen; in the enormous fortunes of some few individuals, and the utter poverty of the masses; the increased self reliance and closer mutual combination of the working classes; as also, finally, in the prevailing moral degeneracy.[22]

In such an environment, the pope wrote, it was difficult "to define the relative rights and mutual duties of the rich and of the poor, of capital and of labor." In fact, "crafty agitators" were taking advantage of the times to "stir up the people to revolt." Instead, a remedy needed to be found for the "misery and wretchedness pressing so unjustly on the majority of the working class." The abolishment of "ancient workingmen's guilds" had left workingmen "surrendered, isolated and helpless, to the hardheartedness of employers and the greed of unchecked competition." The pope wrote bluntly that a tiny elite had burdened the masses of poor with "a yoke little better than that of slavery itself."[23]

It is here, the pope wrote, that socialists entered the fray, using the "poor man's envy of the rich" to their advantage and "striving to do away with private property" by transferring administration of wealth and land to the state. In a lengthy defense of private property, the pope wrote that those who worked the land should rightfully own the fruits of their labor; those who did not own or work directly on the land were connected to it and were paid for their labors through its riches.[24] Private property was in accord with the "laws of nature," including human nature. Furthermore, the pope wrote, socialists would destroy the family by letting the state intrude into the domestic sphere. And their utopian, earthly dreams were dangerous, for to "suffer and to endure ... is the lot of humanity." False promises to the poor would bring forth far worse evils. "Nothing," the pope declared, "is more useful than to look upon the world as it really is."[25]

Instead of anticipating endless conflict between capital and labor, the pope's vision was a cooperative one. Christian institutions could help the classes live in harmony and agreement; indeed, "if human society is to be healed now, in no other way can it be healed save by a return to Christian life and Christian institutions."[26] The state had a duty to protect private property and even break up organizations that sought to seize private property. But workingmen had a concomitant right to form unions; workingmen's unions, the pope asserted, were the "most important" method to protect laborers.[27]

Between the end of his editorship of the *Monitor* in 1898 and the birth, in January 1902, of the *Leader*, Father Yorke skillfully used *Rerum Novarum*, his own writing abilities, and the local San Francisco press to advocate for the rights of labor in the city's Teamster waterfront strike of 1901. In April 1901, a newly formed Employers' Association was defeating small unions one after the other in the city. When employers locked out teamsters after they refused to haul luggage for a nonunion firm, waterfront unions joined forces in a strike. Both sides blamed the other for violent confrontations. When members of the Teamsters' Union approached Father Yorke for his help, possibly to represent them should their struggle be arbitrated, he took time to consult Pope Leo's encyclical.[28] The priest believed that *Rerum Novarum* declared that workers had an inherent right to organize. Yorke first borrowed a tactic from his APA fight a few years before, revealing through articles in the *Examiner* the membership of the Employers' Association (*Examiner* editor Thomas Williams as well as William Randolph Hearst were personal friends of Yorke's).[29] The *Examiner* would remain the outlet for Yorke's commentary on the strike and its developments. In September 1901, the paper listed seven forthcoming articles from Father Yorke and their titles, including "On the Accusations of Violence" and "On Yellow Journalism."[30]

In his third article, "On the Real Question at Issue," Yorke described the employers' changing positions on the strike and, while denying that he in any way orchestrated the strife, alluded to his key role in the conflict. Employers, Yorke wrote, first claimed it was their right to run their businesses as they would; then, that the strikers were dangerous; that armies of nonunion men wished to work but were prevented from doing so; and finally, that strikers themselves wished to return to their jobs but were browbeaten by union leaders. And, Yorke noted, "judging from the welcome abuse of which I am the object in certain sections of the press . . . it would appear that I hatched the strike; that I am maintaining it and that I am the only obstacle in the way of a settlement."[31]

Such distractions, Yorke wrote, diverted attention from the real purpose of the dispute—that is, the Employers' Association, "the rich men's union," was attempting to destroy the Teamsters, "the poor men's union." In between were the middlemen, the draymen, who owned the teams of horses driven by teamsters. The draymen and teamsters had both organized, forming unions and entering into an agreement to employ each other and avoid working for nonunion employers when possible. But when the Employers' Association "threatened to ruin the Draymen by starting a rival draying concern," the Draymen's Association locked out the Teamsters' Union.[32]

Yorke wrote in a simple style, laying out what he called "facts" and letting "the people of California" judge: "Now, in all these changes, in all this turmoil, there are certain facts which stand out clear and distinct. . . . This is a fact that no amount of abuse can get rid of." "Let us come at it again." "Let the facts answer." "This fact cannot be denied." "Here are two great facts that the people of California should face boldly." "Look well on that fact, people of California. It is more than a fact, it is a portent." "A third fact . . . is the keystone of the arch."[33]

This facts-based rhetoric and method is a key marker of Progressive reformers, who sought social amelioration through the "collection, analysis, and dissemination of information to the public."[34] Progressives had great faith that information and its exposure, typically through print publication, was the key to reform. Catholic newspapers responded to nativist charges in a like manner, challenging their adversaries to provide proof in public forums of their claims of Church treachery. Nordstrom sees Progressives as actors "who used the power of information to enact change on the communities around them."[35] Father Yorke was no exception, battling negative portrayals of Catholics and the Irish in print within a framework, journalism, that privileged evidentiary knowledge.

Yet Father Yorke would have never called himself a Progressive. Historians have documented a Protestant and often anti-Catholic cast to the reform impulses of Progressivism. In addition to making the usual charges of Catholics' slavish mentality—taking orders from the pope and thus threatening American democracy—Progressives in their fight against corruption often put in their crosshairs the political machinery and industrial clout of powerful urban Catholics.[36] Yorke's disdain for editor Charles K. McClatchy of the *Sacramento Bee*—Yorke considered McClatchy a traitor to his Irish roots and Catholic faith—demonstrates the late nineteenth-century tension between Progressive reformers and Catholics. McClatchy joined Yorke in taking on the APA, but as he crafted the *Bee* into what one historian calls "a mouthpiece for Progressive reform," he targeted unassimilated immigrant groups and politicians who catered to them and occasionally took jabs at the pope. As explored in greater detail in the discussion that follows, Yorke and McClatchy fought bitterly during the 1898 California gubernatorial campaign, the Teamsters' strike of 1901 (McClatchy supported labor but drew the line at violence, which he saw as coming primarily from the strikers and which he accused Yorke of fomenting), and the San Francisco graft trials of 1906–1909.[37]

Yorke's "facts" in the Teamsters' strike, in any case, were three: that the Employers' Association started the strike by locking out the Teamsters; that the Association began the strike to destroy labor unions; and that the Association refused to meet with the workers and make a deal. He repeatedly called the Employers' Association "the rich men's union," and the Teamsters "the poor men's union."[38]

In the next day's *Examiner* article, "On the Mind of the Pope," Yorke mediated between the pontiff and the city's laborers. What did the pope, according to Yorke, have to say about the rights and duties of capital and labor? He "comes out plump and plain in favor of unions." Unions, the pope believed, existed "of their own right, not by the permission of the employer, or even of the civil government." In fact, as Yorke pointed out, the pope seemed to anticipate employer arguments that no one should speak for individual workingmen—that is, that employers would repeatedly argue that disgruntled employees should simply seek redress with their employers as individuals, not as a collective force. Yorke quoted the pontiff directly: "'Should it happen that a master or a workman believe himself injured, nothing should be more desirable than that a committee should be appointed, composed of reliable and capable members of the labor union . . . to settle the dispute.'" Yet, Yorke said, "this is what the Employers' Association of San Francisco will not do."[39]

Finally, Yorke repeated the pope's words on the special consideration the poor must receive from the state. In assuring equal rights to all, the state must not shirk its duty. "Still," the pope had written, "where there is a question of defending the rights of individuals, the poor and helpless have claim to especial consideration," for "the richer class have many ways of shielding themselves" and therefore need the state less. Yorke charged the San Francisco city government with protecting the rich and leaving the poor to be shot by city police or hired "specials."[40]

The settlement of the strike in October 1901—employers agreed not to discriminate against union men, though they did not agree to a closed shop—was viewed by most as a victory for labor, and union rolls swelled considerably in the months to come.[41] Father Yorke was widely credited with helping earn a victory for labor in the city.

But using an encyclical from the pope to rally Irish laborers was still a risky strategy for an Irish American leader to employ. John P. Irish (his real name), a U.S. immigration officer, agriculturist, and newspaper editor, watched the labor battle and wrote in the *Oakland Enquirer* of the pope and Father Yorke, "Standing at the Antipodes of Rome, I salute that venerable institution (The Papacy) and warn it that the propagation of this Yorke cult in its name in the United States will destroy the religious peace and spiritual prosperity which it here enjoyed under our institutions." Yorke, Irish charged, was introducing the Roman Church into the United States as "a political enemy of the state," and should he continue and gain more support, "the time will come that he and all like him in un-American spirit, will be deported like Chinamen who land on forged certificates."[42] At the beginning of the twentieth century many Americans still cast Catholicism as a foreign religion going against the American grain; Yorke's use of the pope's words to mobilize workers was, to Irish, tantamount to treason.[43]

Not all Irish Americans embraced Father Yorke, of course. Yorke's long-running feud with *Sacramento Bee* publisher Charles K. McClatchy shows how some Irish Americans could embrace Progressive reform efforts and demonstrates the bombastic tone of personality-driven presses of the era. In Yorke's 1896 fight against the APA, Yorke and McClatchy actually helped one another expose shady relationships between the APA and politicians seeking their support. But McClatchy's opposition to church exemptions for property tax brought Yorke's fury down on him. When McClatchy, who had attended Santa Clara University (a Catholic school) but rarely attended church, wrote a series of columns on the Bible, Yorke called them "illiterate." When McClatchy responded that he had no time to determine whether "the name of the Monitor is blown in a bottle before uncorking some of the sunshine and the grace of God" that abounded among all, not just Catholic priests or their publications, Yorke snidely hinted at McClatchy's reputation for drinking. "Tell us C.K. dear, if the sunshine and grace of God abound about you, why is it necessary to uncork them? . . . [D]o they abound about you because you crawled into the bottle and pulled the cork after you?"[44] The two battled most viciously during the 1898 gubernatorial contest between Democrat James G. Maguire, a supporter of Henry George's single tax and a foe of railroad barons and capitalist monopolies, and Henry T. Gage, a Republican linked to the railroads and other moneyed interests. Ever the reformer, McClatchy strongly supported Maguire. But Maguire was linked to an allegedly pro-APA city supervisor and was an ex-Catholic who had criticized medieval popes for colluding with British control of Ireland. This Yorke could not abide, and he denounced Maguire on the eve of the election, possibly throwing the contest to Gage. McClatchy called Yorke a "political haranguer" who had vented his spleen against "honest, manly, God-fearing" citizens because "they would not do his arrogant bidding."[45] He labeled Yorke's subsequent appointment by Gage to the University of California board of regents a payoff.

McClatchy generally supported workingmen but clashed with Yorke again during the longshoreman's strike, particularly when violence erupted. "Clothed with the authority of a Catholic priest," Yorke had acted "not as a counselor, but as a firebrand," McClatchy wrote, accusing Yorke of "distorting" Pope Leo XIII's *Rerum Novarum*.[46] Yorke called McClatchy a "man Friday of capital." The Sacramento editor, he wrote, "unfitted by intellect to understand the dogmas of the Church and by disposition to observe her commandments," had become "according to his own confession a goat."[47] A month later, Yorke wrote of his foe, "His reeling footsteps are on every street. His career smells to heaven."[48]

One final tempest between the two was over the issue of "hyphenated Americans." The Easter Rising of April 1916, an armed rebellion in Ireland against British rule that was quickly suppressed, invigorated Irish nationalism but put Irish Americans in tension with prevailing sentiment in the United States, which increasingly supported Great Britain and France in their World War I battle against Germany. It was during these tensions that McClatchy focused on a local Catholic priest who, during St. Patrick's Day celebrations, had declared Irish loyalty to "the Stars and Stripes of the great Republic," yet added, "But hyphenated we are, and hyphenated we shall be." McClatchy was incensed. "A man is either an American or he is not an American," he declared. "He cannot be a 'German American' nor an 'Irish American.'" Yorke shot back that "at the present time Chump McClatchy" was "rabid on the Irish hyphen" and "throwing fits" and speculated that his surname must be from a long line of Scottish wife beaters.[49]

It was not just Protestants or more assimilated Irish who Yorke as a public figure risked alienating. In citing *Rerum* so extensively, Yorke was perhaps deliberately ignoring another, more recent encyclical from the pope and the dispute it centered around. In *Testem Benevolentiae Nostrae*, promulgated in January 1899, Leo XIII addressed "Americanism," the idea that Catholicism in America was too independent of Rome and too accepting of the separation of church and state. Isaac Thomas Hecker was at the center of the controversy. Hecker, a Protestant convert to Catholicism, one of America's most prominent Catholics, and founder and publisher of the *Catholic World*, was never explicitly condemned by Rome. Rather, a French preface to a translated American biography of Hecker, who had died a decade before, stressed Hecker's individualism and modern thinking. French activist-priests promptly embraced Hecker as well as Catholicism in America, which they believed was more closely connected to the people. They also praised American priests, who they saw as public figures allowed greater individual initiative in their faith and its expression and promulgation.[50] It was these notions, brought together under the rubric "Americanism," to which conservative Catholics in Europe and Rome objected strenuously and which Pope Leo XIII likewise rejected in *Testem Benevolentiae Nostrae*, though with considerably more tact.

In *Testem*, addressed to James Cardinal Gibbons, Archbishop of Baltimore, the pope made clear that individual freedoms could be taken too far in matters of faith; that the Holy Ghost's promptings were not easily interpreted without direction from the Church; and, in a line that would surely have raised the eyebrows of a publisher-priest such as Father Yorke, that the Vatican was wary of the "dangers of these present times," which it defined as "the confounding of license with liberty, the passion for discussing and pouring contempt upon any possible subject, the assumed right to hold whatever opinions one pleases upon any subject and to set them forth in print to the world." All these things demonstrated "a greater need of the Church's teaching office than ever before."[51]

Historians are divided on the effect of *Testem* on Catholic thinking; some see it as drastically deadening Catholic intellectual life, while others insist that few laity or clergy even took notice.[52] It seems likely that Yorke would have read it; a response by New York's Archbishop Michael Corrigan to *Testem* was front-page news in the *San Francisco Call* on May 1, 1899. Corrigan thanked the pope profusely for exposing and rooting out the "so-called Americanism" in Catholic life—and then, in another example of the still somewhat precarious place of Irish Americans in the United States at the turn of the century, professed Catholics' Americanness:

> And now, with our heads held high, we can repeat that we are Americans, as truly as anyone, whoever he may be. Yes, we are, and we

glory in it. We glory in it because our nation is great in its institutions and in its undertakings; great in its development and its activity; but in the matter of religion and the doctrine of discipline, of morality, of Christian perfection, we glory in following implicitly the Holy See.[53]

The quotation exhibits historian Jon Gjerde's "Catholic conundrum." Because in America the Church was largely an immigrant one, Roman Catholics tended to stress elements in American ideology that spoke to a pluralist society. But many Roman Catholics simultaneously believed "theirs was the one true faith." The resulting, vexing question for Catholics: "How could a pluralist perspective that welcomed a variety of beliefs be integrated into these particularist beliefs?"[54]

From the winter of 1898 to November 1899, Father Yorke was traveling and studying in Europe and Ireland; during a trip to Italy, he obtained a private audience with Pope Leo XIII.[55] Yorke appears to have used the meeting, with the help of his relationships to San Francisco media, to strengthen his position in San Francisco and bolster the idea, perhaps against the grain of *Testem*, that priests could be vocal, public figures and publishers. A report in the *Call* a few weeks after Corrigan's response to Americanism described the meeting, gleaned from, the paper explained, "private advices from Rome." Headlined, "Father Yorke Received by His Holiness" and including a subhead, "Pope on Journalism," the article portrayed a frail pope in awe of the journalist-priest from America. The pope took Yorke's hand "in a fond clasp and held it so during the entire audience"; the pope "remained motionless" except upon hearing that Yorke had once spoken to an audience of fifty thousand, at which point "he gesticulated with his hands and arms, throwing them up in the air and wide apart," impressed with "the immensity of this influence for good." The article continued, "'You must wield immense influence,' said the Pope, as he marveled at the audience of one Catholic journalist. He proceeded to enlarge about the power of the Catholic press." The pope's parting words to Yorke were that he should tell his "friends and helpers" that "the Holy Father is deeply interested in your work and that he showed great interest in it when he spoke to you and that he encouraged you with all his heart." The "advices" then give the *Call* a detailed itinerary of Father Yorke's remaining travels.[56] It seems possible, even probable, that the *Call*'s main or only source was Father Yorke himself.

God and Nation

The *Irish World* printed at least one speech of Yorke's during his European travels. After his visit to the pope, Yorke visited his homeland. A speech to

Dublin's Gaelic League on September 6, 1899, demonstrates a kind of Darwinist, religio-racial nationalism that echoes *Irish World* columnist Robert Ellis Thompson's musings on God and nation and foreshadows Yorke's speech to the California Chinese Exclusion Convention a few years later. In Dublin, Yorke was combative, naming names of those in Ireland opposed to the league and calling them "people who thought their highest point of education was reached when they whitewashed their brogue with an English accent." Yorke then warned his audience that those who spoke of "open doors" would open a door to "John Chinaman." He said his audience had "heard a great deal of talk about the Parliament of man and the federation of the world, and other such dreams of the unrealists." It was noble, Yorke said, to think that all men created by God should live in harmony, but "it was quite different to say that all nations should be blended into one hotchpotch." In fact, it was "in the scheme of things that there should be many nations, and that they should be set against one another in the race for higher and nobler aims."[57]

Defending Catholicism in the Philippines

During and after the Philippine-American War, Father Yorke and his *Leader* were particularly vociferous about two issues that preoccupied the Irish American press at the time: the treatment of Catholic priests and Catholic churches in the islands, and how Filipinos would be educated after the war. The *Monitor* ran afoul of General Frederick Funston, charging his troops with looting religious items from Catholic churches in the Philippines and selling them in San Francisco.[58] Later in the war, the *Irish-American* tracked the story of a Catholic priest, probably Filipino, given the "water cure" three times by U.S. troops from Vermont and who died from that torture.[59] Though U.S. censorship of the press during the Philippine-American War contributed to the speculative nature of many reports, Irish American editors were surely correct in their assumption that preserving the nation's Catholic churches was not a top priority among U.S. troops. Senate hearings on U.S. troop atrocities in the Philippines revealed numerous human rights abuses and other violations. A. J. Nicholson, a young San Franciscan who fought in the Philippines in 1898 and 1899, wrote in his diary on July 3, 1898, while U.S. troops and Philippine rebels were still allied in fighting the Spanish, "There are 5 churches in town, and all have their own jails, but they were very badly used up, at the hands of the American gunners, by chance shots, + what they didn't do, the Insurgents finished. In all they were badly destroyed. . . . All the Spanish statues in the town have been beheaded. Some were very fine + also valuable."[60] By February 1899, after Spanish surrender and the beginning of fighting between Filipino rebels and U.S. troops,

Nicholson wrote, "2 companies of Wash. [Washington State regiment] sent accross [sic] river, to burn the shacks on river bank. Church and Priests residence found to be arsenals. Blown up by 6th Artillery. Fire jumps the river, burning several houses on our side."⁶¹ The next day, U.S. troops retreated, "after burning the Church and all shacks. . . . Father McKinnon took an inventory of property in Goudoloupe [sic] church, but Gen. King gave orders to burn it just the same."⁶²

Yorke kept close watch. In an item titled "Priest-Hunting in the Philippines," Yorke's *Leader* reprinted an order from General J. K. Bell that declared "every native priest in the provinces of Batangas and Laguna" to be "a secret enemy of the Government and in active sympathy with the insurgents" and called for priests to be brought to trial "whenever sufficient evidence is obtainable," and even imprisoned and held if "well founded suspicions" but no hard evidence was available. The *Leader* called the order "disgraceful" and compared it to the penal-law period in Ireland.⁶³

Father Yorke, like Patrick Ford and others in the Irish American press, stressed, once fighting had stopped in the Philippines, that the United States should draw on Catholic expertise in administering people in need of uplift. Yorke had made similar arguments before when describing slavery. In an 1896 lecture titled "The Dragon's Teeth," Yorke compared New World slavery as instituted by Protestant England with that of Spain and Portugal. Yorke found English slavery more planned and malicious than that imposed by Spanish crews, which he described as a more ad hoc affair, "what we might expect from rough men cast away from civilization."⁶⁴ The next year, in a response to a personal letter from W. B. Crawley, who asked Yorke about the Catholic Church's role in slavery and in torture during the Inquisition, Yorke wrote Crawley that slavery already existed in Rome when the Church was born and that the Church "did not preach against it like our abolitionists and thereby stir up a great civil war, and do as much harm as good." Instead, the Church told the slave to obey his master and told the master that before God the slave was his equal. "At one blow this destroyed chattel slavery," Yorke claimed. "The slave's marriage was recognized. His rights over his children— his right that the little family be not broken up. His right to a superfluity from his earning, to help him save to buy his freedom. The extinction of slavery after this, is a short task. The task was hurried by the unceasing exhortations of the Church that men should not be held in bondage, and that it is a pleasing act to ransom them."⁶⁵

Yet Father Yorke continued to bluntly call U.S. policy in the Philippines "imperialism" after Roosevelt's declared end to the war. The day after Independence Day 1902, Yorke wrote that "just now" the Declaration of Independence appears to be "a parody," for the "occupation of the Philippines by American troops against the will of the natives of those islands is diametrically opposed to the teaching" of the Declaration. "The principles of imperialism, which now obtain and are defended, are foreign to the theory on which this government was founded. Everybody knows this and most people are ashamed, but the work goes on." Atrocities committed by U.S. troops "would put to shame the most despotic government on earth." The United States "showed its good sense in Cuba. It will do the same in the Philippines. Let it do so quickly."[66] Two months before, Yorke had condemned the war in the Philippines as a "war of extermination" that could swallow "all the good works the United States can do for centuries to come."[67]

By far the biggest issue for Irish American editors during the American encounter with the Philippines revolved around religion and its intersection with education. The debate was in many ways a continuation and revival of midcentury domestic debates between Catholics and Protestants over public education, a "titanic battle," according to historian Jon Gjerde.[68] From the 1840s through the 1870s, American Catholics had charged that public school curricula in the United States were anti-Catholic and taught specifically Protestant religious views and that rather than teach a secularized, pan-Christian curriculum, the state should financially support Catholic schools.[69] A bitter fight between Protestants and Catholics over public education in New York City in 1840 and in Philadelphia in 1844 was followed by relative calm during the Civil War. Then in 1868 in Cincinnati, Catholics challenged the reading of Protestant Bibles in schools. By 1869 cartoonist Thomas Nast had begun skewering Tammany Hall and machine politician Boss Tweed for corruption, and, instigated by Tweed's clandestine placement of a provision in a tax bill that provided funds for Church schools, Nast began his famous series of antipopery cartoons.[70] Gjerde summarizes the outcome of this domestic face-off over public education:

> It did not result in a unified, homogeneous institution that could tutor youth on moral citizenship in urban society as dreamt by the Protestant reformers. It did not provide for religiously separate and state-funded schools as imagined by the Catholic leadership. Rather, it ended with increasingly secularized public schools overseen by a growing educational bureaucracy that provided yet more impetus for Catholic leadership to eschew participation in this very important public institution.[71]

As fighting in the Philippines lessened and U.S. governance began, American Catholics and the Irish American press generally advocated a formal separation of church and state for the Philippines as existed in the United States.[72] But Irish American editors soon became concerned that U.S. plans to institute public education in the Philippines would be dominated by

Protestant missionaries intent on destroying three hundred years of Catholic education in the islands and converting the overwhelmingly Catholic populace to Protestantism.

Irish and Catholic editors targeted the makeup of the Schurman Commission, a five-man civil body formed by President McKinley to make recommendations on governance and education in the Philippines that had no Catholic members. The *Monitor* was convinced that continued insurrection in the islands had something to do with the religious makeup and insensitivity of the commission: "Just why Dean Worcester, who had written a book replete with slanders on the Philippine church, and Jacob Schurman, who has given frequent public manifestations of his bigotry, should have been selected to report on the conditions of a Catholic country is indeed inexplicable." The *Catholic World* agreed, writing, "We always said that it was a mistake" to put men on the commission who had "no Catholic sympathies."[73]

Irish and Catholic fears of Protestant missionary activity were not entirely unfounded. The USS *Thomas* became a kind of icon to American attempts at uplift in the Philippines. The 509 teachers on board dubbed themselves "Thomasites," a term evoking Protestant evangelism that was soon used for all U.S. public school teachers in the islands.[74] Arthur Judson Brown, an influential minister and secretary of the Board of Foreign Missions of the Presbyterian Church of the United States, would in 1903 describe the Roman Catholic Church in the Philippines as a "sore" on the country and the Christianity of the Filipinos as little more than a "veneered heathenism."[75] Brown's vitriol toward the Church was matched by the Presbyterians' chairman on foreign missions, the Reverend George F. Pentecost, who had written in the spring of 1898, shortly after U.S. victory over the Spanish fleet in the Battle of Manila Bay:

> The peace-speaking guns of Admiral Dewey have opened the gates which henceforth make accessible not less than 8,000,000 of people who have for 300 years been fettered by bonds almost worse than those of heathenism, and oppressed by a tyrannical priesthood only equaled in cruelty by the nation whose government has been a blight and blistering curse upon every people over whom her flag has floated, a system of religion almost if not altogether worse than heathenism.[76]

Such writings, combined with alleged anti-Catholic statements by some on the commission, clearly gave American empire a Protestant cast in the eyes of Yorke and other Irish American editors.

In fact, the Schurman Commission recognized that the Philippines was overwhelmingly Catholic, the religion "not only of the majority, but of all the civilized Filipinos."⁷⁷ But it determined the form and quality of the system of primary education set up by the Spanish colonial state to be inadequate.⁷⁸ A survey by the commission in 1900 found that among the Christian population, about half had had some schooling, though often the curriculum was restricted to religious topics. In crafting a new system, the commission had to untangle complicated questions of land and school ownership. The close relationship between church and state under hundreds of years of Spanish rule meant that the Catholic Church claimed ownership of many of the properties that the United States had bought from Spain at the end of the Spanish-American and Philippine-American Wars. U.S. negotiations with Catholic officials in the United States, Manila, and Rome progressed fairly smoothly, even as government officials and their appointments were being pilloried in the Irish American press. William Howard Taft, commissioner of the Philippines and later civil governor, met personally with Pope Leo XIII in Rome and forged an agreement over conflicting property claims in the islands.⁷⁹

When the commission decided that no religious instruction would occur in its new public school system in the Philippines, however, Yorke and others in the Irish Catholic press objected. Taft attempted a compromise involving religious instruction three times per week if requested by students' parents, under the supervision of school authorities.⁸⁰ A rule calling for the dismissal of any instructor who tried to influence pupils' religious beliefs did not placate the Irish American press; the *Freeman's Journal* saw this as an attack on Catholicism, not its protection.⁸¹ When David P. Barrows, superintendent of Manila schools, removed religious objects including crucifixes, statues, and pictures from classrooms, the Boston *Pilot* commented, "It is idle to deny that official opposition to the Catholic religion is at the bottom of all this." McKinley had made that clear when "he appointed no Catholic on the Philippine Commission."⁸²

After McKinley was shot and killed in September 1901, pressure from the Catholic press, especially the Irish Catholic press, around education continued. Roosevelt began to make efforts to ameliorate the situation in 1902, placing more Catholics on the Philippine Commission. When Archbishop John Ireland of St. Paul, Minnesota, who had been instrumental in coordinating Roosevelt's visit to the Vatican to resolve the issue of Church property in the Philippines,⁸³ sided with the president and criticized in press and from the pulpit lay Catholic editors for finding fault with U.S. policy in the islands,⁸⁴ Yorke was furious. Archbishop Ireland, Yorke wrote in the *Leader*, should know that protest from Catholics against U.S. policies abroad "comes not from mere editors or Catholic societies," but "from men as high in the Church as he."⁸⁵ John Ireland was known for promoting the "Americanization" of Catholicism, but according to Yorke, "it is one of the sad commentaries on Americanism of the Pauline kind [a Yorke pun referring to Ireland's home city], that while on the streets it boasts of freedom, individuality, progress, initiative, the spirit of the age and whatnot; at home it rules with a rod of iron and crushes out the slightest symptoms of these qualities." And even if criticisms had come only from the laity and from Catholic societies, "has the ordinary lay Catholic citizen no right to an opinion on the affairs of the nation, especially when they touch on his own interests?"[86] All Catholics, Yorke thought, had a responsibility to make their interests known, and in public forums.

Soon another Catholic, G. A. O'Reilly, was appointed superintendent of schools of Manila in late 1902. Now, Taft wrote to Secretary of War Elihu Root, "I should think that even the wildest Catholic editor ought to curb his fury against you and me."[87] Frank T. Reuter sums up the role of the ethnic press in the debate: Catholic (and Irish) pressure "was not nationally organized, did not represent all of Catholic opinion, and did not get the official support" of the Catholic Church, "yet it succeeded in influencing and changing the educational policies established in the Philippines."[88]

Based on his cautious wording in a foreword he wrote to a book about the Philippines, Taft was still concerned in late 1903 that U.S. governing not be perceived as anti-Catholic (Taft was civil governor of the Philippines until February 1904). Taft wrote that although the book's author, a Protestant minister, had skillfully sought the truth of the situation in the islands, "deductions and inferences made from observations are a matter of opinion and are much affected by one's standpoint." The author "is a Protestant clergyman and looks at the situation from a possibly somewhat different standpoint than that of a Protestant layman or from that of a Catholic layman or a Catholic clergyman." Taft briefly mentions one chapter on the "critical issue as to the friars," which "might present some differences of opinion," before again giving the book his support.[89]

The Press and the Priesthood

By this time, Father Yorke had fallen out of favor with his own archbishop, Patrick Riordan. Documents from the Archdiocese of San Francisco and from Rome demonstrate a relationship between Riordan and Yorke that progressed from "initial cooperation, to conflict, and . . . coexistence."[90] Letters from San Francisco to Rome indicate that Yorke's continued prominence after the APA battle was troubling to the Church and that his character was deemed as lacking prudence.[91] But Yorke's popularity after the APA battle and his key role in the Teamsters' labor fight had made the priest into a kind of spokesperson for the faith, at least in San Francisco. The confusion was enough for the *Monitor* to take steps to clarify the situation in 1906. The paper quoted Archbishop George Montgomery reminding Catholics that Yorke and his *Leader* did not represent Church opinion; only the *Monitor* did.⁹² The fact that Riordan had never publicly repudiated Yorke probably contributed to the mistaken notion that the *Leader* was official Catholic opinion; Riordan himself admitted to an apostolic delegate that among Catholics in San Francisco, the *Leader* was regarded equally with the *Monitor*.⁹³

According to several scholars of the Catholic press, Yorke's *Leader* published during a transitional stage in Catholic publishing in the United States, one of a soon-to-be diminished breed of independent Catholic presses. Not surprisingly, Catholic newspapers grew initially alongside a burgeoning Catholic population, which climbed from six million in 1880 to ten million by 1900. Forty-six Catholic newspapers and ten magazines existed in the United States in 1880; by 1900 the numbers had grown to seventy-three newspapers and eighty-two magazines. Late nineteenth-century Catholic newspapers "evolved from being perhaps the most unfettered of Catholic print media to one of the most religiously partisan."⁹⁴ Many scholars call the first phase of Catholic journalism the immigrant period, when the presses' main function was "to guard the faith of Catholics and to defend the Church against calumnies."⁹⁵ From the twentieth century until World War II, some observers see a "post-immigrant" phase of greater Church control of the press.⁹⁶ John G. Deedy, Jr., describes overexpansion and duplication of the Catholic press in this period and new communications technologies that "did away forever with the isolation not only of cities but of the isolation of communities within cities."⁹⁷ Bishops responded by backing or buying a single publication they could control. "The independent," Deedy writes, "gradually passed away."⁹⁸

Scholars who see the late nineteenth and early twentieth centuries as a time of diminished Catholic intellectual production must take into consideration the Irish American press and its cadre of editor-priests and Catholic laymen and not focus solely on more formal, sanctioned Catholic intellectual production. Donna J. Drucker traces an American priestly culture developing in tandem with a "stifled intellectual atmosphere" within the Church, though she distinguishes between a Church hierarchy and the priesthood itself, which she grants could have been more culturally dynamic.⁹⁹ Examining priestly advice literature in the United States from the 1880s through the 1920s, Drucker finds first an emphasis on duty, conformity, and hierarchy—the priest should be a man set above the laity.¹⁰⁰ (Drucker views advice literature as proscriptive, not descriptive—that is, it describes things as the writer or institution wishes them to be, not as they are. Priestly advice literature, she says, may thus stress conformity due to discomfort over the changing and more public role of priests at the time.) Not until after World

War I does advice literature encourage priests to become part of a "broad priestly fraternity" and engage in public life, weighing in on current affairs.[101] Thomas E. Woods pushes back against the notion of Catholic intellectual conformity in the Progressive Era, profiling three priests whose writings incorporated some Progressive notions but who confronted American pragmatism with uniquely Catholic views—views that match, for example, Yorke's writings on education.[102]

Yorke himself might be described as the foremost editor-priest in the nation around the turn of the century, pulling the Church into discussions from which it might seek more distance or neutrality. Yet early in the *Leader*'s existence, Yorke claimed the paper was not a Catholic one; the "strong point" in a Catholic paper was "deportment," something the *Leader* planned to have none of.[103] In subsequent issues, Yorke carefully distinguished between priest and lay Catholic editors and the challenges faced by each: Clerical editors, on the one hand, were "intellectually capable of bringing out a first rate Catholic paper" but, saddled with duties to their parishes, wound up "trying to do the work of two offices" and doing it badly. Yorke found it "strange" that clerical editors did not know how low-quality their papers were and concluded that "the Catholic newspaper in this country has been made into a kind of sacramental, and, no matter how poor the paper is, the practical Catholic must buy it as religiously as he wears the scapular." Lay Catholic editors, on the other hand, were faced with the task of spreading the faith but knew little of Church history or Catholic theology. In fact, Yorke wrote, Catholic papers were hurt most by these editors, who used them mainly as "mediums of advertisement." "Let us do this well or get out," Yorke concluded.[104]

This Yorke editorial was commented on by the *New World*, a Catholic newspaper that differed from Yorke's *Leader* in two ways: it was edited by a lay Catholic, and it was simultaneously the official organ of the Archdiocese of Chicago. According to an account by Yorke in the *Leader*, the *New World* objected to what it saw as Yorke's suggestion that only Church history and theology were appropriate topics for discussion in a Catholic paper. Yorke rejected such a view as his own, but in an effort to assert the superiority of clerical editors such as himself, he belittled what he suggested were frivolous editorial topics in the last issue of the *New World*.[105] Yorke used his particular position—as editor and priest, but not the head of an official or (in his view) even an unofficial Catholic newspaper—to his advantage. From this vantage point he criticized lay editors for their lack of knowledge of Catholicism, and yet, no longer constrained as head of the *Monitor*, the official archdiocese newspaper in San Francisco, he had the independence to criticize official Church pronouncements and actions as well.[106]

The Long History of the *Monitor*

The origins of the *Monitor* show the multiple interests of a nominally Catholic newspaper and point to pressures that Catholic newspapers put on the faith—as well as the confusing and shifting distinctions between nominally Catholic newspapers, Irish American newspapers, and official church organs. The *Monitor* was started by Catholic businessmen in 1858 and became an official Church organ only in the early 1890s. James Marks, Patrick J. Thomas, and James Hamill, a teacher, businessman, and miner, respectively, were "pioneers of the Catholic Press on the Pacific Coast."[107]

The *Monitor* printed its "prospectus" a few weeks after its first issue: "Although we acknowledge with pride and gratitude that the press of California is in no appreciable measure anti-Catholic; and that it is the most liberal in the whole world, yet we think a Catholic journal free from the rancor of polemics, and devoted to the cultivation of Catholic literature, neither superfluous nor uncalled for." The paper would bring Catholics in San Francisco and the West into contact with their brethren nationwide "as members of the 'Household of Faith.'"[108] The *Monitor* promised a focus on mining, agriculture, and commerce. "With politics," its editors wrote, "we have nothing whatsoever to do."[109]

In fact, with politics the *Monitor* had much to do. During the Civil War, under the editorship of Thomas A. Brady, the paper was perceived by many to be too sympathetic to the Confederate cause; one letter writer to the *Daily Evening Press*, who signed his name "Irish American," called the *Monitor* "treasonable" and demanded that the Catholic Church clarify its relationship to it. The next day, printed in several daily papers, archbishop of San Francisco Joseph S. Alemany disavowed "articles and statements without [Church] sanction or approbation," adding that there were Catholic journals in California that were "not always faithful exponents of the doctrines and wishes of the Catholic Church, which in this diocese has no official organ."[110] The *Daily Alta California* reported that on the day of President Lincoln's assassination, a roving mob in San Francisco stormed many presses and cast "their types and presses . . . into the street." The *Monitor* offices, at Clay and Montgomery Streets, were no exception. "The proclivities of this semi-religious journal are too well known to need explanation here. The office was entered and badly damaged. . . . On the arrival of the Police the same scattering took place as before and the crowd started for another scene."[111] For the next several months, Brady published a paper called the *Universe*; on June 10, 1865, the *Monitor* returned. Brady sued the city for $7,500 for failing to protect his paper from the mob; he described in his lawsuit the newspaper as "a means of permanent and reliable income" to himself. Three years later, the city settled with Brady for $4,200.[112]

As late as 1879, the *Monitor* was still not an official Church organ, though Archbishop Alemany now seemed to have warmed to it: "We cheerfully acknowledge the services the Catholic Press has rendered to religion, and also the disinterestedness with which, in most instances, it has been conducted, although yielding to publishers and editors a very insufficient return for their labors.... We exhort the Catholic community to extend to these publications a more liberal support.... It is our duty to avail ourselves of this mode of making known the truths of our religion."[113]

It was in 1880 that the Reverend John Harrington bought the paper, bringing in other priests to run it. In 1892 the paper was converted into the Monitor Publishing Company and became the official organ of the Archdiocese of San Francisco.[114] But for decades, the accessibility of printing technology had allowed individuals outside of the formal Catholic hierarchy to define for themselves Catholic responses to the issues of the day. Or, as in the case of Father Yorke and his newspaper the *Leader*, at the start of the twentieth century, those within the hierarchy but perhaps stymied in their rise could maintain or increase their influence with lay Catholics through their own personal presses.

Print capitalism's influence on the Catholic Church began long before the nineteenth century, of course; the democratizing force of print culture had been a long-standing tension between the Church and lay Catholics. The Catholic Church of the Counter-Reformation initially tried to review all materials for public use but had abandoned such efforts by the mid-1500s.[115] Bishops in nineteenth-century America had no direct power over publishers of Catholic material, but because canon law required church approval of any religious text or sacred image directed at Catholics, publishers seeking the broadest possible audience often sought such approval, denoted by an *imprimatur*—Latin for "it may be printed"—on the obverse of the title page.[116]

Clearly, Catholic newspaper presses in America were not simple conduits for Catholic doctrine. Invariably, they were shaped by local editors and local disputes; in this sense, the Church encountered contemporary issues that might well foster change in the Church itself. In addition, the lines between official Church newspapers and the broader Irish American press were not easy to discern; an Irish editor's support of certain tactics to achieve an independent Ireland might come to be seen as supported by the Church, whether it was or not.

Newsprint and Catholic Sacramentality

Even as the Church grappled with the conundrums of using the press to spread the word of God, the nature of print, where symbols and images represent real objects in the physical world, may have been slowly changing the faith in another way. Una Cadegan discusses Catholicism's sacramentality, "which maintained the belief that everything in the world was potentially revelatory of God's grace." Books, magazines, newspapers, and other items of Catholic print culture "were enmeshed in a densely sacramental fabric."[117] Yet these media may have subtly affected this aspect of Catholicism even as they spread, bolstered, or consolidated the faith. The ephemeral nature of newspapers—the fragility of newsprint and the reproduction of photography into halftone images—make this medium an unlikely source of sacramentality (Figure 2.2). Touch, for example, seems somewhat degraded through newspapers, as compared to the durability and heft of books, with their robust bindings and embossed covers. Even stand-alone photographs, printed on paper backing, have a three-dimensional nature—that is, they have a reverse side that may contain handwritten notes, preprinted vendor identification, or other symbols. Photography reproduced onto newsprint via the halftone, however, is essentially two-dimensional. A photographic print is typically private or domestic in nature; the halftone inhabits a public, commercial space, and multiple viewers may interpret it differently or ignore or even discard it.[118] Though the sacramental nature of Catholicism is hard to define, measure, and track, it seems likely that newsprint helped to convey some aspects of the faith but was a poor medium with which to convey Catholicism's emphasis on materiality.[119]

Figure 2.2 An image of sacred vestments allegedly looted from a Catholic church in the Philippines, from "Church Desecration in Philippines," *Irish World*, December 9, 1899.

Yorke and the Chinese

There was one way many Irish Catholic editors on the West Coast found to fill in the fault lines in their American identity: they broadened and generalized both religion and race, emphasizing a common Christian heritage to downplay their religious differences with the Protestant mainstream, and pushed a "white race" conception that encompassed European immigrants who, earlier in the nineteenth century, had commonly been described as separate races. The Chinese on the West Coast were key in this process, serving as a foil, a nonwhite heathen "other."[120]

Irish and other immigrant laborers were at the forefront of agitation against the Chinese throughout the western states, especially in the 1880s. Patrick Ford's dedication to black civil rights had in all likelihood strongly influenced the openness toward African Americans of the Knights of Labor and its chief, Terence Powderly, an Irish Catholic machinist and former mayor of Scranton, Pennsylvania. Powderly became vice president of the American Land League in 1881 and was well acquainted with Ford and his *Irish World* and radical economist Henry George. Powderly's vigorous denunciations of racism against African Americans attracted some sixty thousand blacks to the Knights. Yet he matched Henry George in his virulent anti-Chinese bigotry; in the West, the Knights "stood at the center of what was called an 'abatement campaign' to forcibly drive Chinese workers out of the region's lumber and mining camps."[121] Ford, as noted in Chapter 1, tried to distance himself from anti-Chinese racism while praising the passage of the Chinese Exclusion Act in 1882. At the turn of the century, Yorke added his own support for continued Chinese exclusion without any of Ford's racial egalitarianism.

Just weeks after Yorke's battle for the Teamsters had concluded in a labor agreement, laborers and politicians met in San Francisco at the California Chinese Exclusion Convention of November 1901.[122] The meeting was called to promote the extension of the 1892 Geary Act, which had made more stringent and extended for ten years the 1882 Chinese Exclusion Act.[123] Examination of Yorke's speech at the gathering provides further evidence of the intersection of race and religion in the establishment of American citizenship and the importance of the circulation in print of racially demarcated notions of citizenship in the nineteenth century, particularly on the West Coast.

Yorke was the last to address the convention and, rising, claimed he was asked to speak "just a few minutes ago." He described himself as "one who is sincerely in sympathy with your efforts," who believed that times were "fraught with the greatest and most momentous consequences" to California. Just as Romans had demolished a bridge to protect their city from Etruscans, Californians had gathered "to take counsel with regard to this threatened invasion from the West, which invasion threatens our civilization, threatens our institutions, and . . . if this country is to be saved to Christianity and to the white man, 'The bridge must straight go down.' (Applause.)"[124]

Two things, Yorke said, make a country "civilized or uncivilized." One was "the way men have of looking at life"; the other, "the way we have of treating those who work."[125] The American way of looking at life was "unreservedly committed" to "the Christian idea." America was not a colony of Asia or Africa; Europe was its "motherland," whose races were "practically all of the same blood." They may differ in "languages," "institutions," and "laws," but "hardly do they enter the gates of Castle Garden[126] than they are fit to take their places in the civilization of America," and these immigrants' children "cannot be distinguished from the children of those whose ancestors have been here for the sixth and the seventh generation." Yorke declared that, "although we may look back with a certain love and sentiment to the land from which we are sprung . . . when we come here we come here to be Americans in the fullest and brightest sense." Yorke might fight passionately against Irish assimilation or stress Irish difference as integral to a kind of American tapestry, but here he would stress (white) American unity through comparison to the alien Chinese.[127]

"Now, then," Yorke continued, "we are face to face with an immigration which is emphatically not Christian. I have nothing to say about the ideals or about the morality of the Chinese. They may be very good in their own place, and this is in China (laughter), but, as somebody has defined dirt as matter out of place, so we may say that the virtues of the Chinese, be they never so great, and never so fitting for their own country, are out of place in this. (Laughter and applause.)"[128]

"Their thoughts are not our thoughts; their blood is not our blood; their outlook is not our outlook," Yorke continued. And though obviously inferior, their sheer numbers meant they could act by "brute force" to create something "entirely contradictory to our institutions." Americans across the land must "demand that a wall be built up against Chinese immigration."[129]

Yorke sought to bring labor into a definition of American citizenship, and by this he meant more than the dignity of work. His second civilizational element was "the condition of labor." Yorke told the crowd that a rich man in China was no different than one in America; the wealthy were "the same all the world over. . . . What rich men do, what rich men eat, what rich men drink, what rich men wear, have nothing at all to do with civilization. The test of civilization is how the laborer is treated."[130] These were the requirements for a workingman to be a free man: "that he be not the property of any lord of labor, that he be not owned by any man, that he be free to give his labor, or not to give it, as he wished, and that he have some say in the condition of the country." If Chinese labor were to be amassed in America, laborers who "will not strike and who don't want to strike," "who will work for very small wages and who will live on things that the rats would starve on," would "create great fortunes for certain people." Freedom-loving people must keep out those "who do not believe in the rights of free men, who do not believe they have a soul to call their own, and who do not care what becomes of this great white civilization that has been built up with such care, with such expenditure of brains and energy.... (Applause.)"[131] To Yorke, Chinese willingness to work for paltry wages was an indication not of desperation or of global disparities in wealth that made the wage attractive to Chinese but of immorality.

Yorke filled his speech with biological metaphors. "When a man is in good health, if a foreign body lodges in his anatomy, immediately it sets up an inflammation, the warning of its presence ... it must be sought for and cast out. And so it is with this agitation now against the foreign body in our body politic, it is the sign to the whole country that there is something there which is dangerous to our civil life, and which must be cast out."[132]

A few labor unions added statements of support to the proceedings at the Metropolitan Temple. The laundry workers union No. 55 of Alameda County wrote that, "should the bars of Chinese immigration be lowered and our Golden State invaded by hordes of Mongolians, it is fearful to contemplate the destitution, misery and want that, as a consequence, would naturally follow in its wake."[133]

Race hatred and a desire to strengthen one's American identity were tangled up in fears about the threat to working-class livelihoods that the combination of profit-seeking employers and cheap, available Chinese labor could represent. Nearly 5,800 Chinese arrived in California per year between 1861 and 1865; the Chinese were the largest foreign-born population in the state in 1860, just edging out the Irish at 9 percent (34,933) of the state population. While the majority of Chinese arrivals worked outside cities in mining, agriculture, and railroads, one-third found employment in urban areas. By the 1860s and 1870s, Irish in San Francisco had watched Chinese move into several areas of unskilled or relatively unskilled labor such as digging and grading, restaurants, laundry, and domestic work. Work that paid $1 an hour in 1850 paid as little as $2 a day in 1875.[134] The city's growing industrial sector saw Chinese employed in cigar making at less than $1.40 per day, excluding the Irish and threatening the jobs of East Coast Irish cigar rollers. In 1870 the Chinese manufactured one-half of all shoes and boots made in San Francisco.[135]

Gauging the effect of an end to Chinese exclusion on San Francisco's economy in the early twentieth century is beyond the scope of this book; certainly wages in several occupations might have been threatened by Chinese labor, as Irish prosperity in the city still depended on the maintenance of relatively high compensation for low-skilled work.¹³⁶ Undoubtedly, new economic opportunities for U.S. citizens as a whole were also created through Chinese immigration. But Yorke and other labor advocates used racism as more than a simple tool to catalyze Irish labor solidarity.

These activists participated in the construction of what Kornel Chang calls a "militant, racialized class consciousness" that cut across ethnic and even national boundaries.¹³⁷ In Washington State and in British Columbia, for example, after the 1880s immigrants formed a majority of the region's settlers, coming from continental Europe, the British Isles, Anglophone settler societies, and Asia. According to Chang, Europeans of diverse national origin responded to this multiplicity of identities by creating a new one, by "fixing on their whiteness, intensifying their racism," and "abstracting their ethnicity." Whiteness in this formulation becomes "the first and most essential marker of social responsibility."¹³⁸ All these elements are strong in Yorke's 1901 speech. Chang and other scholars have shown how practices, theories, and identities traversed globally from one white settler colony to another, carried most frequently, according to Chang, by English, Scottish, Cornish, and Irish skilled miners, some of whom became known as experts on "coolie labor" or the "yellow peril."¹³⁹ Anti-Asian racism was key to the formation of this transnational white working-class identity on the West Coast. "White labor leaders and workers crisscrossed the western U.S.-Canadian frontiers to engage in race riots, lobby for immigration restriction, and establish anti-Asiatic organizations, forging racial and class bonds across national boundaries."¹⁴⁰ Yorke was more sedentary, but his notions of civilization and its constitutive elements of whiteness, religion, and working-class vigor echo Chang's transnational actors. Yorke would express these notions again in his own newspaper, the *Leader*, a few months after the exclusion convention: "The exclusion of the Chinese is absolutely necessary for the preservation of the white man's civilization on the Pacific coast."¹⁴¹

The Star Press, run by James H. Barry, printed the proceedings and speeches of the anti-Chinese convention. Barry ran his own newspaper, the *Weekly Star*, which he founded to fight government corruption, and was an early supporter of the secret ballot, the referendum, and public ownership of utilities. He was also staunchly opposed to Asian labor. While running for the U.S. Senate, James D. Phelan, San Francisco's former Democratic mayor (and the opening speaker at the exclusion convention), thanked Barry for positive coverage in the *Star*: "I shall keep our State . . . a white man's country, free from the grinding competition of Oriental coolieism," Phelan wrote the publisher.¹⁴²

Historians have noted that earlier in the nineteenth century, when there was less labor competition between the Irish and the Chinese, there was less ill feeling between the two. Still, the consistency of, for example, the *Monitor*'s anti-Asian sentiments is remarkable and long-standing, across many different editors and decades. In May 1868, for example, the *Monitor* reprinted an editorial from the *State Capital Reporter* that it called "judicious." The *Reporter* wrote of "the danger our state would be in were it to invite the vast hordes of Asia to settle in our midst, and at the same time give them control of the Government. Ours is a Democratic government, relying for its stability, progress and preservation upon the masses of the people—the laboring classes." To fill the country with "an inferior race of semi-barbarians" was "dangerous."[143] A few weeks later, in an editorial titled "Coolie Immigration," the *Monitor* stated that "some 700 Celestials arrived in the *New York* recently, and another ship-load is expected shortly.... [C]oolie labor may be as efficient in preventing white immigration to the Pacific slope as negro labor has proved in keeping it out of the South."[144] The newspaper was a forceful advocate for white West Coast labor from its inception.

Nearly four decades later, in 1906, now an official organ of the San Francisco archdiocese and with Thomas A. Connelly editing, the *Monitor*'s stance toward Asians had changed little. "Some Eastern Methodist ministers have put themselves on record against the anti-Asiatic sentiment of the Pacific Coast," the newspaper wrote. "The brethren are unsparing of adjectives in condemning the brutal and un-Christian attitude of the California whites who unreasonably object to being crowded off the map by the little pagan brown men, whose standards of living and morality are a menace to Caucasian civilization on this rim of the continent. The same preachers, it may be remarked, are usually among the most ardent advocates of putting up the bars against white immigrants at the Atlantic ports of entry."[145]

A Tricky Quest for Acceptance

Irish Americans in the late nineteenth century faced the complexities of a paradox: asserting their difference might increase their case for acceptance as part of the American grain in a country that told itself it valued pluralism and welcomed immigrants. But emphasizing difference, particularly their religion, could foment backlash in a land where Anglo-Saxon and Protestant heritage still claimed normative status. Father Yorke and other Irish Americans responded, in part, by emphasizing their Christian whiteness through shared notions about Asian racial inferiority and heathenism.[146] Yorke's racist rhetoric directed at the Chinese and Japanese encouraged European-heritage workers to unite around a white supremacist identity. His words and analogies, particularly concerning an Asian "invasion" of the U.S. body politic, essentially condoned violence against Asians. That Catholic Church publications on the West Coast had been printing similar views for decades is important context but does not take away from the viciousness of Yorke's contribution to racial strife around the turn of the century.

Yet, simultaneously, Yorke remains a compelling figure for positive reasons. He helped win key victories for labor in San Francisco when employers were uniting to destroy the power of unions. His energy and creativity in pushing back against the APA is rightly admired. The success of nativist publications in the Midwest several years after the APA controversy and the endurance of anti-Catholic agitation well into the twentieth century suggests that the APA, at least nationwide, was no paper tiger. In the field of education, one Yorke historian criticizes Yorke for failing to use his position as a University of California regent to bring more Irish Americans into a growing university.[147] These criticisms have merit, and Yorke's tenure as a regent was marked by his silences and his typical absences at regent meetings and university functions. Yet here, too, criticism of Yorke misses some of the consistency of his sympathies and even the prescience of some of his positions. Yorke fought for the least of his fellow Irish Americans and imagined a religious education for them in specifically Catholic schools. His priority was not large secular universities. There, he raised his voice only when he thought the public university was acting in a specifically Protestant way.[148] The best education for Irish Americans was to focus first on faith and character, not professional skills: "To train the reason and neglect the will is not education, and a university that is compelled to set aside that ancient and only efficacious training of the will, namely, the inculcation of a definite religious belief, is deprived of half its power." A university, Yorke wrote, "is not a department store. It must have its professional schools, but its real work is done not there, but in arts."[149]

Popular accounts of newspapers in the late nineteenth century stress the power of William Randolph Hearst's yellow journalism in pushing the nation toward war in Cuba and the Philippines, but Yorke, Ford, and other Irish American editors demonstrate the considerable clout of the ethnic newsweekly during this time. Though the anti-imperialism of many Irish American editors could not keep the United States from claiming the Philippines as a possession, personal presses such as Yorke's and Ford's threatened to embarrass the Roosevelt administration on the issue of public education in the islands. The administration responded by appointing Catholics to prominent positions in hopes of silencing the guns of the Irish American press.

When considering the relative vigor of Catholic intellectual production during the late nineteenth and early twentieth centuries, scholars must include the contribution of Catholic editors, lay and clergy alike, Church-sanctioned or not. Lay Catholic and clerical voices were empowered by newspaper technologies, which extended and simultaneously challenged Church control of Catholic messaging. Newspapers made Catholics, including Catholic priests, increasingly public figures, presaging changing notions of a more public and vocal priesthood. Yorke and Ford each found in Catholic theology and papal encyclicals a rich source of support for their own particular intellectual and activist positions. In some ways, Ford, though not a priest like Yorke, may have felt more pressure to conform his paper's stance to Catholic Church prerogatives, as he lived and worked closer to powerful East Coast bishops and dioceses. The more maverick Yorke, however, could retain much of the stature of a Catholic priest even as he might embarrass and defy the West Coast Catholic hierarchy.

Irish Catholic editors might be associated with Progressive reform, like the *Sacramento Bee*'s McClatchy. But when top Progressive reformers criticized Tammany Hall for putting in power "a crowd of illiterate peasants, freshly raked from Irish bogs," Yorke, for one, felt he knew that "reform" surely meant attacks on the Irish poor.[150] Yet Yorke, Ford, and other Irish American editors employed many of the same journalistic practices as Progressive muckrakers in their own campaigns, privileging the collection and dissemination of "facts" as they probed the weaknesses of their opponents' arguments. That such emphasis on evidentiary knowledge might sit incongruously with more spiritual ways of knowing did not seem to bother Yorke at all.

II

THE AFRICAN AMERICAN PRESS

Flexibility in the Fight for Freedom

THE BLACK PRESS had been agitating for African American rights for many decades before T. Thomas Fortune and James Samuel Stemons began their newspaper odysseys. The first African American newspaper, *Freedom's Journal*, was published in New York in 1827 by Samuel Eli Cornish and John Brown Russwurm. Its editors sought to provide an authentic black voice, for others had "too long spoken for us."[1] Disagreements over colonization led to a split between the editors; Russwurm, in fact, would soon leave for Liberia. Cornish, a free black Presbyterian minister, would go on to lead several black newspapers, including the *Colored American*. Samuel Ringgold Ward, a Congregationalist minister, ran the *True American* and the *Impartial Citizen*; he served as a corresponding editor for the *Aliened American* from 1852 to 1856.[2] Many antebellum black newspapers had a sense of mission that one scholar terms "chosenness": the belief that God had tasked slaves and freemen with bringing about mankind's liberation.[3]

At midcentury, Frederick Douglass's more secular *North Star* garnered circulation of about three thousand after its start in 1847; in 1851 it became *Frederick Douglass' Paper*, perhaps to capitalize on Douglass's fame as an abolitionist lecturer. In the latter half of the century, the long-lived Washington, D.C., *Bee* (1882–1926) was edited by the contrarian William Calvin Chase. T. Thomas Fortune's storied newspapers would employ at least two black female journalists and editors, including Victoria Earle Matthews and

Ida B. Wells-Barnett. The Indianapolis *Freeman* tried to incorporate visual elements within its pages.

By the turn of the century, Booker T. Washington had become the foremost African American leader and began asserting his influence over many black newspapers. Washington, born a slave in southwest Virginia in 1856, would not directly challenge disenfranchisement and segregation; white and black, he said at the 1895 Cotton States and International Exposition in Atlanta, Georgia, could live peacefully in the South as African Americans focused on economic empowerment: "In all things purely social we can be as separate as the fingers, yet one as the hand in all things essential to mutual progress," he told the Atlanta crowd.[4] Washington worked quietly behind the scenes to fund civil rights cases, but the political machine he built could ruin the careers of aspiring black writers and editors if they strayed too far from the Tuskegee vision.

Since Garland Penn's *The Afro-American Press and Its Editors* in 1891, the first historians of the black press have generally described it as a "champion" of an "oppressed people," as a "fighting press."[5] Vishnu V. Oak wrote that no other black institution "has helped so whole-heartedly in the acceleration of the social, economic, and political progress of the Negro as its press."[6] Later scholars looked more closely at black newspapers' role in black communities and found greater room for criticism. "The people who publish and write the Negro newspapers belong to the upper class," Gunnar Myrdal wrote in 1944.[7] To Myrdal, this gave the Negro press an "essential conservatism." He appears to mean in social matters, however, for the reliance of the black upper classes on lower-class readers and consumers gave the press, according to Myrdal, a politically and economically "radical" stance. "The importance of the Negro press for the formation of Negro opinion . . . for Negro leadership and concerted action generally, is enormous." Myrdal called the black press an "educational agency" and a "power agency" that promoted "an intense realization on the part of the Negroes of American ideals" but simultaneously "makes them realize to how small a degree white Americans live up to them."[8]

Other studies also described most nineteenth-century black editors as economic and cultural elites compared to the masses of black Americans. African American sociologist E. Franklin Frazier labeled the press the "mouthpiece" of the black bourgeoisie and key to the propagation of a "myth" of a secure black middle class.[9] The black press, in Frazier's view, touted the achievements of this small, economically and psychologically anxious class in an attempt to compensate for this group's collective insecurity.[10] Albert Lee Kreiling viewed the black press through the cultural or anthropological lens of media theorist James W. Carey, seeing newspapers as "arenas of symbolic action."[11] The black press, Kreiling said, was a major force in creating race consciousness and in "making The Race into a symbolic entity with a life of its own.... [A] personal identity rooted in the nationwide collective life of The Race has joined the identification with church and local community life characteristic among southern blacks immediately after Emancipation."[12] Kreiling criticized the Northern black press for painting too pretty a picture of Northern freedoms but thought the press successfully reoriented small-town African American migrants toward a broader collective black identity in a rapidly urbanizing, secular society.[13]

Historian William G. Jordan focuses on black newspapers during World War I, a little over a decade following T. Thomas Fortune's Pacific quest and just after James Samuel Stemons's newspapering, and he accurately describes many rhetorical techniques and notions characteristic of Fortune's and especially Stemons's publishing efforts. Jordan seeks to move beyond "accommodation/protest" and "Booker T./Du Bois" dichotomies, for a "profound ambivalence" marked the black press as a whole in this time period, as well as idiosyncrasies and indeterminacies. Black ambivalence is not cloudy thinking or indecision in this view; rather, "it flowed from writers' efforts to use language to motivate powerful white readers to attempt to improve race relations in America" without promoting white backlash. In this ever-shifting field, black journalists should be "judged by the impact of their words rather than by the logical consistency of their arguments." Editors cast themselves as arbitrators between black and white worlds and were accepted as such.[14] Late nineteenth- and early twentieth-century black newspapers developed "a balance between militancy and accommodation shaped by . . . [the] personality and ideology of publisher, the state of race relations in the local area, the relationship of the publisher to local political parties, recent events, and the requirements of a particular situation or moment." Jordan finds that Southern black papers did become less militant and more interested in individuals' social and economic advancement after withdrawal of federal troops in the South. Three factors contributed: Jim Crow, the ascendancy of the ideology of industrial capitalism (and its individualism), and the escalation of vigilante violence.[15]

Stemons did hope to become an arbitrator between black and white, and some of his thinking straddled the protest-accommodation divide that Jordan wisely critiques. Fortune's militancy made him an unlikely partner of Booker T. Washington, yet he, like Stemons, rejected much of W.E.B. Du Bois's agenda. Seeing Stemons or even Fortune as "elites," however, is problematic. Stemons's single-minded determination to make his own mark in reform efforts, to establish himself as an expert on black-white relations and the Negro Problem, does fit well with analyses of the late nineteenth century as a time of heightened individualism. Fortune, too, seems concerned with his legacy. And both men do seem to be trying to make sense of and capitalize on the dislocations of Kreiling's modern cityscapes. But as we see in the next chapters, the drive to be heard involved entering into prevailing discourses of race and poverty, which sometimes weakened each man's critique of personal and institutional white racism. And the newspaper medium itself exerted aesthetic, ideological, and economic agendas that editors and publishers could not ignore.

3

FORTY ACRES AND A CARABAO

T. Thomas Fortune, Newspapers, and the Pacific's Unstable Color Lines, 1902–1903

We stand largely where they stand—outside of the American Constitution, but under the American flag. The hazards of war make strange bedfellows, but none stranger than this of the Afro-American and Filipino peoples.
—T. THOMAS FORTUNE, statement to a gathering of African Americans in Washington, D.C., 1903[1]

What is liberty for a race, and how is it to be obtained?
—BOOKER T. WASHINGTON, "The Educational and Industrial Emancipation of the Negro" (1903)

In the spring of 1903, one of the nation's foremost black journalists paused in the humid air of northern Luzon for a photographic self-portrait. Dressed in explorer's garb, T. Thomas Fortune struck a manly pose (Figure 3.1). Bandits and cholera stalked the countryside as the Philippines struggled to recover from two years of brutal warfare between Filipino guerrillas and the U.S. Army. Yet Fortune had bravely marched northward from Manila accompanied by two black U.S. soldiers, a "Capt. Wormsley" and Robert Gordon Woods, the latter considered an expert on the islands. As a temporary agent of the U.S. Treasury Department, Fortune was determined to gather information on trade and labor conditions in two of America's recent possessions; just weeks previously he had completed a calmer and much more cordial visit to Hawaii. In the back of his mind lay the strained finances of his *New York Age*, his tense friendship and collaboration with Booker T. Washington, and his struggle with alcohol. At the front was the question of whether these new territories might make a good home for African Americans seeking a fresh start away from the violence and poverty of the U.S. South.

More than forty years ago, Fortune's biographer, Emma Lou Thornbrough, looked briefly at his journey, reconstructing it primarily through the

Figure 3.1 T. Thomas Fortune in Luzon, from *Voice of the Negro*, March 1904. (Courtesy of the Schomburg Center for Research in Black Culture, New York Public Library.)

papers of Booker T. Washington and Fortune's own writings.[2] Despite rich new scholarship on race and empire and newly accessible digital newspaper archives in Hawaii, only a few contemporary scholars have briefly revisited the trip. One historian describes Fortune as consistently militant in the Philippines, making common cause with Filipinos and calling out white racism wherever he saw it.[3] Most others see Fortune's close relationship with Booker T. Washington at this time as constraining his radicalism, though few go as far as W.E.B. Du Bois, who in 1907 would describe Fortune as a "fallen" genius, "groveling in the dust" because of his association with the Wizard of Tuskegee.[4] To one historian, Fortune abroad is a carrier of masculinist imperialism, "swept up in romantic ideas about empire."[5]

Washington's already-mixed reputation, too, seems to have suffered further as a larger body of recent scholarship has probed Tuskegee's overseas projects. Going further than Louis Harlan, who found that Washington's internationalism remained "provincial," at least one historian charges the Tuskegee leader, in conjunction with sociologist Robert E. Park, with helping create a "global South" by adapting Jim Crow politics to West Africa and beyond "in a manner that appealed to powerful imperial interests across the global North."[6]

While acknowledging the strength of such scholarship, this chapter finds a more complex process of African American accommodation and resistance. By viewing Fortune's trek along with other African American editors' responses to U.S. imperialism, I attempt to gauge how black journalists and activists capitalized on the fissures that empire and its contradictory ideologies and iconographies opened in America's racialized borders of belonging. Examination of Washington's speeches and letters in the years leading up to and simultaneous with Fortune's journey as well as Fortune's own words and writings reveals that, at least around the turn of the twentieth century, both men hoped U.S. expansion and African American participation in it might expose not only the power of race but also its instability and vulnerability. Fortune did indeed preach the Tuskegee line of respectability and self-help as he traveled in Hawaii and the Philippines and contemplated a refuge for African Americans; Washington is no doubt part of the story of the global economic restructuring of slave labor into something that remained, and remains, racialized and exploitative. But both men, along with other black newspaper editors, also imagined transnational alliances along lines of color that might destabilize a strengthening Jim Crow system at home. Fortune in particular seemed to hope that new emancipatory cultural and racial mixings, channeled and empowered through "newspaper organs," might emerge from America's encounters in the Pacific. Fortune's own power as a black publisher is difficult to gauge; it was neither illusionary nor deep. His renown in the medium helped him secure the government appointment in the first place and likely contributed to his cordial reception by Hawaii's planter class. Yet at the end of his journey, he was as financially strapped as at the start. Furthermore, vibrant and ethnically diverse presses in both territories had their own competing conceptions of race and citizenship and dogged the renowned black journalist during his visit even as he tried to use the newspaper medium to advocate for African American citizenship and opportunity.

How did T. Thomas Fortune, founder of early black civil rights organizations and a constant gadfly against white racism, wind up in the Philippines? Fortune was born into slavery in Marianna, Florida, in 1856, the third child of two slaves, Emanuel and Sarah Jane. His parents each claimed African, European, and American Indian ancestry.[7] After emancipation, Fortune's family was terrorized by white supremacists (Emanuel was active in Reconstruction politics) and fled to Jacksonville in 1869. Fortune's education included time in a Freedmen's Bureau school and two school terms at Howard University in the 1870s, but he would always cite his work as a printer's assistant for several newspapers as key to his intellectual growth. Printer's offices, he said, were "wonderful schools."[8] He founded the *New York Globe* in 1881; the paper would become the *Freeman* and later the *Age*. His editorials were often militant; he called on African Americans to resist white violence with deadly force and demanded that the government uphold African American social and political rights. He appears at least once in Patrick Ford's *Irish World*, in an 1890 news item about a Young Men's Industrial League that worked to secure employment for African American youths.[9]

In fact, as Fortune made a name for himself as a foremost agitator for black civil rights, he often looked toward Irish nationalists and their organizations as models for African American resistance. In 1884, during his most militant period, he published *Black and White: Land, Labor, and Politics in the South*, in which he strongly affirmed the rights of African Americans as American citizens; advocated, as Washington would, a practical, industrial education for blacks; and joined Patrick Ford, Michael Davitt, and radical economist Henry George in calling land ownership key to the rise of the downtrodden. The "Afro-American," Fortune wrote, "is, like the Irishman in Ireland, a stranger in his own land."[10] Fortune was perhaps the first to propose a national black civil rights organization, in 1887, which he modeled after the Irish Land League; in 1890 he spearheaded the National Afro-American League, which collapsed by 1893 for lack of funds. He admired the fighting spirit and organizational abilities of the Irish. "We know what oppression is," Fortune wrote in his *Freeman* in 1886, and African Americans "sympathize therefore with the Irish, who at home are in political and industrial slavery; and we rejoice to see the day of their deliverance drawing nigh."[11] When he criticized African American leadership, he sometimes contrasted black leaders to those of the Irish. "Have we ever produced a man in any way comparable to Charles Stewart Parnell? Have we a man to-day in any respect his peer?"[12]

However, more typical in the black press during Fortune's lifetime were expressions of mistrust, hostility, and revulsion toward the Irish. They were "the most prejudiced race of all toward the black man," according to a writer in the Indianapolis *Freeman*.[13] In 1845 Frederick Douglass found his two-year lecture tour of Ireland inspiring, and Irish crowds and Irish leaders, including the pro-abolitionist Daniel O'Connell, treated him with great warmth. But Douglass frequently made clear his distaste for the U.S. Irish, who were longtime supporters of the Democratic Party and perpetrators of mob violence against African Americans. Irish Americans "are instantly taught when they step upon our soil to hate and despise the Negro" and see him as labor competition, he wrote.[14]

But Douglass, too, supported home rule for Ireland, and some black editors went beyond simple editorials in their support of Irish independence—newspaper networks occasionally interfaced. Black papers in San Francisco and Trenton, New Jersey, kept their readers informed about the doings of local chapters of the Land League and the Ancient Order of Hibernians.[15] J. E. Brown of the San Francisco *Vindicator* offered readers a joint deal: four dollars for a year's subscription to both his black weekly and the *United Irishman* of New York. When Ford and some other Irish nationalists sought Republican Party support for their newspapers and lined up behind James G. Blaine in 1884, some African Americans foresaw the Irish finally abandoning the Democratic Party. One black reader wrote to Fortune's *Globe* that "it would appear that we are entering the Millennium . . . when there shall be no North, no South, no East, no West . . . no sectarian prejudices, no color or race prejudices, but all Freemen under God. . . . Yes, let us welcome with all our hearts the Irish American" into the Republican Party.[16] (A Protestant minister's quip about the Democrats being the party of "rum, Romanism, and rebellion" helped squash any Irish migration toward the GOP.)[17] Black and Irish relations remained paradoxical, as the Irish, for African Americans, modeled both good and bad behavior. Other immigrant groups learned from the Irish the harsh racial rules of the United States; African American activists like Douglass and Fortune envied, emulated, and feared Irish organizational clout.

By late 1902, Fortune's best days as a race advocate seemed behind him. He was broke, in debt, and in near-daily communication with Booker T. Washington, for which some black leaders fiercely criticized him.[18] That summer, Washington had helped place Fortune at the head of the Afro-American Council, and many black newspaper editors were dismayed, predicting, with some accuracy, Tuskegee's takeover and blunting of the early civil rights group's activist edge.[19] Fortune felt his work as a race man entitled him to a political appointment, perhaps as minister to Haiti, but Roosevelt had repeatedly rebuffed him.[20] Finally, he got a placement of sorts: General James S. Clarkson, a white old-time abolitionist and Republican leader, arranged Fortune's appointment as a temporary special immigrant agent of the Treasury Department to study racial and economic conditions in Hawaii and the Philippines.[21]

Fortune described his purpose to Booker T. Washington a month before his departure, writing, "[I] had in mind the shunting of our surplus labor to the Orient if I found the conditions such as to warrant such recommendations." He also wanted to get out of the country and "make enough money to pay [his] debts and start fresh in purely literary work," an astonishing statement for the famed journalist (and considerably less-famous poet) to make. He assured the Tuskegee leader that he had stopped drinking for good and that Washington "need no further fears on that score."[22] Washington wrote President Theodore Roosevelt that Fortune's appointment had given him "the greatest general satisfaction," which suggests that he, along with Clarkson, bent Roosevelt's ear.[23]

The *Washington Post*, however, linked Fortune's journey to the colonization schemes of Alabama senator John Tyler Morgan, notorious for his racial extremism even in a time of vigorous white supremacy.[24] Morgan, the paper claimed, had told Secretary of War Elihu Root and Philippine commissioner William Howard Taft that although Southern farmers still believed they needed the Negro, soon enough "millions" of African Americans might emigrate, be given "homesteads of about twenty acres each," and be found "working out their own salvation" in the Philippines. Morgan told the *Post* that his plan would not deprive African Americans of their citizenship—they would "still be under the flag" in a climate "better suited to them"—and that Taft and Root were impressed with his idea.²⁵ Scholars have not uncovered any correspondence between Washington, Fortune, and Morgan, and such an alliance seems unlikely, for Fortune had long locked horns with the senator and ex-Confederate general.²⁶

In the years before his overseas journey, Fortune appeared skeptical but not wholly opposed to voluntary black migration outside the United States. In *Black and White*, he rejected white-run colonization schemes, and as late as 1901 he was still sharply critical of Bishop Henry McNeal Turner's calls for mass black migration to Africa on the grounds that Afro-Americans were by now culturally American and foreign to Africa.²⁷ However, in the fall of 1891 in the *New York Age*, Fortune pushed back at a white journalist critical of schemes by Turner and Edward P. McCabe to settle African Americans in Liberia and Oklahoma, respectively. Fortune agreed that such efforts would likely be fruitless but objected to the journalist's scorn at "improvident Negroes" eager to get to "some promised land where there is no work to do." "Why improvident?" Fortune asked. Had it not always been the case, for both black and white, that "discontent, caused by hard social conditions," motivated emigration?²⁸ Fortune may also have considered black emigration a way to reduce white mob violence in the South. In an 1899 letter to the *New York Sun*, Fortune included a lengthy passage from his longtime friend William A. Pledger, who wrote that, "as a solution to the difficulty" of mob rule, a group of African Americans, "thoroughly imbued with American ideas," would prove "a positive acquisition" to the Philippines.²⁹ Pledger's statement and Fortune's possible endorsement of it hint at two other ideas that Fortune would return to on his journey: that African Americans could help Filipino society develop and that Tuskegee, or Fortune himself, might help furnish the right black population.³⁰

Fortune arrived in Honolulu from San Francisco on the steamer *Doric* on December 16, 1902, landing on a tropical island with an astonishingly vibrant newspaper scene. Hawaii in the late nineteenth and early twentieth centuries was home to establishment papers, oppositional presses, independent actors, and in-language ethnic presses. The alliance of missionary descendants and white business interests, mainly planters, who overthrew Queen Liliuokalani in 1893, constituted much of the newspaper press; newspapers quoted in this chapter and not denoted as "nationalist" or "independent" are such establishment, oligarchy-supporting journals. But many outspoken oppositional and nationalist newspapers, published in English, Hawaiian, or both, and staffed by native, mixed-race, or white journalists, still existed when Fortune visited the islands. These were accompanied by in-language ethnic newspapers as well as independent pro-labor newspapers. By 1909 Hawaii had about one hundred publications in print, and a full 30 percent were published in languages other than English, including Chinese, Japanese, Portuguese, Korean, and several Filipino languages.[31] Fortune was intrigued; one Honolulu paper reported shortly after his arrival that he was "greatly interested in the newspapers of the city, asking many questions about them."[32]

If Hawaii's newspaper scene was healthy, its sugar economy was not. As he toured the islands with representatives of the planters' association and the chamber of commerce, "even the hack drivers talk sugar to me," Fortune told the press, "and the paramount idea is how to get sugar planting back to the old time basis when everybody, according to all accounts, carried round a hundred or so in his pocket just for change to rattle."[33] Planters suffered from a shortage of labor and were desperate to find the "right" kind of worker. A report from U.S. Commissioner of Labor Carroll D. Wright put it bluntly: "Hardly a locality exists in the world where there is a surplus of unskilled labor that has not been visited and investigated by Hawaiian labor agents."[34] As they brought in workers from abroad, planters hoped they could find a way to gain an exemption from Chinese exclusion for Hawaii and thus import Chinese laborers, thought by many to work the hardest and with the least protest.

In exploring possible black emigration to Hawaii, which one paper reported was part of Fortune's personal advocacy work for African Americans and "in no way connected to his mission,[35] Fortune was forced to engage a planter discourse in the oligarchy's press that racialized labor. Finding the right laborer was tantamount to finding the correct racial group, whose members were thought to naturally—via biology, culture, or some combination of the two—possess the proper attributes to handle the difficulties of reliably harvesting cane. It was a long-standing discussion in the islands' best-funded presses. Two years before Fortune's arrival, for example, the *Maui News* described labor strife on a plantation: Japanese at Kahului were striking for better wages and shorter working hours; by a combination of "threats and coaxing" and "the foolish terror of the Hawaiians," they convinced some native Hawaiians to join them; then workers at the Spreckelsville mill joined in. Fortunately for the plantation owner, the *News* reported, "a large consignment of negroes and Italians had recently arrived"; they were put to work "with gratifying results."[36] Yet by the summer of 1901, after a black laborer on Maui reportedly stabbed a Japanese man, planters' opinion of African American labor had soured.[37]

Commissioner Wright's 1903 report was filled with more explicit race/labor typologies: the Japanese were vain "like children" and had to be flattered into working; the Chinaman was, by contrast, "a sort of agricultural automaton."[38] Puerto Ricans were apt to carry weapons, drink, and fight but were slowly settling down and having families as a result of their possession of "the heredity of the Caucasian."[39] Planters, Wright wrote, still desired Chinese workers the most and wanted to "play off" the Chinese against the Japanese to make labor more "tractable."[40]

When members of the same racial group were perceived as acting in disparate ways, Hawaii's planter press simply divided the group into subtypes, often based on region. One editorial less than three years before Fortune's visit, noting that Kohala planters were to "experiment" with African American labor, advised, "it matters very much where you get your negro from." Those from the agricultural sections of the United States were "sober, quiet and industrious"; if they came with their families, "we could educate their children in our schools." But there was a "class" of African American from "the vicinity of the towns" who had "no home life, but moves about from one job to another, sometimes working, sometimes loafing, sometimes stealing, poker playing, crap shooting and drinking." The paper suggested direct recruitment of the best class of black man by those who sought him, rather than relying, remotely, on a labor agent.[41] Though it could be argued that these statements refer to supposed cultural and not imagined racial characteristics, these traits are frequently described, as in race-based notions, as essential and unchanging.[42]

Rather than resist these race/labor typologies, in laying out his plan for African American labor on the islands, Fortune often echoed them. He told the Builders and Traders meeting, "'I do not think . . . that those who object so strongly to the introduction of negro labor here have seen the true plantation laborer.'" He continued:

> There are one or two Southerners here who know the class of people I mean, and they will uphold me as to their fitness for the work. The true negro is a different individual from the half-breed tinctured with the ambition of the white united to the natural shirking responsibility of the negro. It makes a bad combination. And in a milder degree this is true of the class that has come here and which has been culled from barbers, waiters, touts, dock hands and the riff raff of Southern cities spoiled for work by their closer association with white man's ways which they imitate but do not emulate.[43]

In other remarks at the Builders and Traders meeting, Fortune told the audience of businessmen that because of organized labor's success in "the coal strike"—in all likelihood the 1902 anthracite coal strike in eastern Pennsylvania, which Roosevelt had mediated—the power of organized labor to keep Chinese workers out of the United States and all its territories would likely increase. But Chinese exclusion was happening at a time when "discontent among the negro laborers of the South was never greater." Though Fortune stressed that he had "no fixed opinion on the subject" and had "come to learn," he laid out his vision: "I believe that from 20,000 to 300,000 negro laborers, not the vicious from the slums, but men who are workers all the time, could be secured to work in the fields of Hawaii and the Philippines and that they would prove the best kind of labor." Cuba's and St. Thomas's sugar industries, after all, had been "built up by black labor," in contrast to the "failure" that resulted when Italians were brought into Louisiana for the same purpose.[44] Like Father Yorke, Fortune described labor as a key plank of citizenship rights for his group. Unlike Yorke, whose readership might be protected by powerful, racially exclusionary unions and the wages they could command, the work on Hawaii that Fortune sought for African Americans was low-wage and grueling.[45]

Fortune posited himself as the expert who could find the right kind of black laborer for Hawaii, a link between the fields of the U.S. South and those of Hawaii. The "true negro agriculturist," Fortune said, would "not be easily persuaded to leave" the United States, "but it is a possibility, if you go at it the right way and get men like Booker Washington, myself if you like, and others who have the interests of the race truly at heart, to get the supply for you."[46]

Journalism as a practice is tied up with the formation of these race/labor typologies. Fortune's stated expertise on different "types" of black laborers resembles newspaperman James Samuel Stemons's (discussed in Chapter 4) similar observations about types of African Americans as well as *Freeman* publisher Edward Cooper's words: "No class of men know the Negro so well as the editor. . . . Who knows the vain woman, the dude, the barber or the crooked preacher so well? He knows them all for he has dealings with them."[47] Cooper's urban black editor seems to walk city streets in a kind of detached, classificatory mode reminiscent of Walter Benjamin's *flâneur*, "a nineteenth-century social type known for his roving forms of urban spectatorship."[48] Newspapers and newspapering flattered editors that theirs was a particularly privileged viewpoint from which to understand the world (see Figure 3.2).

If Benjamin saw the *flâneur*'s willingness to seek out new and even shocking sights as a sign of his modernity, other scholars studying nineteenth-century manners have found countercurrents: the city's crowd could be perceived as a threat, and middle-class conduct manuals, for example, recommended visual withdrawal and tighter differentiation. James W. Cook stresses "the chronic semiotic confusion sparked by rapid demographic mobility, market expansion, and urbanization across the nineteenth century," which produced "a brave new world in which traditional systems

Figure 3.2 "Specimens of Afro-American Statesmen," by Moses L. Tucker, from *The Freeman* (Indianapolis), September 20, 1890.

of visual identification (based, for example, on dress or bodily comportment) no longer seemed to signify in consistent and reliable ways."[49] Newspapers—through editorials, where the editor shared his wisdom on the city; columns that divided life into news, interests, sports, and leisure; and especially images, whether of cartoonish types or documentary-style "news" photography—attempted to make sense of this brave new world and helped encourage the recognition of types and classes of people. Newspapers helped train the eye in particular ways of seeing.

Newspapering seemed to give Fortune some clout with Hawaii's mainstream press; the *Gazette* wrote upon his arrival that "perhaps no negro publicist and orator is better known in the United States."[50] Reaction to his hopes for African American labor on the islands, however, was mostly negative. Several articles in various Hawaiian establishment papers criticized the proposal; most claimed that black labor was tried before, on Maui, with disastrous results.[51] The *Hawaiian Gazette* printed eleven one-paragraph responses from eleven major sugar planters to Fortune's suggestion of African American labor; almost all rejected it outright. J. A. Gilman of Castle and Cooke said that African Americans "who would come from so far away are always the undesirable ones." F. A. Schaefer and several others noted that the "experiment" failed in the past; W. M. Giffard, for example, said that African

Americans had shown "a tendency to fight" with each other and not associate with Hawaiians. W. O. Smith, secretary of the planters' association, told the paper that such efforts had taken place since 1872 and had always been futile. Perhaps, he said, it could work if whole black communities, along with their preachers, were brought in, so that "they might build new homes."[52] Even Fortune's African American friend T. McCants Stewart, a former emigrant to Liberia who was practicing law in Honolulu in 1902, told the *Evening Bulletin* that Hawaii could only attract the worst elements of black labor, as only "40 Acres and a Mule," an impossibility on Hawaii, could attract the best black plantation laborers.[53] The most sought-after racial group for labor in the fields remained the Chinese.

Fortune's own views toward the Chinese are hard to decipher from press reports of his visit. He would write upon his return to the United States that the Chinese were among the "best and most sympathetic and reliable people" he had met on his journey.[54] However, in a third *Gazette* report on Fortune's arrival, Fortune told those gathered that his fight against "race distinctions" caused him to "take issue with Prof. Jenks over his recommendations that Chinese be permitted to enter the Philippines."[55] The paper provides no information on Jenks, who is in all likelihood Cornell political economist Jeremiah W. Jenks, a frequent visitor to Asia who was complimentary of Chinese entrepreneurialism. In other Asian lands such as Ceylon, Burma, Java, and Sumatra, Jenks wrote, Chinese immigrants' "diligence" and "thrift" had been "practically indispensible" to development. For natives, the Chinese had "raised their standard of living" by "doing the work they were unwilling to do."[56] Another intellectual, Frederick Wells Williams, agreed, writing in the *American Historical Review* that Americans must "dismiss old prejudices and learn to consider the Chinaman in our Eastern dependencies as an indispensable means to their economic development." The Chinese were "one of the most expert and subtle peoples on the globe."[57] Despite these positive views of the Chinese, however, in the mid-1800s, Republicans and reformers had equated the coerced labor of the "coolie trade" with slavery, and their efforts to stop the importation of indentured labor helped pave the way ideologically for Chinese exclusion later in the century. This may help explain how in 1902 Fortune and Patrick Ford could each position themselves as both fighters for racial equality and supporters of restrictions on Chinese migration.[58]

Hawaii's independent, nationalist, but nonnative press similarly mixed pro-labor and anti-Asian sentiments in a "race-inflected antimonopoly populism" common to the time.[59] Fortune's visit was watched by at least one such newspaper known for lambasting the annexationists and calling the planter oligarchy "an American mafia." The *Independent*—at the time of Fortune's visit owned and operated by ardent Hawaiian nationalist F. J. Testa, one of seven signers of an anti-annexation letter to President McKinley in October 1897—urged Fortune to explore the "general inhumanity" of the way in which field labor was employed on the island. If he looked closely, Fortune could surely produce a plan that would "forever remove the Asiatic blot on the industrial progress of this Territory" and help the general community. "Search the methods of the 'sugar barons,' Mr. Fortune ... and obtain a story yet uncompleted of the how and wherefor of the transmutation of Chinese labor passage money into Hawaiian Territory Treasury warrants." A concern with corruption and the inhumane treatment of workers seems to slip inexorably toward excluding "Asiatics." Yet Testa also defended the Chinese community in Hawaii from charges that its neighborhood was a breeding ground for disease.[60]

Native Hawaiians, too, watched Fortune's visit. At least one Hawaiian-language newspaper commented on his arrival, and several had addressed U.S. race relations prior to his journey. The *Home Rula Repubalika*, run by Robert William Kalanihiapo Wilcox, who was nearly hanged for his armed revolt against the white oligarchy, expressed sympathy toward African Americans in 1901, when Booker T. Washington's visit to the White House sparked Southern outrage. Roosevelt had said he would make himself president of the entire nation, the paper wrote, so why all the fuss? The Republican Party in the United States, after all, was known to be friendly to dark-skinned people. But on Hawaii, "our Republicans are not like that. They are highly racist against the dark-skinned. Yet they still claim the rights of the Republican name," something the paper called a "fraud."[61] But the *Ke Aloha Aina*, founded by Joseph Kahooluhi Nawahi, a native Hawaiian legislator and publisher, commented during Fortune's visit that "it would be outrageous if this dirty labor race is introduced to us in Hawaii in place of the Chinese," and, the paper warned ominously, "it would not only be us who would witness the bad things of these people."[62]

Faced with Hawaii's complicated racial politics, Fortune attempted to turn some of it on its head at the expense of whites while simultaneously performing his duty as a government agent. After a few weeks on the islands, Fortune told the *Hawaiian Star* that he understood why planters desired Chinese labor so strongly: the Chinaman "sleeps on a mat, he wears clothes that cost less for a year than most men's monthly laundry bill.... He smokes no expensive cigars, buys no twenty-five cent drinks, entertains no friend and has got the white man, who spends half his income [on] clothes, entirely out of the race as regards labor competition." (The Japanese man, Fortune said, also had a "disposition to dress up and be a bit of an American dude, which costs money.") On the U.S. mainland, laborers feared the Chinese and had "placed a prohibitive tariff, so to speak"—Chinese exclusion—"against this competitive labor." Fortune said he did not think planters would get their exemption to Chinese exclusion.[63]

Short of Chinese labor and besides black labor, what else might help Hawaii? Fortune recommended the islands diversify their agriculture and grow coffee and vanilla at higher altitudes and consider rubber and cacao, too. Fortune may not have forgotten his past beliefs in the importance of land; the *Star* reported that he was "looking largely into the lands which are open for homesteading" for African American workers.[64]

Racial Discord at Home and Abroad

As Fortune was completing his Hawaii investigation and preparing to set sail for Manila, race relations were deteriorating rapidly in the U.S. South. Attention to the domestic front reveals connections between American empire and a rapidly advancing Jim Crow system and philosophy, its expression and dissemination through newspapers, and provides clues into Booker T. Washington's and perhaps T. Thomas Fortune's global thinking in the early 1900s.

Washington wrote Fortune in February 1903, from Tuskegee, hoping his friend had not suffered seasickness during his travels and then stating, "I must confess that we are passing through a rather severe trial in the South just now."[65] At least three things had inflamed Southern politicians and newspaper editors: President Roosevelt had followed Washington's recommendations and appointed William D. Crum, an African American, to the position of collector of customs in Charleston, South Carolina; black public officials in Washington, D.C., had attended a judicial reception at the White House; and, in early January, Roosevelt had shut down the Indianola, Mississippi, post office after local politicians forced out, because of her race, its postmaster, Minnie M. Cox, an African American woman and a McKinley appointee.[66] Perhaps as troublesome and vexing for Washington was that Secretary Root, just back from the Philippines, had delivered a peculiar speech on African American rights. "The whole situation is very much mixed and there is a good deal of unrest among our people," Washington wrote Fortune in mid-February. "Secy. Root's speech in New York a few weeks ago, which nobody seems to understand, further complicates the matter."[67]

Root had spoken at the Fortieth Anniversary Meeting of the Union League Club in New York City on February 6. (Blacks, whites, and sometimes both races together had formed union leagues that became "the political voice for impoverished freedmen" after the Civil War.[68] By 1903, however, few such clubs retained their activist edge.) Root began by honoring the "Gentlemen of 1863" present, who had helped end the "curse of slavery." But now, Root told the gathering, three "problems almost immeasurable" challenged the younger generation: a widening gap between rich and poor, which corrupted politics and threatened through envy to provoke a "war of classes"; ever-more powerful unions, which hurt American meritocracy by protecting "sloth," "incompetency," and "stupidity"; and the so-called Negro Problem, though he never named it as such. Here, Root questioned the entire Reconstruction project to grant African Americans full citizenship. "I fear we are compelled to face the conclusion that the experiment has failed," he told the gathering. He described the loss of black suffrage rights in the South and hinted at his exasperation at Southerners' "loud outcries" against Roosevelt for appointing African Americans when the president had in fact made fewer such appointments than his predecessor. Soon, Root said, "white men will succeed in excluding blacks from all offices in the southern States." Root repeated that the country must "face the failure of the plan . . . to lift the blacks" after emancipation through the strategy of voting rights.[69] A vexed Washington wrote Fortune, "The President seems to be standing squarely and so far as I can get information directly or indirectly, he is with us."[70]

Two weeks following Root's speech, his words appeared to be on Washington's mind as Washington spoke to a Bronx audience and pointedly addressed freedom, race, and empire. After reciting famous groups in U.S. history that revealed the "desire for liberty that is natural in every human breast," such as the "Cavaliers of Jamestown" and the "Puritans of Plymouth Rock," Washington complicated freedom, bringing the concept into increasingly incongruous situations. Through the Monroe Doctrine, the United States would not only "contend against the world for its freedom, but for the freedom of all governments upon the two American continents." Next, the former slave described the Civil War as a Confederate leader might: "Half a century later we find the Southern section of our country entering into a political and physical war in a contention for freedom in the control of domestic and state policies." As for the recent Spanish-American War, "we [found] ourselves demanding, at the point of the sword, the freedom of our neighbors, the Cubans."[71]

Washington then put this problematic "freedom" into conversation with race. "During all the period that the majority and dominant races were contending for the most complete and perfect freedom and independence," he continued, "there were living by their side two other races, different in color and different in history—the Indian and the Negro." Whenever and wherever whites and Indians met, "there either was war between the two or injustice and oppression shown [on] the original American." When encountering other races on a quest for freedom, Washington told his audience, "you have so far practiced absorption, colonization, or extermination." Yet "you have got the Indian out of the range of your vision. And in this country it seems to be the fashion to consider a problem solved when we get it out of our sight to such an extent that its existence is unobtrusive and our consciences are eased."[72]

But now, Washington said, a new "experiment in the way of race accessions" loomed, and the Filipino would soon be classified "as a black man or a white man":

> Just now the Filipino seems to be going through the interesting process of being carefully examined. If he can produce hair that is long enough and nose and feet that are small enough, I think the Filipino will be designated and treated as a white man; otherwise he will be assigned to my race. If I were to consider the question purely from a selfish standpoint, I should urge that our new subjects be classed as Negroes; but if I were to consider unselfishly the peace of mind of the Filipino himself, I should hope that he . . . will not struggle through all future generations considered and looked upon as a problem, instead of a man.[73]

The speech is fascinating not only for its scarcely veiled anger at white America. What was the "selfish" reason Washington cited for imagining the Filipino as black? Did he hope Tuskegee might be called on to work not only in Africa, where its employees were mediating between indigenous Ewe farmers and German colonialists in the growing of cotton, but in the Philippines, too? Or was it a numbers game—that is, could more allies in a struggle against discrimination tip the scales toward racial justice?[74]

The two possibilities are not mutually exclusive. It is the contention of this chapter that both Fortune and Washington were attempting to position themselves as brokers for African American labor and coordinators of Tuskegee-style native uplift in the territories and hoped that American empire might destabilize a white racial order and present new opportunities for black advancement at home and abroad. According to the *Hawaiian Star*, Fortune had international connections as a kind of agent for the exportation of black labor. The *Star* reported that he was attempting to supply black labor to "a big rubber plantation on the Congo in West Africa."[75] Earlier in 1902, Fortune and Washington had discussed the Congo with each other and, for Washington, with investors. In June, Washington had written to Fortune, "I also have your circular letter of June 7th asking my opinion regarding the possibility of getting 100,000 Afro-Americans to go to the Congo. I would say briefly that I feel very sure that if you could get Bishop Turner, Col. Pledger and Rev. W. H. Heard to go to the Congo and settle there that you would have little trouble in getting the remainder to follow. What do you think of this scheme?"[76] By mid-February 1903, Washington was being recruited by the powerful Lord Grey of the British South Africa Company in Rhodesia to tour the nation for six to nine months and recommend how best to "raise, educate, and civilize the black man."[77] Newspapers reported the offer, and Washington consulted with Roosevelt before deciding that, according to Harlan, "his primary responsibility was to his institution and the American Negro."[78]

But perhaps, Washington must have thought, Tuskegee could both participate in American empire and advocate for people of color. In 1900 Washington had informed readers of the *Century Magazine*, the widely read successor to *Scribner's Monthly*, that what Tuskegee had accomplished in the U.S. South "under most difficult circumstances" could be attempted in Cuba and Puerto Rico. Tuskegee was training "a few of the most promising men and women from these islands" to replicate the institute's "industrial" methods in their lands. But historically, Washington wrote, white Cubans and white Spaniards had treated black Cubans with near-equality. "In only a few instances [was] the color-line drawn. . . . Certainly it will place [the United States] in an awkward position to have gone to war to free a people from Spanish cruelty" only to "treat a large proportion of the population worse than did even Spain herself, simply on account of color." To Washington, a U.S. encounter with Cuba's fainter color line might highlight and unsettle sharply drawn racial segregation at home.[79]

But Washington was also correct that the Filipino was being "carefully examined" by Americans, including American cartoonists, who seemed confused about how to characterize men from Southeast Asia. An 1899 illustration in *Judge* shows Uncle Sam as a barber, with scissors of "education" and "civilization," having just given a trim to figures representing Cuba, Hawaii, and Puerto Rico—all drawn in the typical minstrel form of racial ridicule. Sam announces, "You're Next!" to a fourth figure, the Filipino, who appears as a hybrid of African American and American Indian stereotypes. This literal drawing of the Filipino mirrors race scientists' actual confusion with how to classify and understand the "Malay race." Uncle Sam as civilizer appears in many guises in *Puck* and *Judge*; one of the most common is as a headmaster, schooling his newly acquired students in the finer arts of civilization. (And, because President McKinley had called on America to "Christianize" Catholic Filipinos, one can understand why the Irish in America were so vigilant in battling for Catholic education and Catholic commissioners in the islands: Catholicism must not be included among the list of pagan dangers to America that so many in the mainstream anti-imperialist camp feared as blowback from U.S. adventures abroad.) Many American scholars and politicians looked to Hampton and Tuskegee Institutes to provide this civilizing uplift in the Pacific.

In Honolulu, as he would in Manila, Fortune stressed Washington's educational philosophy and a kind of politics of respectability as he toured the islands. At the Honolulu YMCA, Fortune delivered a talk titled "Self-Respect and Its Basis."[80] In that speech, according to a lengthy write-up in the *Pacific Commercial Advertiser*, Fortune spoke to an "unusually large audience" and "drew graphic word pictures" about the lives and character of the three men. Fortune described Lincoln's humble upbringings in a Kentucky log cabin and the lack of opportunities for "religious culture" or "mental development"; yet, through his mother and through contemplation of "nature and nature's God," Lincoln rose and became the Great Emancipator. While the nation mourned his assassination, another man, Samuel C. Armstrong, "stood on the prow of a vessel headed from Mexico" and "pondered . . . what was to become of these millions of freed blacks." Arriving in Virginia and "remembering what his father taught in Hawaii before the war," Armstrong created the Hampton Institute, educating "head, heart, and hands." Fortune said, according to the paper, that he counted himself lucky to have been acquainted with Armstrong and gave Hawaii credit for "the part which she has played in the education of the negro race of the southern states through the indomitable courage, sacrifice, and philanthropy" of Armstrong and his Hampton Institute. Finally, Fortune said, Booker T. Washington "walked 300 miles to Hampton Institute from the wilds of West Virginia" and later toiled day and night to build Tuskegee and "carry out the work of Lincoln and Armstrong." Fortune ended with words on character, whose basis was "in the home, in the school, in the church," and without which "no one could have respect."[81] At least in public, Fortune and Washington were in synch ideologically in 1902–1903.

Armstrong, who died in 1893, had written that "from 1820 to 1860, the distinctively missionary period, there was worked out in the Hawaiian Islands the problem of the emancipation, enfranchisement, and Christian civilization of a dark-skinned Polynesian people in many respects like the negro race."[82] Historian Gary Okihiro notes incisively that an 1882 letter from Hawaii's Bureau of Immigration to Armstrong, which asked the famed educator about the feasibility of black labor on Hawaii, reveals that "the ideas of native education and servile labor for the ostensible uplift of subject races migrated between island and continent, and a seed first cultivated in Hawai'i and transplanted in the American South had found its way back, full circle, to the Islands."[83] Fortune's trip to Hawaii surely represents the continued circulation of educational philosophies intimately tied to racialized notions of civilization and labor and embraced by expansionists as a method for integration and control of subject races at home and abroad.

Yet for Fortune and Washington, coexisting with and possibly cloaked by these conservative philosophies and pedagogies lay more subversive hopes, critiques, and perhaps agendas. "If the American flag remains in the Philippines," Fortune would soon write, "Afro-Americans will have to be drafted to hold it up."[84] As he prepared to leave Hawaii, he switched temporarily from journalist to poet, publishing a verse in the *Evening Bulletin* titled "The Kanaka Maiden." The maiden was Hawaii herself, "made for love, and not for labor." But her "towering hills" and "slumberous vales" were no longer her own; instead, a "stranger lords it now on the hillsides," and "even on the restless ocean tides / Are nothing seen but alien sails."[85] Fortune's rebellious poem and its newspaper placement may echo Hawaiian *mele* (chants, songs, or poems) that Hawaiians, according to Amy Ku'uleialoha Stillman, increasingly printed in late nineteenth-century Hawaiian-language newspapers as a way to voice political and nationalist desires.[86] The same romantic style that helped disguise the poem's subversiveness, however, also constrained its critique. "The Kanaka Maiden" evoked a nostalgic view of a lost land that dovetailed with late nineteenth-century sympathies for indigenous peoples as "dying races." (The poem recalls the "pipe of peace/piece of pipe" Irish American postcard shown in Chapter 1, Figure 1.7; social Darwinist thought ranked perceived racial groups and cast them in a winner-take-all fight for survival.)

As Fortune was preparing to leave Hawaii for Manila, Washington wrote him again: "I advise you to be very careful about what you say to newspaper men, especially in the Philippines, as they are rather treacherous."[87] His remarks, as Fortune would soon discover, were prescient.

The Philippines in the Black Press

By February 1903, when Fortune arrived in the Philippines, the black press in the United States had already engaged for several years in a lively debate about the Spanish-American and Philippine-American Wars. Many black newspapers stood staunchly against the conflicts. Some drew affinities along lines of color; the Salt Lake City *Broad Ax* declared that "no Negro possessing any race pride can enter heartily into the prosecution of the war."[88] Others stressed the hypocrisy of bringing democracy to Asia while African Americans were being disenfranchised at home, as the *Richmond Planet* did when it editorialized, "A man who is not good enough to vote for a government is not good enough to fight for it."[89] In an editorial titled "Reflections," editor Sol C. Johnson of the *Savannah Tribune* worried that war was unifying white people at home and abroad:

> The Spanish American war has drawn the Anglo Saxons together. The Union can scarcely be called national alone but international as well. All of the branches of this great race felt a deep sympathy for the American branch of the family in her armed contention with Spain. . . . The stars and stripes and the Union Jack are blended to-

gether on festive occasions and men's faces grow red and their throats hoarse in exulting and exhilarating utterances of love, friendship and union for the united race.[90]

The *Tribune* feared that Anglo-Saxons were "intoxicated with the wine of success" and had forgotten that "victory belongs to the American people, not to the Anglo Saxon race." The outburst was "pernicious, full of mischief and broods no good to the republic."[91] Johnson and some other black editors had supported U.S. intervention in Cuba or the Philippines from the start, pushing for African American enlistment and fighting for black soldiers' fair treatment. But now the *Tribune* saw race and nation merging treacherously.

Black soldiers in the islands also wrote letters home to the black press, using African American newspapers as a forum to express their opinions on the war and occupation. Black newspapers reprinted letters originally printed in other papers, circulating opinions on life in the Philippines from a black perspective. Fortune would have surely followed these soldiers' letters, which showed a range of responses, from pride at serving one's country to outrage at white soldiers' racism toward black U.S. troops and Filipinos.[92]

The contours of black editors' critiques of Anglo-Saxonism and the extent of the affinities they felt with Filipinos and with southern Africans in the Boer War were shaped and constrained partly by their domestic fight against Bishop Turner and other advocates of black migration to Africa. In describing both Africans and Filipinos, the black press could critique the racialized binary of civilization and savagery but might also employ that framework with little modification to stress, for example, how unsuited African Americans were for migration schemes to "savage" Africa. The Indianapolis *Freeman* wrote in February 1899 that Filipinos were "possessed with much pride and independence of spirit and have some notions of government," but "the bushmen of today cannot be the legislator of tomorrow" and hence must be under U.S. control until "the staying hand of America might be withdrawn."[93]

Though subject to segregation and marginalization in all regions of the country in the late nineteenth century, African Americans could still be expected to hold biases similar to those of other Americans. To some extent, these prejudices may have been augmented by black newspapers' routine use of "patent back" material—ready-made text and images purchased by weeklies, often from the Associated Press newswire, to bulk up the paper. Fortune and other black editors hated seeing such material reprinted in the black press. "By means of plate matter and patent-backs selected and prepared by white men," one correspondent wrote to Fortune's *Age* in the early 1890s, "our own newspapers become oftentimes a circulating medium for error and wrong."[94] *Freeman* owner George Knox prided himself on printing little patent material, yet the close-up of the illustration "Native Insurgent Soldiers" (Figure 3.3) is from the *Freeman*. The identical illustration appears in both mainstream and ethnic media of the time (see, for example, the June 9, 1898, *Salt Lake Herald*), suggesting strongly that it originated with a news service, possibly the Associated Press.[95] The date "Native Insurgent Soldiers" appeared in the *Freeman*, May 14, 1898, was just two weeks after Admiral George Dewey's decimation of the Spanish fleet in Manila Bay and several months before U.S. and Philippine troops would clash—a tense period of U.S. occupation of Manila, when both Philippine rebel leader Emilio Aguinaldo and the United States were engaged in "competitive state-building."[96] The illustration essentially explains "the Filipino" to the newspaper's readers, with accompanying text that resembles the anthropological rhetoric of a natural history museum diorama (the Filipino is "coarse and ugly," though "tractable and docile when well treated"). The illustration along with reprinted maps of the Philippines with accompanying text dovetail with a popular rhetoric of national manhood and aggressiveness common at the turn of the century.[97]

Figure 3.3 "Native Insurgent Soldiers," from *The Freeman* (Indianapolis), May 14, 1898.

How can we understand the appearance of "Native Insurgent Soldiers" in the *Freeman*? The editor's decision to reprint the illustration appears to mark in a straightforward manner this "race paper's" support of U.S. imperial efforts and ideology. The *Freeman* did back U.S. annexation of the islands and merely urged Philippine independence as soon as the United States deemed Filipinos ready for self-rule. Though the late nineteenth-century imperial drive held a strong component of white superiority, it also contained other notions, such as American exceptionalism, which some African Americans might embrace. Darwinian ideas about competition between living organisms were frequently applied to human society at large, and this, too, might have had some appeal to many black writers and thinkers—that is, an emergent black middle or upper class especially might flatter itself through notions of a kind of societal "survival of the fittest." Efforts to appear modern might involve distancing oneself from "dark" or "heathen" parts of the world.

Yet even the most pro-war black newspaper at least critiqued justifications for expansion, especially notions of a "white man's burden." The *Freeman*, for example, reprinted a letter from Private Fulbright in the Twenty-Fifth Infantry, who wrote, "If we are to unfurl our flag on these islands let us make these natives joint heirs in our citizenship."[98] The "Native Insurgents" image and text sits uncomfortably with these messages of support for Filipino rights. Furthermore, how the *Freeman*'s readers interpreted this image may have been complex. Sometimes African American editors reprinted outrageously racist excerpts from mainstream newspapers with little or no accompanying commentary or perhaps with ironic headlines. Editors trusted that readers could decode these passages for themselves. The black press, pro-expansion or not, like much of the liberal white press, routinely turned the discourse of "savage" versus "civilized" peoples around, noting that atrocities in the Philippines or, at minimum, lynchings in the U.S. South brought into question who was civilized and who was not. Johnson, editor of the *Savannah Tribune*, particularly liked to suggest that white Southerners, through their lynch mobs, were degenerating into "cannibals";[99] Knox was no exception. Thus, loyal readers might supply their own quotation marks around the terms "savage" and "civilized" that appear beneath the "Native Insurgents" illustration, for this discourse had already been extensively problematized in the paper. The possibility the image presents for dual perspectives, of racial identification or a more class- or culture-based dismissal, mirrors T. Thomas Fortune's hybrid rhetoric in his *Voice of the Negro* articles (discussed later), where he alternately attacked Anglo-Saxonism or elevated African Americans over Filipinos by asserting blacks' membership in a broader American cultural superiority.

Fortune's own views on Western imperialism were complex. In Atlanta, Georgia, in 1895, concurrent with but overshadowed by Booker T. Washington's famous "Atlanta Compromise" speech at the same venue, Fortune spoke to Methodist missionaries and African American leaders on "The Nationalization of Africa." Fortune described European imperialism as bloody and cruel but also claimed it would produce a stronger, more unified and better-governed continent, helping Africa escape the "demoralizing heterogeneousness" of so many "savage" tribes. Yet racial diversity and hybridization, by contrast, would strengthen Africa, and Fortune predicted that Europeans would in fact be assimilated and absorbed into the continent, producing a new and glorious civilization.[100] A similar cosmopolitan mix, he would soon write, could happen in the Philippines.

The Newsweekly "Lions" of Manila

When Fortune, en route from Hawaii, reached the elegant Hotel de Oriente in Manila late one night in February 1903, he found that an American porter had left on his table "a large batch of Manila newspapers, saying that . . . he was sure I would find many things in them to interest me." Their racist vitriol shocked the journalist.[101] Examination of the *Manila American* and other American-run newspapers available at the National Library of the Philippines reveals a different expression of white supremacy from that which Fortune encountered on Hawaii, one contained and disseminated by a unique newspaper press that Fortune would characterize as "Southern" in character.[102]

Shortly before Fortune's February arrival, the *Manila American* published an editorial titled "Chinese Are Wanted, but No Negroes" that linked Senator Morgan with Roosevelt and "special envoy" T. Thomas Fortune. On Hawaii, the paper reported, Fortune had "told the planters that 100,000 southern negroes could be landed . . . within six months."[103] "We do not want any more negroas [sic] in the Philippines," the *Manila American* declared. "He is here now, and we are having all sorts of trouble with him." Though "quite a number" of African Americans on the islands were "shining examples" of success, too many had become "vagrants," exploiters of Filipina women, and members of "bands of highwaymen . . . commonly called 'ladrones.'"[104] The *Manila American* called on its readers to "meet Mr. Fortune upon his arrival in the islands, and vehemently protest against the importation of negroes."[105]

The Manila *Freedom*, though it did not comment directly on Fortune's visit, also favored Chinese labor, because of what it characterized as the racial inferiority of Filipinos. "We are here, supposedly," the paper wrote around the time of Fortune's arrival, "to help the Filipino climb up the ladder of success. . . . We have seen their shortcomings so often that we have rather grown to despise the little brown man, with his timid ways.... The Filipino is a Malay, and will never get over that crowning misfortune."[106] To the *Freedom* and most other white American newspapers in Manila, any attempt to uplift Filipinos was futile.

Fortune explained the American media's aggressiveness toward him as a function of what he claimed were its practitioners' roots in the American South. The newspapers were "as violently Democratic and race-hating as those of Memphis or Atlanta," because of President McKinley's "fatal weakness for appointing Southern Democrats to controlling positions in the civil and military establishments in the insular territories."[107] He fired off a letter to Booker T. Washington: "No southern white man should be allowed to hold office in the Philippines.... The Filipinos hate the whole tribe of southerners here, and so do I."[108] He said the "open-armed hospitality" with which he was greeted on Hawaii, by contrast, was due to the "descendants of New England missionaries, who had planted there a civilization based on the Christian virtues in which race prejudice had no part."[109] On the mainland West Coast, however, evangelical Protestants had largely abandoned a multiracial vision of Christian social harmony by the late nineteenth century.[110] Yet some such hopes endured, and the Hawaiian Islands could inspire them. A writer in the *Missionary Review of the World* of November 1900, after discussing in positive terms Hawaii's "five principle races" (Polynesian, Japanese, Chinese, Portuguese, and Anglo-Saxon), declared:

> The brotherhood of man, the fact that of one blood God has made all the children of men to dwell together upon the face of the earth, seems to be one of the lessons to be taught on Hawaii. And there is no spot where the race question is being more happily solved—none, where a man is more regarded for his inherent qualities, rather than for his race affinities; none where the races mix with greater harmony in social, business, and political circles.[111]

The *Review* went on to speak with admiration of Chinese reformer "Leung Chi Tso" (Liang Qichao), who was staying temporarily in Hawaii while "lecturing to his countrymen in Honolulu." Establishment Hawaiian newspapers, too, typically spoke respectfully of Liang, who was regarded as a modernizing force.[112] Contemporary historians may also note a unique Hawaiian culture, though very few would go as far as Fortune and describe missionaries as free of racism. Even Western notions of the "multicultural" can hide imperial histories; a multicultural society, for example, may not come into being "until conquerors conquer and until workers around the world are imported."[113]

What about Fortune's notion of Manila as a kind of outpost of Dixie? A Southern Democrat, Luke E. Wright of Tennessee, would succeed Taft as governor-general in 1904. A few years later, the then governor General William Cameron Forbes would likewise attribute discrimination against Filipinos to the large "proportion of Southerners found in the Government service of the Philippine Islands."[114] Yet troop regiments in the Philippines came from all parts of the United States, as did, of course, racist attitudes toward African Americans. Top posts in the Philippine Commission—also known as the Taft Commission, the legislative body appointed by the president to govern in the Philippines—were not dominated by Southerners.[115] Many black soldiers did indeed chafe at white Americans' racism; one wrote to the *Richmond Planet* that "the whites have begun to establish their diabolical race hatred in all its home rancor in Manila." The soldier did not distinguish whites by region, however.[116]

Yet the long shadow of the Civil War likely stretched outward toward the territories. The American press in Manila may have feared that greater black presence in the Philippines could, as Amy Kaplan suggests, reopen, instead of heal, the wounds of the Civil War, recasting it as a "global race war" and destroying the sense of white unity that the *Savannah Tribune* editor had described.[117] In the recently ended war with Filipino rebels, a small number of African American troops did defect, including David Fagen of the Twenty-Fourth Infantry, who became a captain in the rebel army and led several guerilla attacks on U.S. troops.[118] Philippine rebels appealed to African American soldiers to join the insurgency and, their eyes on the U.S. South, implored black U.S. troops to "consider your history," "take charge that the blood of [Georgia lynching victim] Sam Hose proclaims vengeance," and defect.[119]

Fortune was not the only target of the American press in Manila. These newspapers were aggressively opposed to the Philippine Commission. In fact, the American press appeared as much a thorn in the side of the Roosevelt administration as the Irish American press, before Yorke, Ford, and other Irish American editors were at least partially appeased by the addition of Catholics to the commission and to the Manila school system. The diary of Daniel R. Williams, personal secretary of Philippine commissioner Bernard Moses, shows the commission government's frustration and inability to control American newspapers in Manila. Williams wrote on August 11, 1901, that the "American papers of Manila" had from the start "antagonized and obstructed the work of the civil authorities." Objecting to the appointment of Filipinos to government posts, they had called the natives "treacherous, untrustworthy, etc." Williams called Filipinos "morbidly sensitive to criticism" and wrote that he hoped they could learn that "the attacks of a few disgruntled American papers do not express American sentiment."[120]

Two years later, head commissioner William Howard Taft echoed Williams's assessment, lashing out several times at the "young lions of the American press" in a speech before the Union Reading College in Manila on December 17, 1903. These editors had "no patience with the policy of attraction, no patience with attempts to conciliate the Filipino people, no patience with the introduction into the government as rapidly as their fitness justifies of the prominent Filipinos.... They insist... that the welfare of the Americans and American trade should be regarded as paramount."[121]

It was the close relationship between the military and "those venturesome business spirits that thrive best in times of trouble and excitement," Taft said, that accounted for these attitudes. Because military men had fought a guerilla war marked by "treachery and cruelty," current and former soldiers held strong grudges against all Filipinos. "The Anglo-Saxon is not noted for his courtesy" or "for his consideration for races which he considers inferior to his," Taft said. With seventy thousand troops in the Philippines in 1900, merchants found profits "very great indeed" from selling food and drink. "It was only natural that the newspapers, whose editorial staffs were largely composed of men recently in the battlefield and whose subscription lists were largely swelled by the names of soldiers, whose advertising columns were filled by the advertising of these American merchants, should reflect the opinion which the American merchant and the American soldier had of the Filipinos." And as long as business was good, there was no need to "cultivat[e] the taste or the good-will of the Filipinos for business purposes." But now, Taft said, with the American army reduced to fifteen thousand men, "the pinch is being felt," and "with the lack of logic, so characteristic of human nature," the merchant blamed the civil government and its policy of "encouraging the native as far as it could."[122]

Manila editor William Crozier's reminiscences about his days at the *Manila American* support Taft's view of close ties between merchants and soldiers. Crozier's memories are replete with journalists' nicknames, practical jokes, battles with the censor, and other war stories, some of them literal, since much of the paper's staff were current or former U.S. soldiers. (Crozier described a tense moment when the paper ceased production in February 1899 while its soldier-journalists were called on to push back a Filipino rebel attack on Manila.)[123] In addition to race hatreds they arrived with or seized upon during months of brutal guerilla warfare, American newspapermen in Manila may have felt the need to defend American merchants' territory from a slowly growing Filipino-led government. The *Cablenews American* wrote that "benefits afforded the Filipinos are proper as long as these do not coincide with American rights in the islands."[124] Crozier and his cohorts resemble Donna Gabaccia's "mobile Americans": investors, businessmen, and missionaries who developed American empire as they pursued private agendas and interests abroad and clung to their own customs, languages, and religions.[125] Whether or not Fortune could pin Manila's aggressive racism on Southerners, he seems close to the mark on the importance of regional differences in the projection of U.S. power abroad. Different histories and different media landscapes contributed to unique racial politics in two of the nation's new territories.[126]

Gauging Afro-Asian Affinities

Despite his unfriendly reception among whites in Manila, Fortune still took time to poll Filipinos on their opinion of black emigration. Though long discussed in the 1800s, the concept of public opinion had emerged anew by 1903 out of the fields of social psychology and strategies of market research. Writings of the time sometimes speak of it as something mysterious and powerful that might be discovered and tapped; English investigative journalism pioneer W. T. Stead had argued that the telegraph and the printing press could return nations to direct, participatory democracy, like the Greek agora of old.[127] Fortune's questionnaire was reprinted in the Spanish-language *La Democracia*, a Filipino newspaper that advocated for gradual independence for the islands, as opposed to others, which were more forceful.[128] Fortune's first four questions were for identification purposes; the next five got to the heart of the matter:

5. What, in your opinion, are the needs for workers in the Philippines?
6. Are you pro Chinese immigration?
7. Please name your reasons.
8. Are you pro immigration of negroes to the Philippines?
9. Please give all your views.[129]

La Democracia, in an editorial on Fortune's questionnaire and plan, strained to remain polite toward the struggle of African Americans in the United States but, when it came to opening their nation to black emigrants, admitted a "rare stupification" (*nuestra estupefaccion raya en lo insolito*) at the thought of how "we Filipinos shall be entitled to the blessings of humanity by the work of redeeming a people." Fortune's poll came at the worst time possible; famine still loomed, and Filipinos were struggling to address basic necessities—not to mention "vital political questions." Fortune had "ponderously stoked the fire of racial discord" (*atizar muy ponderosamente el fuego de las discordias de raza*).[130]

Before leaving the Philippines, Fortune embarked on a dangerous six-week trek through northern Luzon as a cholera epidemic raged, a trip "few

Americans had ever attempted."¹³¹ Two African American soldiers, Captain Robert Gordon Woods and Captain Wormsley, accompanied him. Throughout the journey, recounted a year later in a series of articles for *Voice of the Negro* and in one article in the mainstream journal the *Independent* a few months after his return, Fortune alternately employed and sometimes critiqued the prevailing civilizationist discourse of the times. His photography, some of which is described in this chapter, also seems to simultaneously sit within, and critique, racialist anthropological aesthetics.

Fortune frequently adopted an orientalist frame toward Asia, starting with his first installment on his trip for *Voice of the Negro* in March 1904.¹³² Fortune began by praising poetry, which called forth the "finer feelings" and could be an antidote to "the worries of bread-winning and the relentless strivings after place and power," perhaps echoing his letter to Washington about his plans to drop journalism and write poetry instead. "'Ah for some retreat / Deep in yonder shining Orient,'" Fortune wrote, quoting Lord Tennyson's "Locksley Hall," though he stopped before the line, "I shall take some savage woman / She shall rear my dusky race."¹³³ He then quoted Lord Byron's "The Bride of Abydos" ("Know ye the land where the cypress and myrtle / Are emblems of deeds that are done in their clime?") and wrote that "the Orient is wrapped in mystery . . . its people . . . have no thing in common with the strong thinking and death killing efforts after material things of the whiter races: for they think languidly and labor only when is necessary."¹³⁴ Yet he then defended Filipino work habits, which he said were the most-discussed topic among whites in the islands, who constantly denounced "the laziness of the Filipino." Fortune recounted breaking into one such conversation and silencing it: "'I have been in the Philippines two months and have not seen a white man working with his hands; they were all working with their mouths,'" he told a group of white Americans on a "coastwise steamer." "'Why do you expect the Filipino to do what you will not and cannot do?'"¹³⁵

Still, in Fortune's third installment in *Voice of the Negro*, he complained that "the average Filipino appears to have been born tired."¹³⁶ He described the incredible dusk-till-dawn din of Manila—roosters crowing, brass bands playing in the early morning, church bells pealing—and concluded that Filipinos must have no nerves. "People without nerves do not think much, rapidly or profoundly, and the basic elements of their character are superficiality." That he then attributed the same characteristics to "eighty percent of American negroid people" and much of mankind in general softened the blow only a little.¹³⁷ Fortune stood uncomfortably within dominant, racialized discourses of civilization, attempting to adopt aspects that might bolster his standing as an American sent to assess and possibly help the Philippines while also scrambling the logics of white supremacy. Of one white general in Luzon with whom he and Captain Woods stayed, who was uncomfortable around Fortune's "brothers in black and yellow" and who was later convicted of embezzling public monies, Fortune wrote, "His race prejudice will wear itself out in Bilabid prison, where he must consort on terms of equality with all the race colors of the globe."[138]

Black Newspapers and a New Technology

Along his trek Fortune used photography to document his travels. Sometimes his photos seem to sit within a kind of imperialistic photographic aesthetic, a classifying, anthropomorphic gaze that freezes the subject in an inferior position with respect to the photographer. Three photos in one of Fortune's *Voice of the Negro* articles relating his journey, "A Filipino and His Rooster," "Native Mode of Transportation," and "A Typical Filipino Cart," seem mildly objectifying, the first photographed straight-on, the latter two showing simple vehicles drawn by a cow and a water buffalo (or carabao), respectively. But at times Fortune may attempt to subvert this genre. He (or his *Voice of the Negro* editor) captioned, for example, his self-portrait (see Figure 3.1) with the phrase, "Photo taken in Northern Luzon by a Filipino," which may deliberately imply cooperation between Filipinos and African Americans, Fortune's hoped-for brothers in black and yellow.

Like the mainstream press, Fortune and other black periodical editors experimented with photography during the late nineteenth century. The halftone revolution of the 1880s—when photographs could be cheaply reproduced onto inexpensive paper such as newsprint—did more than increase Americans' exposure to circulated visual images.[139] It contributed to an ongoing anxious, gendered debate about art and perception. Examination of a series of hybrid portraits in the Indianapolis *Freeman*—for a time in the early 1890s, the newspaper printed halftone photographs of African Americans surrounded by an engraver's depiction of laurels, curtains, and other paraphernalia—reveals newspapers as a site of aesthetic and possibly occupational tension.

Edward E. Cooper founded the *Freeman* in 1888 and published it until 1892, when he sold it to George Knox. Knox, a former slave and successful black businessman, wanted a "national race paper" and, partly because of successful job printing, achieved a circulation of sixteen thousand in 1903.[140] Booker T. Washington was close with Knox and provided occasional financial support. Knox supported the Tuskegee leader's industrial education program. He nonetheless maintained much editorial independence from Tuskegee; he rarely hesitated to criticize lynching, for example.[141]

The masthead of the *Freeman* (Figure 3.4), which described itself as "a national illustrated colored newspaper," as well as that of the *Colored American* demonstrate the "cluttered eclecticism" and "densely decorative style" of middle-class homes in the late Victorian era.[142] The *Colored American* in particular resembles the popular *Harpers Weekly* in its depiction of books, a globe, a telescope, and possibly a compass or sextant.

Figure 3.5 shows the *Freeman*'s typical front-page illustration style before the onset of halftone photographs. The *Freeman* usually ran engraved portraits of African Americans within drawn picture frames, the picture itself set on a table. Figure 3.6, three years later on October 21, 1893, is one

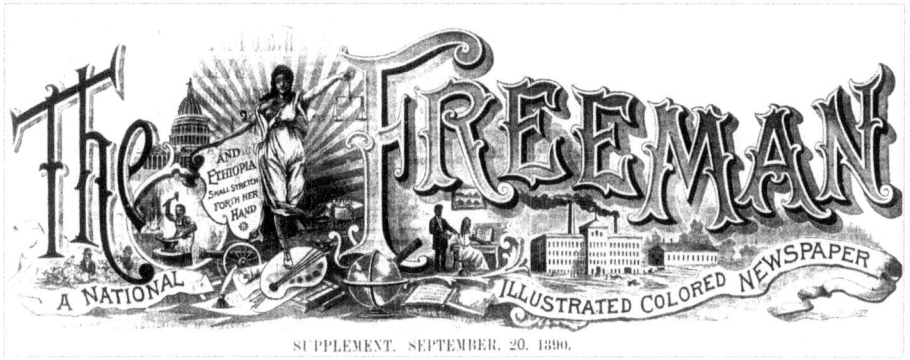

Figure 3.4 The masthead of the Indianapolis *Freeman*, September 20, 1890.

Figure 3.5 A typical front-page illustration for the *Freeman* before its use of halftone photographs, August 30, 1890.

Figure 3.6 An early halftone photograph printed in the *Freeman*, surrounded by illustrations, October 21, 1893.

of the first halftone photographs in the paper. The *Freeman* has continued its long-standing style of surrounding a portrait with the accoutrements of taste, refinement, and intellectual bearing. Here a halftone photograph merely replaces the art of the illustrator, who himself may have worked from a photographic portrait of an African American leader in political or cultural life.

To modern eyes, this hybrid or mash-up of illustration and photographic reproduction appears jarring. Another halftone on the cover of the *Freeman* three weeks later (Figure 3.7) uses less illustrated accompaniment but still surrounds its halftone with garlands and other paraphernalia of respectability. Does this show a discomfort with a new technology—as if the halftone

Figure 3.7 Less illustrated material accompanies this halftone photograph in the *Freeman*, November 11, 1893.

alone cannot transmit an individual's gravitas? Or, to be more cynical, is the illustrator hanging onto his job for dear life, arguing visually about his worth to a newspaper in danger of adopting a more "realistic" medium for its portrayal of race leaders?

Those are difficult questions to answer for several reasons. Commentators and critics did argue about photography and its use and nature in the late nineteenth century, and engravers and other illustrators did fear the threat that the new technology posed to their professions. Nancy Martha

West explores the gendered anger and alarm of engravers in the mid-1880s. "The most talented engravers," wrote engraver W. J. Linton in 1884, "are hampered and crippled by [photography] . . . they waste their powers on an effeminate excess of fineness and other girl-nonsense. . . . Only the artist-engraver, while he upholds the dignity of his manhood, can assure the future of engraving. Beware of photography!"[143] Linton objected to engravers working from a photograph rather than a drawing; photography, he thought, privileged accuracy over the symbolism and spirit of an original artwork, which demanded translation from the engraver, not mechanical reproduction. English art critic John Ruskin and English novelist and poet Thomas Hardy were two influential Victorians who similarly feared that "art had lost its object, its privileged methods and categories, and its institutional security" to photography.[144]

In these three *Freeman* images, the power of the portrait in the nineteenth century is suggested; it projected propriety, self-control, and self-possession. African Americans, particularly race leaders who hoped to push back against racist portrayals, embraced photography and portraiture. Frederick Douglass was optimistic about photography's potential to empower African Americans even while recognizing its power to promote false imaginings. Douglass and other African Americans, behind or in front of the camera, increasingly challenged representations of blacks in the late nineteenth century. Ginger Hill finds Douglass deliberately and self-consciously posing for numerous portraits. He guarded his respectability religiously, carefully regulated the angles of his sittings, and on the lecture circuit always received from his wife, Anna, a freshly pressed shirt, sent ahead.[145] Shawn Michelle Smith dissects W.E.B. Du Bois's photographic exhibit on African Americans for the American Negro Exhibit at the 1900 Paris Exposition, finding conscious subversion of the format of scientific race photography—the exhibit begins with the full frontal and side portraits common to anthropological and phrenological studies of "savages" and moves from there into nuanced, dignified, and particularized profiles of African American families.[146] Michael Scott Bieze and Marybeth Gasman have begun to detail Booker T. Washington's artistic philosophies and endeavors, including his interest in Ruskin and the Arts and Crafts movement. Bieze sees Washington's work as presaging the Harlem Renaissance. Washington did not shy away from photography in the slightest, employing A. P. Bedou and other black and white photographers for various Tuskegee projects.[147]

Americans did not immediately rush to use photographic images to depict the world "realistically" in the 1800s. Scholars of Victorian aesthetics suggest that our current taste in photography is a conservative one, stressing realism and seeking an "honest" use of the medium. Nineteenth-century

Americans, by contrast, reveled in the many forms photography could take, one moment embracing its ability to seemingly freeze and portray reality and the next celebrating its ability to create fantasies or trick the eye.[148] In this respect, the *Freeman*'s mixture of photography and engraving may not have perplexed its readers at all, who were used to seeing photography employed as an expressive rather than an unembellished medium.[149]

Another African American portrait from the Philippines also suggests African Americans' conscious attempts to imagine and bring into being, through photography, an opportunity for a dignified life in America's new possessions. The *Colored American* newspaper of Washington, D.C., presented a profile on Lieutenant David J. Gilmer (Figure 3.8), declaring that "colored officers speak well of the treatment they received" in the Philippines, from both "natives" and white teachers and civilian clerks alike. The latter "seem to forget their American prejudice, when they meet a colored officer, and are usually glad to talk with him. The race question is rapidly solving itself in the islands, is the verdict of those capable of judging."[150]

The photograph serves to reinforce the claims of the text accompanying it. The Philippines is presented as an escape from American racism, where African American talent and manhood are freely expressed and adequately rewarded, and where white Americans forget their racial animus. That there may be opportunities for African Americans abroad is reinforced on the same page by an advertisement from the Tuskegee Institute that describes a whirlwind of opportunities for African American men trained in scientific agriculture, both domestic and "in several foreign countries."[151] Scholars now know many of the details of Booker T. Washington's efforts in West Africa to assist German colonialists in the growing of cotton. The year 1904 would be approximately midway through that eight-year experiment, a time when German desire to diversify its cotton imports, so as not to rely so exclusively on the United States, and Washington's desire to make African Americans indispensable to world markets coalesced.[152]

In both Fortune's and Gilmer's Philippine portraits, each man stands in front of a painted backdrop. Media scholars Lisa Gitelman and Geoffrey Pingree note that the sale of such backgrounds in Sears and Roebuck catalogs of the early twentieth century for portrait photographs "suggests the wide circulation of different and uniquely personal portraits, all with identical, impersonal backgrounds." Gitelman and Pingree suggest that the mass marketing of these painted screens can help focus scholarly discussions of the "age of mechanical reproduction" by troubling assumptions of the uniqueness of painting versus the mass production of images "or that painting and photography always form antithetical sources of meaning."[153] In this book, the self-conscious, constructed nature of these photographs and their placement in black periodicals aligns with the personal use of newspapers to

OUT IN THE PHILIPPINES.

Lieut. David J. Gilmer Makes a Good Record, and is Promoted.—Natives Friendly to the American Negroes.

A recent letter from the Philippines tells many stories of the achievements and success of the colored Americans in those far away islands. There are now quite a number of commissioned officers of the U. S. Scout regiments, who are winning spurs and who are adding lus-

[photo]

LIEUT. DAVID J. GILMER,
Nueva Caceres, Camerines, P. I.

ter to the already proud record of col? ored soldiers. Last August, September and October, Lieut. David J. Gilmer was on duty at Bato, commanding a detachment of soldiers stationed there to protect a lake or rather the fishes in it. In October Lieut. Gilmer was appointed quartermaster and commissary officer by Gen. Jesse M. Lee, Third Brigade, Department of Luzon. On leaving Bato to accept the new duties, Lieut. Gilmer was honored by a grand ball given by Judge Forteno and the Mayor of the town,

Don Sirrionalla. The elite of the town was at the ball. Upon entering the ball room the wife of the Judge and the Mayor received Lieut. Gilmer and pinned a beautiful boquet of tropical flowers on his left breast, while the band played the "Star Spangled Banner," in his honor.

The colored officers speak well of the treatment they received there, and the cordial relation existing between them, and the natives. While ninety-nine per cent of the teachers, (male and female)

the civilian clerks that come to the aisles are all white, these same people seem to forget their American prejudice, when they meet a colored officer, and are usually glad to talk with him. The race question is rapidly solving itself in the islands, is the verdict of those capable of judging. The mosquitoes and ants are very bad, and while we in this country are doing all in our power to keep warm, the people in the Philippines are doing their utmost to keep cool.

The song-service at the Metropolitan Church last Sunday evening, drew out a large audience and was very fine. The trios and choruses were all especially well done under the masterly leadership of Prof. John T. Layton. Rev. O. H. W. Scott is a brilliant success as pastor of this important church.

The Emery family, of Ohio, have, within the last twelve months, given the money for the erection of a large brick dormitory for boys, at the Tuskegee Institute, and within the last few days have informed the Trustees that they have decided to erect a second dormitory for the Tuskegee Institute.

EDUCATIONAL.

THE COLORED BUSINESS
Preparatory and Elementary . . .
Night School

IN THE
OLD *TRUE REFORMERS HALL.*
Cor. Fourth and N Sts., N. W.
AN OPPORTUNITY FOR ALL.

Special courses—Business, Preparatory, Elementary, and Lecture. Shorthand and Typewriting.
Free information given from 4 to 5 p. m. Subjects—Arithmetic, Algebra, Geometry.

J. W. BOTTS, A. B., Ph. B.,
Manager.

HOWARD UNIVERSITY,
Washington, D. C.

TEN distinct departments, under one hundred competent professors and instructors—Theological, Medical, Legal, College, Pedagogical, Preparatory, English, Agricultural, Industrial, and Musical. For information address—
Rev. J. E. RANKIN, D. D., LL. D., *President.*

THE MARYLAND AGRICULTURAL AND INDUSTRIAL INSTITUTE, LAUREL, HOWARD CO., MD.

Situation beautiful; climate unsurpassed; work thorough and efficient. Courses: English, Normal, Agriculture Practical and Scientific, Stockraising, Dairying, Sewing, Cooking, Laundering, Domestic Science, Carpentry, Mechanical Drawing, Dressmaking and Millinery. $7.00 per month covers tuition, furnished room, heating, lighting, washing and board. Fall term opens October 1, 1903. Winter term opens December 28, 1903. Further information, address M. J. NAYLOR, A. B., Acting President, Box 199 Baltimore, Md.

OPPORTUNITY FOR YOUNG MEN.

The demands in all parts of this country, and in several foreign countries, for well trained men of our race in the direction of scientific and practical agriculture are so great that this institution is willing to offer exceptional advantages to young men who wish to come here and take either a regular or post graduate course in agriculture. We cannot begin to supply the demands that come to us for trained men in the direction of agriculture. The positions for which these trained men are wanted are those in most every case which pay high salaries.

A good education before coming here, and are ready to enter upon a thorough course of agricultural training.

For further information address,
BOOKER T. WASHINGTON,
Prin. Tuskegee Institute,
Tuskegee, Alabama.

All Nations welcome except Carrie Nation
EDWARD GREEN
Fine Wines and Whiskies
Cigars and Tobacco
Private Entrance for Ladies
S. W. Cor. Cameron and Fayette streets
ALEXANDRIA, VA.

HOTELS AND RESTAURANTS.

The Albany Hotel.

Has been enlarged and newly outfitted with modern improvements for the accommodation of Guests so as to furnish firs. class services with Bar, Dining Room, Private Parlors and first class Sleeping Apartments.

Arthur Webster, steward; William Leonard and William Hall, mixologists; Henry Johnson, manager, and Auto Scott, clerk.

CALEB A. SIMMS, Prop.

331 W. 37th St. New York

The Porters Exchange Hotel
BROWN & SMITH,
Proprietors.

Newly rebuilt and elegantly furnished.
Meals at all Hours.
Electric lights, bells, steam heat, hot and cold baths.
High grade Wines, Liquors and Cigars.
The coldest Beer in the city.
103 and 105 Sixth Street, N. W.
Handsome rooms, $1.00 & up.
Phone 1733 Y.

THE WOODSON HOUSE.

First-class, newly furnished and decorated, unsurpassed cuisine; convenient to all cars. Only half square from Pennsylvania depot.
467 MISSOURI AVENUE.
HENRY WOODSON, - - *Proprietor.*

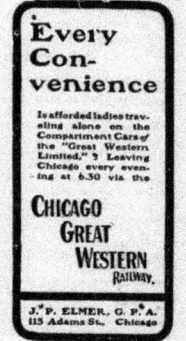

Every Convenience

Is afforded ladies traveling alone on the Compartment Cars of the "Great Western Limited." Leaving Chicago every evening at 6.30 via the

CHICAGO GREAT WESTERN RAILWAY.

J. P. ELMER, G. P. A.
115 Adams St., Chicago

Phone East 347.   Rooms 5 and 6
WM. L. POLLARD.
ATTORNEY AND COUNSELLOR-AT-LAW

Collections, Real Estate and Insurance.
All matters given prompt attention in the District of Columbia.
Member of the Washington Real Estate Exchange.
609 F St. N. W., - Washington, D. C.

"WE MOVE EVERYTHING"
Douglas Baggage and Furniture Express
1533 14th Street N. W.
R. T. DOUGLAS, Manager

Figure 3.8 Lieutenant David J. Gilmer, from *Colored American*, January 16, 1904, p. 7.

produce meaning and assert one's self while advancing the well-being and future of one's race.

The tools of the newspaper trade, of course, could not automatically eliminate racial animus. Fortune's Philippines journey almost ended in ignominy when, upon returning from his Luzon trek, he, Captain Woods, and possibly as many as three other African Americans were arrested after a dispute with police, described with equal parts glee and contempt in the *Manila American*. The newspaper claimed Fortune stopped his carriage in the middle of the street to speak with another African American, blocked traffic, and talked back to a police officer. The *American* claimed that Fortune, taken to the police station, kept yelling, "I am T. Thomas Fortune. I am the special agent of the U.S. Treasury. That's who I am." The newspaper dubbed Fortune, "T. Thomas Titmouse," though two days later it reluctantly acknowledged that Vice Governor Wright had intervened to get the case dismissed.[154]

Fortune would sum up his recommendations for the Philippines in his final installment for *Voice of the Negro*. Luzon's rich farmland was not being exploited by Filipinos, who "do not seem to care to work"; the land could support up to seven million more people, five million of whom "could be Negroes." "The Negro and the Filipino get along splendidly together," and emigration from the Southern United States, "where [African Americans] are wronged and robbed . . . would be good for them, good for the Filipinos, who badly need rejuvenation of blood, and good for the United States," which could "take a long step in solving the Filipino and the Negro problem" and avoid coming bloodshed on both accounts. The United States had not given the black man "life, liberty, and the pursuit of happiness" and in fact "seems now to be on a policy of crushing out entirely his manhood and citizen rights." He was owed. "Give the American Negro a chance in the Philippine Islands, if he wants to go there," Fortune ended.[155] That the voluntary nature of the migration needed to be stressed demonstrates the dire situation of African Americans, especially those in the South, in the early twentieth century.

Upon his return to the United States on June 24, the Treasury Department informed Fortune that his appointment had been only for six months and had been terminated on May 16. He would not be paid for his final weeks of travel. He protested, withholding his final report on the trip; there is no evidence it was ever completed or published.[156] Aside from his three *Voice of the Negro* articles, Fortune did publish an essay for the national journal the *Independent*, wherein he described three major political groups in the Philippines: the main group of nationalist Filipinos, who he said regarded Taft as their "saint"; white Americans on the islands, dominated by a Southern mentality; and a tiny, heterogeneous third group composed of "the best

Filipinos," a few white Americans and Europeans, and all three hundred African Americans. This third group, which in its cosmopolitanism recalled Fortune's 1895 speech on a "nationalized" Africa, was the Philippines' only hope for a harmonious and prosperous future, for it believed that the islands should be governed "in the interests of all the people, native and foreign born, with justice for all and special favors for none." Fortune hoped it would succeed, though he admitted that—reflecting his continued interest in the interplay of media and publics, civil rights and readership—the tiny group had "no acknowledged leader and no newspaper organ."[157]

Tangled Color Lines

Fortune's and some black newspaper editors' attempts to imagine and promote a better life for African Americans in Hawaii or the Philippines were not necessarily naïve or deceptive. Lieutenant Gilmer, the dignified black soldier pictured in Figure 3.8, may have found in Manila some relief from American racial mores and perhaps obtained real opportunities for professional advancement. The *Colored American* certainly thought so.[158] Optimists like Washington could take heart in the letters of some black soldiers in the Philippines who wrote home without mentioning race at all. Another, Chaplain T. G. Steward of the Twenty-Fifth Infantry, when cursed by three white privates on a street in Manila, seemed to revel in his apparent authority to stop, intimidate, and reprimand his antagonists: "I . . . read them a lecture."[159] In this particular case, military rank seemed to maintain its power across segregated military units and trump social rankings based on skin tone.

Fortune's guide for his Luzon trip, Captain Robert Gordon Woods, seems to have had a long and relatively successful career in administrative positions with the Philippine Constabulary and Army. Woods appears decades later at the close of World War II in a profile in the Chicago *Afro-American* newspaper. Age seventy-two in 1945, Woods was still living in the Philippines. At the start of Japanese occupation, according to the *Afro-American*, when first approached by a "hissing, bowing Jap," Woods survived the encounter and his eventual imprisonment by "playing dumb." Woods might remain in the islands after the war, the *Afro-American* wrote, "because he has come to love the little brown people."[160]

The *Afro-American*'s profile, along with the derogatory comments about black labor by one native Hawaiian newspaper, reflect the various racial discourses available to African Americans and Asians encountering U.S. imperial agendas—each group might draw on different strains of a contradictory ideological mix to make claims for their worth or sophistication. The accessibility of an orientalist discourse to African Americans in the late nineteenth century is shown in Fortune's writings in *Voice of the Negro*, where he often posited himself as a Westerner visiting the strange, indolent East. In the ideology of the Hampton Institute, in fact, African Americans were expected to help "civilize" Native Americans—even as the tenets of industrial education "situated the black labor force at the bottom of the Southern economy."[161] Hawaiians and Filipinos, of course, could employ and circulate in their own presses the tenets of race science or popular biases to assert their own civilized nature in opposition to blacks. Perhaps someone translated the *Ke Aloha Aina* article for Fortune, for he wrote upon his return to the United States that the "Hawaiian Kanaka" was like the American Indian, "think[ing] himself better than the black man."[162] Though Fortune would write that Filipinos did not seem to share other nonwhites' disdain for African Americans, a Filipino student publication at the University of California at Berkeley two years after Fortune's return printed as filler at the end of an article on education a short poem about a "little nigger" and a crocodile.[163] Perhaps its editors consciously sought respectability in America through racial putdowns, or maybe the periodical medium, wherein "white space" between articles was often quite literally an Anglo-Saxon territory filled by convention with ethnic jokes or minstrel sketches, dictated editors' decisions more automatically. Either way, in 1903 and beyond, any moves toward Afro-Asian solidarity faced racial bigotries flowing in multiple directions. Fortune's hopes for black labor abroad also seem stymied in part by an early belief in a racial association between African Americans and crime, which is explored further in Chapter 4.[164]

Two years after his journey, Fortune was still optimistic about empire's possible unintended effects on domestic race politics. Back at the helm of the *Age*, Fortune printed an article from a frequent correspondent in Chicago. Riffing on the U.S. policy of tutelage for Filipinos, the writer described a group of Filipino emigrants to America who, "believing that 'benevolent assimilation' means what the term implies," enrolled in a state college in Illinois. The chilly reception the "innocent, dark-skinned" students received at the school must be, the students decided, "one of the peculiarities of benevolence." Believing that "all things would work out benevolently," the young Filipinos got haircuts at a barbershop in town; outraged white students threatened to boycott the business. "It mattered not that the students from the Orient were Malay, not Negroes; it was sufficient grounds for objection that they had the color of the American Negro." The *Age* correspondent concluded, "There are hopeful signs that the battle of the 'color line' is not to be fought out by the Negro race alone."[165]

4

J. SAMUEL STEMONS'S ONE-MAN PRESS

The Act of Newspapering in Black Philadelphia, 1906–1907

We have weeklies that lasted a week and a daily that had a name though the paper itself never came.
—WENDELL P. DABNEY, *Cincinnati's Colored Citizens* (1926)[1]

It is really remarkable. . . . There is a great big sign under the window: "The Pilot, James Samuel Stemons, Editor." The same sign hangs overhead; the same is . . . on three doors. Graham's name only appears in the paper—in one place, and yet he comes daily to my office, and works like a slave—and advances all the money.
—JAMES SAMUEL STEMONS, letter to Mary Stemons, March 4, 1907

James Samuel Stemons (1870–1959) was not one to set his sights low. Just two years after T. Thomas Fortune's return from the Philippines, the former farm worker, railroad track layer, and janitor was convinced he was on his way to becoming a major force in African American life. As a Philadelphia newspaper editor and race activist, he would solve the Negro Problem. Neither the agriculturally focused and separatist vision of Booker T. Washington nor W.E.B. Du Bois's emphasis on higher education and political rights appealed to Stemons, who instead imagined blacks working alongside whites in skilled industrial jobs at decent wages. The question, to Stemons, was how to get whites to open both their hearts and their union shops to allow African Americans entry. He was convinced he had the answer and the means to promote it in print and in person in Philadelphia and nationwide. By the end of the 1910s, he would cross paths with Fortune, correspond briefly with Booker T. Washington, and be visited by other well-known African Americans. Yet very few historians have written about him.

The papers of J. Samuel Stemons are fairly extensive. Several boxes of materials, mainly handwritten and typed letters between Stemons and his sister, Mary, in Kansas, afford a rare inside look at the nuts and bolts of operating a weekly black newspaper in the early twentieth century. Historians in their investigations of both mainstream and black and ethnic presses have tended to examine newspapers with extensive runs to track changes in opinion or emphasis on particular topics through time. Less studied are the many hundreds of newspapers, mostly weeklies, that lasted a year or two, or perhaps just months or even days—despite the fact that these short-lived papers are increasingly representative of contemporary publishing patterns. Stemons did not become a leading figure in debates over the Negro Problem, and no known copies of his two brief newspaper efforts, the *Courant* and the *Pilot*, exist. But for a very brief time through these newspapers and the pamphlets and essays that he circulated, Stemons successfully branded himself an expert on African American affairs and attracted interest from some of the leading lights in black politics and culture. He also kept writing books throughout his long life. Precisely because he does not fit perfectly into historians' theories about the purpose and function of the black press, Stemons's experience can be used to probe the utility of those theories. Ultimately, his political views and his strategies for success in print cannot be separated, and thus he provides clues about the influence that print as a medium and an economy had on questions of race in the early twentieth century. His experience also points to black newspaper weeklies, even those that lasted only a few years or months, as unexpected but trenchant nodes of African American writing and thought in the long nineteenth century and beyond.

Called to Help His Race

Stemons was born of former slave parents in 1870 in Clarkesville, Tennessee; when he was six, he and his family moved to Kansas.[2] Little is known of Stemons's early years, but in 1893, after he was apparently refused a job because of his race, he decided that his life's calling was to advocate on behalf of African Americans. He set out toward Boston on a journey of speaking to church congregations and publishing in local newspapers. Stemons's calling appears to have been spiritual in nature; in at least one letter to his sister later in his life he mentions seeing a bright light before this journey.[3] From Boston in 1894 he traveled for three years through New York, Pennsylvania, and Ohio, delivering addresses that focused on the industrial discrimination blacks faced in the North. Stemons estimated that he made more than three hundred speeches, mostly in white churches.[4]

From the start, Stemons sought to be both a speaker and a writer, and for several years churches would be an important but problematic venue for his reform efforts. Stemons reported that when he did secure speaking engagements with white clergymen, he was usually treated respectfully. Financially, however, he barely kept body and soul together. In Cleveland, from 1895 to 1896, "through the voluntary contributions that were made at my lectures," Stemons recounted, he typically earned less than two dollars, with about one speaking gig per week. Considering "that I had to dress, pay my lodging, subsist, and send a little money, at least once a month, to my aged parents and a sister at my home in Kansas . . . the fact will be better appreciated that my entire work among the white churches of Cleveland was retarded, and finally abandoned," Stemons wrote, speaking of his inability to raise twelve dollars to print even the bylaws of an organization he wished to start.[5]

Stemons (Figure 4.1) kept himself going by working as a waiter for $4.50 a week and typically ate "either a pound of broken crackers or a stale loaf of bread" each day. For two to three months in the spring of 1895, he was forced "literally to take to the proverbial tall timber," sleeping in various forests "with a bunch of leaves for a bed and a fire of broken branches to prevent [his] freezing."[6] He struggled to keep a respectable appearance, washing himself and his clothes in forest streams. Stemons reported that one white pastor "placed his hand affectionately on my shoulder and said: 'Mr. Stemons, you must not feel in any way humiliated by what I am about to say, for you are doing a very noble and heroic work. . . . But tell me; am I right in believing you to be on the verge of starvation?'"[7]

Stemons spent the winter and spring of 1897 in Buffalo, New York, noting that it was "one of bitterest and most depressing periods of my entire life." Journalists there seemed to like him—the Buffalo *Express*, Stemons said, followed his efforts and editorialized "on the necessity of diversified employment for Negroes"[8]—but most clergymen gave him the cold shoulder. One sympathetic pastor, however, himself "a publisher on a small scale," agreed to finance the printing of Stemons's manuscript *A Cry from the Oppressed* in booklet form (the race of the pastor is not mentioned in Stemons's account but was presumably white). Stemons called the booklet a "flat failure," but by selling it door to door he paid back the publisher and raised enough money to leave Buffalo. His sights set on Philadelphia, he stopped over in Rochester, where he received excellent newspaper coverage and secured several speaking spots in area churches, both black and white. Stemons claimed several reformers of both races in Rochester begged him to stay, but he moved on.[9]

Philadelphia, like Buffalo, was unwelcoming, at least at first. White pastors would not let Stemons speak to their congregations, and although black preachers were more receptive, Stemons claimed "their universal custom of excluding all secular topics from their pulpits on the Sabbath" prevented him from gaining "an adequate hearing among the colored people."[10] Although his vision for change did not involve agitating for immediate social and political equality for African Americans, Stemons's confrontational

Figure 4.1 Cover of James Samuel Stemons's *A Cry from the Oppressed: A Plea for the Industrial Rights of the Colored Race in the Northern States*, E 185.8 .S834x, Historical Society of Pennsylvania, Philadelphia.

stance against racism in the workplace may still have put him at odds with many black churches after Reconstruction. By the late nineteenth century, churches were "the largest and most powerful institution in the black community," owning property worth $26.6 million in 1890 and more than twice that by 1906.[11] Church membership among African Americans grew from 2.6 million in 1890 to 3.6 million in 1906. One historian of the black church in the South writes that although it remained a source of emotional and material support and a "theme of protest" could still be detected, the black church overall in the early Jim Crow years did not resist the prevailing values of separation and accommodation and "came to be seen more and more as a social rather than a political institution."[12] Yet different denominations had different characteristics; Robert Gregg explores black Methodist churches in Philadelphia, one of which Stemons would work with, and finds a complex uplift ideology that could encompass both accommodation and protest.[13] For Stemons, Philadelphia churches would remain a source of both support and frustration.

A Philadelphia Home

Despite his initial poor reception in Philadelphia, Stemons made his stand there and became for a short time a known reformer in the city. Philadelphia in the late nineteenth century had one of the largest populations of African Americans of any city in the nation and was home to a liberal Quaker tradition as well as black institutions catering to black migrants from the South. In fact, Stemons's association with one black Methodist church newspaper would place him amid an area known for its crime and poverty—as well as its zeal for experiments in social reform.[14]

The bulk of the letters in the Stemons collection begin with Stemons's acceptance of the position of editor in 1906 at the *Courant*, a church newspaper that until then had focused only on church affairs. Before Stemons took the helm, the *Courant* had been edited by A. P. Caldwell, who ran what Stemons called "perhaps the strangest colored church in the city." (It is uncertain what Stemons found so strange about Caldwell's church, Wesley A.M.E. Zion. Started in 1820, "Big Wesley" was one of the city's largest black churches, with a congregation of around two thousand in 1907.[15] At Fifteenth and Lombard Streets, it lay within the Seventh Ward, home to one in five Philadelphia African Americans around the turn of the century and the focus of W.E.B. Du Bois's famous sociological study, *The Philadelphia Negro*.)[16] Stemons said he sought the *Courant* out "because it has no real personality; it is no positive force and has no positive character behind it. Yet, strange to say it has pretty good backing." Caldwell, Stemons wrote

Mary, was an impressive young man, but "he has utterly failed to infuse The Courant with the force which is so manifested in him as an individual."[17]

Frank Luther Mott, in a study of U.S. journalism, called the late nineteenth century the age of "personal journalism."[18] Nineteenth- and early twentieth-century black weekly newspapers would have shared many structural similarities with their white or mainstream weekly counterparts. Thomas Clark writes of Southern "country editors" after the Civil War and up to the early 1900s:

> Just as no extensive education was necessary in the editing of a weekly, so also only a limited amount of mechanical training and equipment was needed. It was possible to compose and print a paper in a remarkably small building space. A single room was frequently adequate housing. A Washington or Franklin hand press, a few cases of type, a foot-treadle job press, a pair of type sticks, a couple of iron chases, one or two galleys, a proof press, a supply of ink, a bundle of ready-print pages, a roller towel and wash pan were sufficient equipment.[19]

But how accessible was newspaper publishing to someone like Stemons, marginalized because of his race and of very limited means? The economics of the black press mystified even Booker T. Washington, who carefully watched and in many cases partially funded and shaped the black press. In one revealing letter, Washington wrote in the summer of 1904 to Robert Curtis Ogden, a white philanthropist who sat on the board of the Hampton Institute. Ogden appears to have been interested in funding the *Colored American Magazine* but had balked. That summer Washington was engineering the ouster of Pauline Hopkins from the magazine's editorship, to be replaced by Fred R. Moore, who was much more of a Tuskegee loyalist.[20] Washington attempted to reassure Ogden that the venture, with his backing, could work out. "Permit me to say that I appreciate the advice which you have given [Moore], but I do not think you know all the circumstances," Washington wrote. "In the first place, the magazine has been kept alive for six or seven years and already has a circulation of between four and five thousand." Washington thought Ogden might have been "unconsciously" comparing "the cost of such a magazine as Mr. Moore is publishing with the white magazines. It would surprise you to know how cheaply many of the publications are published and kept alive; just how it is done in all cases I confess I do not know." Washington speculated that because Moore had his own printing press and frequently paid nothing to contributors, "I am of the opinion that the figure which he gives would put the magazine upon its feet."

Washington closed by mentioning T. Thomas Fortune and his *New York Age*, which "started years ago with practically no capital behind it. At the present time that paper clears above expenses about $50 a week." Perhaps, Washington wrote, the fact that African American publications have "not as severe competition as among the whites may have something to do with their opportunities of succeeding."[21] Washington's view might have been too rosy or designed to appease a potential investor who was getting cold feet, for Fortune's *Age* was frequently in financial trouble.

Washington's nemesis, W.E.B. Du Bois, also struggled to secure funding for a black periodical. In the summer of 1903, he and renowned black author Charles Chesnutt discussed the idea of a national black journal. "What the Negro needs more than anything else," Chesnutt wrote Du Bois, "is a medium through which we can present the case to thinking people, who after all are the arbiters of our destiny." Chesnutt also thought a national black newspaper would be a good idea.[22]

Du Bois tried to get financing from white banker Jacob Schiff, but Schiff may have spoken with Washington, who may have nixed the project.[23] Washington did not directly control editorial content at many, or possibly any, black publications; black newspapers that took some funding from Tuskegee, for example, often criticized lynching in the strongest terms possible, while Washington was much more circumspect on the issue. But Washington's money gave him influence over editorial direction, and he stymied some black publishing ventures and black journalists with which he disagreed by redirecting white philanthropy elsewhere. Because Du Bois, in 1905, had charged that Washington subsidized several black newspapers and that their editorial independence had been compromised, when word got out that Du Bois himself was seeking support from wealthy whites for a race journal, Fortune was quick to accuse the intellectual of hypocrisy.[24] The *Moon* failed by the summer of 1906; four years later Du Bois would continue to make his mark on history in part through his editorship of the *Crisis*, the magazine of the National Association for the Advancement of Colored People (NAACP).

The J. Samuel Stemons Papers provide further clues to how black newsweeklies thrived, failed, or just scraped by in this period. To take the helm of a newspaper in early twentieth-century Philadelphia, Stemons would need the support of either churches or white investors. Stemons started his editorship of the *Courant* with no set salary. "I will receive but little remuneration for my services to the *Courant*, at first, and that will be on a percentage basis," he wrote Mary. But Stemons, demonstrating a high, sometimes haughty self-confidence found throughout his letters—he often told Mary that he would soon be the most prominent spokesperson on the race issue—predicted that he would shortly be making at least $10 a week, "based on the increased circulation which my work on the paper will bring." He expected to "spend every moment, night and day writing editorials" and correcting those written by Caldwell.[25]

A month later, Stemons wrote Mary that he tried to sever his relationship with the *Courant*, but Caldwell pleaded with him to stay. So Stemons submitted a proposal—he would receive 75 percent of the net increase in the money from circulation and advertising since he came aboard, with an income of $10 a week; 50 percent of the increase until income amounted to $15 a week, and 10 percent of all increases over $15 a week. Later, Stemons would similarly have to tie his *Pilot* salary to his abilities to grow the paper.[26]

Yet just a few weeks later, even with church sponsorship, the costs associated with publishing the *Courant* appeared to stymie its growth. Stemons and Caldwell agreed to seek funds from white philanthropists to expand circulation. "We are just sending out a letter to a number of moneyed white men asking them to grant me an interview, in order that I may interest them in my work on the Courant, and my desire to make of it the mouth-piece of the colored race, and also a medium for giving employment to colored youth," Stemons wrote his sister in March 1906, reflecting his continued interest in diversified employment for African Americans. Stemons hoped he could borrow at least $1,000 from these men to add to the funding of the printing press. "Of course if I succeed, this will be enough money to give me a controlling interest in the Company, and will also enable me to devote my entire time to newspaper work." Stemons told Mary he would rather ask to borrow the money, so as not to be "handicapped by charity."[27]

The Experience of Ida B. Wells

Achieving part ownership in black newspapers had worked for some black journalists and reformers. It was precisely the strategy of antilynching activist Ida B. Wells, who found great synergy between lecturing and journalism. Born a slave in Mississippi in 1862, Wells became, at age fourteen, the head of a household of six children after her parents died of yellow fever. She became a schoolteacher and moved her family to Tennessee and continued to teach. Wells took courses at Fisk University and began writing for local newspapers and church weeklies under the name "Iola." Journalism did not yet pay the bills, but it did become an important part of Wells's identity: "The confinement and monotony of the primary [teaching] work began to grow distasteful," she wrote in her autobiography. "The correspondence I had built up in newspaper work gave me an outlet through which to express the real 'me' and I enjoyed my work to the utmost."[28]

Yet when offered a staff writing job in the local Memphis *Free Speech and Headlight* in 1889, Wells, in a move she would make more than once in her life, refused and instead bought one-third ownership in the paper and became its editor (she soon shortened its name to the *Free Speech*). "[Every] chance she got," writes Barbara Diggs-Brown, Wells "leveraged these offers into equity investments in publishing organizations."[29] She more than doubled subscriptions to the *Free Speech*, traveling across the Mississippi Delta to solicit subscribers and correspondents. "In nine months time I had an income nearly as large as I had received teaching and felt sure that I had found my vocation," Wells wrote in her autobiography. "I was very proud of my success because up to that time very few of our newspapers had made any money."[30] For Wells, written work and public speaking worked in tandem; when Frederick Douglass was unable to raise enough funds to produce a book protesting the denial of African American participation in the Chicago World's Fair of 1893, Wells raised the funds on the lecture circuit.[31] In 1892 a white mob in Memphis, Tennessee, destroyed Wells's newspaper offices after she wrote that many lynchings for the crime of rape in fact happened after consensual sex between white women and black men. T. Thomas Fortune immediately gave her a job on the *Age* and printed many of her subsequent antilynching articles.

Stemons and the *Pilot*

Stemons, however, continued to struggle to earn a living in the print world. He soon fell out with Caldwell and the *Courant*, and in early April announced his split.[32] But by late 1906 he wrote his sister about a new venture, the *Pilot*, which he would produce along with a white benefactor. Stemons estimated putting out an eight-page paper would cost about $85 per week, "and that by securing ads, the paper might soon be able to bring in a little more than that weekly." The investor agreed to put up all the money to run the paper for three months, "about $3,000," Stemons estimated.[33]

Stemons was thrilled at the prospects of independence from a church publisher and eager to make his mark on the world, telling Mary of his new partnership with "Warren C. Graham, attorney at law (white)," nephew of ex-Philadelphia district attorney George S. Graham, a Republican and reformer.[34] Initially, through Graham's financial backing, it appeared that Stemons would earn a salary. "At first my salary will be but $15 a week, with raises dependent on business," Stemons wrote his sister. "I have at last been taken up and placed on my feet on the strength of my individual worth."[35] In the next letter, however, the terms appear worse—Stemons would receive no salary at all but get half the profits of the paper for two years, "at the end of which time, the same contract can be renewed."[36] Stemons described the contract as "a most excellent arrangement, because the paper ought to soon be making a big profit," though he admitted, "it may not run more than a month or two." Still, that would be enough time to "do much good, and to do much to change public opinion on the race and other questions." Ever optimistic, Stemons told Mary that he had quit waiting tables. He reflected on his long fight to reach his new position and thought back to his itinerant days in the Northeast: "Through all this I look back to that light which I saw years ago, and think of the feeling which then possessed me that there was great work laid out for me to do. Through what thorny and stony paths my bleeding feet have since been led, no mortal will ever know. But, unworthy and unfaithful as I have been, I still feel that I have been piloted by the God of Nations."[37]

The paper launched sometime in January 1907. In early February, Stemons wrote Mary, "Mr. Graham is just as proud of the *Pilot* as I am, and spends from two to six hours in the office every day working right by my side." The *Pilot* was bringing in "$18 a week from our advertising. Of course this does not begin to pay our expenses. But we have two men in the field all the time, one of whom does little besides solicit advertisements." Stemons described the paper as "creating a great sentiment throughout the city, and, I suppose, in every place where it is known. But I see there is a disposition on the part of all would-be leaders to freeze me out." Stemons sent subscription letters "to every colored preacher in the city" but none had yet replied.[38]

A week later he noted, "Subscriptions are coming in slowly, a few every day—not as fast as we expected, but comparatively fast. Better, I am sure, than any other colored paper does. But I had thought the unusual qualities of the Pilot would make people subscribe for it much more rapidly than they do." Yet, in the next sentence, as if to renew his confidence, Stemons wrote, "But the people read it. They buy it off the newsstands. Its fame is rapidly spreading." One problem, Stemons wrote, is that people may "fear we do not intend to continue after the February election," a clue that, although the age of newspapers as political organs may have waned, campaign material masquerading as newsprint still circulated.[39]

Just a few weeks into publication, Stemons feared he might not see any money from the paper. As it turned out, "the terms of the agreement is that I receive no money till after all money paid out by Graham is recovered. We now have a deficit of about $200.00. Our total expenses for publication are in the neighborhood of $50.00 a week. Our income from the paper is now about $25 a week." Stemons wrote that he could, as a last resort, borrow money from Graham for living expenses.[40]

What were Graham's motivations in this business arrangement? Mary must have written Stemons about Graham, perhaps being too complimentary of him for Stemons's tastes, for in late February Stemons wrote Mary that she was "very, very much mistaken with reference to Mr. Graham," who was "connected to this paper for business reasons, pure and simple."

(Stemons's response also reads logically if Mary had suggested that her brother was too trusting of Graham.) Graham, Stemons wrote, has "no special regard for the colored race." If Graham did not foresee a profit, "he would not continue in it one week." Despite this, Stemons wrote, he rather enjoyed being associated with someone "who appreciates the fact that my talents have a commercial value."[41]

By the beginning of March, Stemons wrote Mary that the *Pilot* was "just paying expenses."[42] Graham desired a printing press to achieve financial viability. According to Stemons, a printing press cost about $2,000, and it cost about $20 a week to have the paper printed, "so it can be seen that a press would pay for itself in one year, to say nothing about the job work we would do on the side." Graham would borrow money from his uncle to get the press. "He is still elated with the prospects of The Pilot. It is really remarkable when one comes to think. There is a great big sign under the window: 'The Pilot, James Samuel Stemons, Editor.' The same sign hangs overhead; the same is ... on three doors. Graham's name only appears in the paper—in one place, and yet he comes daily to *my* office, and works like a slave—and advances all the money. There are but few colored newspapers which have their own plants—but I think we will be almost sure to get one."[43]

Job Printing

Graham's desire for a printing press makes sense. Publishers who owned their own printing presses ran many of the most successful and long-standing black newspapers in the nineteenth century.[44] In this way a newspaper could be funded in large part by profits brought in from printing for outside clients a wide variety of forms, including handbills, accounting ledgers, notices, tickets, and timetables. Job printing, according to a 1904 survey of the publishing industry, accounted for 30 percent of all profits (newspapers and other periodicals were 50 percent and books and pamphlets just 11 percent). By the late nineteenth century, however, job printing had become increasingly specialized, requiring different printing technology and techniques than newspaper printing.[45] Still, the capacity to print pamphlets and other materials could have made the difference for Stemons.

By June 1907, Mary had apparently suspected that the *Pilot* had folded (it had not; "Oh, ye of little faith," Stemons admonished his sister). "I did have to borrow $25 from W. C. Graham to-day," Stemons admitted, "or I would have been in trouble about my rent and the paper too."[46] It appears that Graham had either already left the paper or would soon; Stemons got a new African American investor, W. W. Rourk, around mid-June 1907.[47] Stemons agreed to give Rourk half ownership of the paper for several installments totaling $300 and a long-running advertisement that would pay Stemons $10 a week. The *Pilot* was still alive in October of that year; Stemons was working full time at the U.S. Postal Service (he had taken the civil service exam a few months previously), which made finding time to work on the paper exceedingly difficult. It did, however solve his financial problems; Stemons, who fought in vain for good jobs in the private sector for African Americans, apparently worked for the U.S. Postal Service for most of the rest of his long life. He immediately promised Mary he would resume sending her money.[48]

Pamphlet Publishing

The desire to further spread his ideas and profit from their circulation led Stemons to pamphlet publishing, another example of the print economy of the late nineteenth and early twentieth centuries. Here, the church connections forged through his reform work were vital. In May 1907, Stemons breathlessly wrote his sister, "I have just written the crowning article of my life so far—THE NORTH HOLDS THE KEY TO THE NEGRO QUESTION." Stemons sketched out for Mary the economics of distributing his text. "I can have 1,000 printed for less than $10, perhaps for $5. I can sell them in churches, that is I can have agents. Dr. Tindley will sell 500 in his church in little or no time, and there are other preachers who will do the same. Then I will have agents in this and other cities." Stemons was upbeat; he thought the article would surely "revolutionize thought on the race question," adding, "It follows a line of reasoning never before, so far as I know, taken up by any other person."[49]

About a month later, Stemons informed Mary that he had chosen a syndicate to distribute "The Key." "There is as you doubtless know, syndicates who place all kinds of reading matter before the traveling public—in depots and railway trains," Stemons wrote. "In Philadelphia that syndicate is known as the Union News Co." Stemons had visited the manager, who had offered him about five cents a sale. But this manager, Stemons wrote, stressed that the pamphlet would be "in the hands of no less than 250 agents . . . in all railway depots in charge of the Union News Co. . . . [and] placed directly in the hands of every traveler by the news boys in trains."[50] Though Stemons was optimistic about the Union News Co., he told Mary that too many "petty white news dealers . . . turn up their noses at the book as soon as they see it." Stemons saw "a giant conspiracy throughout the country among newspaper and magazine editors to foster sentiment against the Negro." He had received a letter from "one of the best known white editors in the country," who he said intimated to him, confidentially, that white editors would no longer publish anything sympathetic to black rights.[51]

Could this have been true in the "nadir" of African American rights, marked by the end of voting rights in the South, lynching, and the birth of

Jim Crow?[52] Though it would be hard to define a particular "worst" year for African Americans during the period, the end of 1906 shattered many black hopes for strong federal action in defense of civil rights when President Theodore Roosevelt summarily dismissed black soldiers dubiously accused of fomenting a riot in Brownsville, Texas.[53] A search of "the negro problem" in Google's Ngram Viewer, which uses a database of approximately 1.16 million books published in the United States between 1800 and 2000,[54] shows that the frequency of the phrase skyrocketed in print in the early 1900s, reaching a preliminary peak in 1907 and topping out in 1911. Other search terms such as "negro," "the negro race," and "negro citizenship" all show peaks in the early twentieth century right around 1907 (other high points are predictably during the Civil War and during the civil rights movement), the very moment of Stemons's forays into newspaper publishing. Google's Ngram Viewer makes a strong case for the year as a high point for sheer volume of writing about African Americans, at least in book publishing. Evidence from the previous chapters also suggests a broad-based cultural and legal crisis point in African American citizenship sometime during the first decade of the twentieth century. As discussed in Chapter 3, Secretary of War Elihu Root reached his own turning point with respect to African American rights around the time that a racist senator's plan for relocating blacks to the Philippines seems to have gotten at least a hearing at high levels of government. Roosevelt, even before the Brownsville troop dismissal, had changed his story about the fighting prowess of African American soldiers on San Juan Hill (he initially praised them but later claimed they were aimless or cowardly). Chapter 1 describes how Patrick Ford's *Irish World* backtracked on black rights in a series of columns by Robert Ellis Thompson. Perhaps sensing an ominous moment but one also full of possibility, Stemons would try to lift his own ideas about black-white race relations to prominence over others.

Politics in an Economy of Words

What were Stemons's ideas for African American success and improved race relations? Stemons's letters, books, and occasional articles printed in other newspapers reveal his arguments during the heyday of the so-called Negro Problem.

Stemons's vision was different from that of Booker T. Washington and W.E.B. Du Bois, the leading—and conflicting—African American thinkers and activists of the time. Stemons objected to the demand for immediate political and social rights for African Americans, and in this way he supported part of Washington's vision against that of Du Bois. Such protests would spark white backlash; they would "only result in increased friction between the races." Stemons had always said, he wrote Mary, that African Americans must "withdraw from politics in some parts of the south" or "race hatred and riots would be the inevitable result. . . . Time has proved that I was right." Furthermore, placing political rights before the economic put the cart before the horse, according to Stemons. Like Washington, Stemons believed that earning a livelihood and creating wealth were the only things that could secure full citizenship rights for African Americans.[55]

Yet the separatist aspects of Washington's vision repelled Stemons. Attempting to advance African American economic well-being in a sphere outside the mainstream U.S. economy struck Stemons as absurd. "The strange and pernicious doctrine that Negroes should create their own opportunities, instead of seeking to share in the common opportunities of a common country, has spread with such frightful rapidity as to make it appear presumptive and far-fetched to urge for Negroes any opportunities other than such as they personally create," Stemons wrote in the Chicago *Broad Ax*.[56] Stemons continued:

> The fact that the gifted few among Negroes have not the means . . . to thus in one generation, or in a dozen generations, develop industries and enterprises sufficient to furnish adequate employment to the millions who are not gifted, matters not to the voteries of this perversive doctrine of race exclusion, separation, and self-sufficiency—a hardship which no one even thinks of entailing upon the nearly one million of aliens who annually come to these shores. Indeed, so well have an element of Negroes succeeded in establishing the idea that they are a distinct and separate part of the social fabric that the average philanthropist, employer or what not, feels that he has fulfilled his highest possible duty to the race when he gives a few hundred, or a few thousand dollars to some Negro institution, any opportunity which he may offer the Negro of working to make an honest living being regarded by him as a superfluity.[57]

Jobs in industry would save African Americans; the seemingly endless debates over what type of education blacks should receive—Washington's agricultural and vocational curriculum versus Du Bois's classical schooling for a "talented tenth"—were, to Stemons, a distraction. "The hypothesis that education and a certain degree of civil and political freedom must of themselves either convert the Negro into a high and noble type of citizen or prove conclusively that he is incapable of attaining to such development," Stemons wrote in a 1907 essay, "is a sophistry which seems to be gaining in popularity."[58] Stemons sought African American advancement in stable, secure, and fairly reimbursed jobs with white Americans in, for example, manufacturing;

this would uplift the race and differed from the "industrial" focus in Tuskegee's curriculum, which was designed to train teachers to teach farming and various trades.

Stemons saw one opportunity for industrial jobs for African Americans when the steel industry in Pennsylvania put out a call for more workers. In the spring of 1907, as he was busy at the helm of the *Pilot*, Stemons clipped an article from the *Philadelphia Public Ledger* (daily, 1846–1942) concerning an offer to Pennsylvania working men from steel magnate Charles M. Schwab, the owner of the Bethlehem Steel Company. Schwab proposed to "pay apprentices living wages while [they received] technical training at the steel works"; he sought to create "the greatest manual training school in the world." In the same article, Archibald Johnston, president of Bethlehem Steel, urged young people in Pennsylvania's Lehigh Valley to take up Schwab's offer and move into financial security, "equipped to hold [their] own against the best workers the rest of the world can produce," lest they "become the poorly paid store clerk, the common laborer, one of that vast army of men whose pitiful story of poor wages, restricted opportunities, with the far more dreadful story of little children forced into mills and sweatshops, is all summed up in the few words, 'He has no trade.'"[59] Stemons's own long, difficult hours as a waiter and janitor no doubt shaped his beliefs in the importance to African Americans of just such opportunities. Stemons wrote Johnston on April 29, according to a letter in the Stemons files dated May 4. Stemons must have asked Johnston if he could arrange for young African Americans of Philadelphia to attend such a school, for Johnston's assistant wrote back, "There being practically no Negroes in our community, I am afraid that the surroundings would not be any too congenial to the boys of your race."[60] No positions, supposedly, could be given to African Americans because few African Americans lived nearby, a racial catch-22 that Stemons no doubt anticipated.

Stemons and the Politics of Respectability

Though Stemons's background was hardscrabble, his ideas could be elitist. Stemons's key to getting Northern industry to hire blacks involved encouraging better behavior on the part of a certain element of the black community; if such people could become more respectable or could be isolated so that whites could distinguish them from the majority of upright African Americans, Stemons believed, whites would be more likely to hire blacks. Chapter 13 of Stemons's *The Key* is titled "The Obtrusive Negro." Stemons considered the charge that "a class of American Negroes" have "an irrepressible fondness for attracting attention and making themselves obnoxiously conspicuous" and concluded that it is "persistent and, it must be admitted, well founded." Who in the North, Stemons said, has not seen "a crowded street car hushed to everything save the vociferous babblings of a half-dozen ignorant and uncouth Negroes?" Taking these observations as a given and separating this class from the "quiet and well-bred deportment" of the "intelligent Negro," Stemons asked why some African Americans should act in such a fashion. He blamed race prejudice; the consistently polite "European Negro," after all, "regards his social freedom as a matter of course," while "three centuries' serfdom" had taught black Americans that they were viewed as inferior to whites. This caused an uncouth element of African Americans to "feel called upon to be ever on the alert to force the impression that they are the equals of white men." This was an entirely human reaction, Stemons concluded; if the tables were turned, white men kept down for ages would similarly puff up their chests and declare their manhood when given new freedoms. In a qualified call for change, Stemons wrote: "So long as [the African American's] social status (and the word *social* is here used as applied to democracy) alternates between absolute segregation and the most scant and reluctantly accorded freedom, so long will he revel in and exploit that freedom in a way repulsive to those who have never known such restraints."[61] Stemons fingered white racism as the cause of such obtrusiveness, but his division of African Americans into good and bad groups blunted his critique, which veered toward the essentialism of the era's race science even as it underestimated the strength and durability of white racism. Stemons assumed that behavioral change on the part of blacks would be enough to cause whites to share power.[62]

Stemons's parenthetical caveat in the preceding quote already suggested he would not push for "social equality" and would instead be willing to leave much of Jim Crow intact. In fact, his next paragraph, the penultimate paragraph of *The Key*, is ambiguous; Stemons called again for white men to make "rigid distinctions" between two classes of Negro, the "vicious" and the "upright," the "refined" and the "uncouth," which would stress to African Americans that "any recognition of their race . . . is a recognition solely of individual worth" until "the time when all distinctions because of race or color shall be relegated to the dark and dismal past."[63] The passage reflects the ambiguity of the era's politics of respectability, a discourse in which Evelyn Brooks Higginbotham finds both accommodation and resistance. In her study of black Baptist churchwomen from 1880 to 1920, Higginbotham shows that in addition to chastising the poor for immoral behavior, the laity, in their focus on respectability and propriety, could challenge white power structures for their failure to live up to their professed ideals of equality and justice.[64]

Khalil Gibran Muhammad, one of a few historians to write about Stemons, focuses on his 1909–1910 activism, after his newspaper editorships ended and he engaged in what Muhammad calls a kind of hybrid campaign for both black economic empowerment and crime reduction in black communities. Muhammad writes that Stemons's rhetoric about, essentially, good and bad African Americans, "crossed the line into criminalizing jobless and underemployed blacks, diluting the strength of his attack on industrial repression."[65] He writes:

> For black writers and reformers . . . highlighting black criminality was a double-edged sword. At the same time that it carved out space to create a dialogue with liberal whites about racism's consequences and middle class blacks about their duty to the race, it defended the conservative self-help solution that dominated the pace of racial reform before Washington's death in 1915 and the onset of the Great Migration. This conservative edge was not what Stemons or Du Bois had intended to use.[66]

Stemons was not the only black thinker to alternate between racialist thinking and an emphasis on more environmental and economic explanations for black poverty and crime. Scholars have long noted the same in W.E.B. Du Bois's early writings. In *The Philadelphia Negro*, written less than ten years before Stemons's writings explored here, Du Bois alternately echoes and attacks aspects of social Darwinist thought. "The Negro is as a rule," he writes at one point, "willing, honest and good-natured; but he also is as a rule, careless, unreliable and unsteady." The comment echoes Fortune's remarks about most Filipinos' and African Americans' superficiality in the previous chapter.[67]

While Stemons may have indeed contributed to what Muhammad describes in his book as the association of crime with blackness,[68] Muhammad may still underplay Stemons's vigorous, long-standing belief that distinguishing between upstanding and venal African Americans was the key to improved race relations, producing greater white acceptance and hiring of blacks that would lead to economic empowerment. As late as 1941, Stemons retained a strong attraction to racial and ethnic stereotypes. In that year he published *As Victim to Victims: An American Negro Laments with Jews*. Describing in the first pages his decades-long battle for better race relations, Stemons summed up his two-part vision: justice for African Americans must include "economic freedom"; that freedom, in turn, would "hinge largely on the ability of Negroes to confute and confound their traducers" by "mak[ing] themselves synonymous to all that America means in human happiness and social advancement"—an allusion to some combination of societal conformity and bootstraps-pulling self-help.[69] Indeed, the key to black advancement lay in African Americans addressing their two greatest faults: "obnoxious and often deliberately insulting deportment in public" and blind involvement in the country's most "vile, corrupt, and conscienceless political machines."[70] Stemons wrote that his two biggest foes had always been, on the one hand, "those who insist the Negro has no legitimate place in the American scheme of civilization" and, on the other, "those who insist he ought to be accorded an immediate and unqualified share in all that America has to offer." (The most "unscrupulous" and "blind" opposition to Stemons's vision, he wrote, came from African Americans themselves, though he noted that black clergy had often been an ally.)[71]

In *As Victim to Victims*, Stemons related at some length others' critiques of anti-Semitism, including a long excerpt from black communist James W. Ford,[72] and found he agreed in general that anti-Jewish arguments were absurd, especially the "floundering" and "blind" suggestion that Jews were simultaneously the world's most rapacious capitalists and its most nefarious socialists.[73] But in a chapter titled "Evaluations," he still found "pro-Semites" too glowing in their description of Jews. They were "determined to ignore all except the most flattering facts regarding these sorely distressed people."[74] His solution to anti-Semitism was similar to his approach to the so-called Negro Problem: Jews must "take an inventory of their most objectionable features, and make a move to remedy them."[75] Stemons saw this approach as realistic and not derogatory of Jewish Americans. Anticipating opposition, Stemons related socialist newspaper editor Abraham Cahan's insistence that, as a Jew, he would "not be held responsible for the shortcomings of individual Jews, any more than other groups are held responsible for the antisocial forces among them." This, to Stemons, was "just, sane, and logical," but "history and experience" showed that Jews and Negroes would indeed be "judged and dealt with" based on the "lowest" among them.[76] After a lengthy recounting of his positive and negative experiences with Jewish merchants—some Jews, according to Stemons, had cheated him—Stemons concluded that Jews, too, should "draw a line of demarcation between themselves and the element which provides anti-Semitism with the food on which to thrive."[77]

As Victim to Victims received at least one mainstream review, by Richard Dewey, a sociologist at Butler University. Dewey found "refreshing" Stemons's suggestion that blacks and Jews find reasons within their own control for their respective groups' "unfortunate positions in American society." Dewey found Stemons's black typology appealing and listed the types of African American "offenders" in Stemons's crosshairs: "the political pawn, the prostitute, the exploiting gambler" and those who offend by their "blatant deportment in public."[78] Stemons's and his sister's apparent attempts to develop an African American doll (alluded to in his letters to her) suggest attempts to put forward positive portrayals of African Americans, but his classificatory regime matched white notions of (oftentimes derogatory) black types.[79]

As Chapter 3's look at T. Thomas Fortune suggests, black newspaper editors might describe other African Americans, particularly those in both the cities and countryside, in a manner informed by illustrated caricatures of African Americans (especially in the minstrel style) printed in the press. Furthermore, the newspaper medium seems to have encouraged stereotyping of nonwhite "others" through intimations of the editor's privileged gaze. Though it is not known whether Stemons incorporated illustrations in the *Pilot*, we can examine the work of black illustrators in the black press to understand their sometimes compromised efforts to strike back at racial ridicule.

African American Cartoonists and a Tricky Aesthetic

On June 8, 1889, the *Freeman* introduced, with some trepidation, cartoonist Moses Tucker's debut:

> The work of Mr. Moses L. Tucker which appears in this issue does not do him justice. His special work on the "Georgia Cracker" was the caricaturing of colored people, and his ability in this line has been thoroughly demonstrated. While we are averse to "poking fun" at the Negro, still there are many traits and characteristics which will bear criticisms, and which should be eliminated. This phase of the race problem will receive more attention hereafter and Mr. Tucker's gifted pen will do a share of it.[80]

The *Freeman* was sensitive to white ridicule of African Americans, yet its uplift ideology sought the elimination of certain "traits and characteristics" embarrassing to the race.

Little is known about Moses Tucker's life. He was born in 1868 in Fulton County, Georgia. By 1889 he was living in Indianapolis, where at the *Freeman* he joined cartoonist Henry J. Lewis, who left the paper soon thereafter. In 1910, when Stemons was an anticrime activist in Philadelphia, the census lists Tucker as an inmate of the Marion County Hospital for the Incurably Insane in Indiana. The date of his death is unknown.[81]

Figure 4.2 is a kind of visual representation of minstrelsy, with Tucker essentially performing in blackface—that is, portraying with ink and paper white Americans' imagined and desired ideas of blackness. Two black men stand in front of a closed bank; one dresses in floppy clothes while the other is a black dandy complete with top hat and cane. Not only the clothing but the back-and-forth dialogue of these Tucker cartoon characters match the minstrel genre, where an interlocutor, a kind of straight man, would com-

Figure 4.2 "Just Like White People," by Moses L. Tucker, from *The Freeman* (Indianapolis), September 20, 1890.

monly ask questions of a blackface performer, whose daft answers provided the humor. (Tucker's "Uncle Sam and the Negro," in the September 13, 1890, *Freeman*, repeats this style.) Eric Lott calls "cultural appropriation" the "central fact" of the minstrel show, though he detects strains of white (particularly working-class) sympathy and envy for African Americans' talent, culture, and physical embodiment.[82]

Yet the minstrel aesthetic was still somewhat "pliable"; in "Just Like White People," much of the joke is on white people and the series of financial booms and busts of the 1890s.[83] In this fashion, minstrel-like cartoons in the black press could be called a reworking of a cultural appropriation. Pearls of wisdom delivered by exoticized "black" performers were not uncommon to stage minstrelsy; the performance genre could accommodate some agency and intelligence on the part of its typically debased black characters. Class may be at work here, for the illiterate and ragged African Americans of minstrelsy may have been largely alien to a black editorial elite, as they mostly were to the white Northerners who developed blackface minstrel shows. It seems possible that the black bourgeoisie could enjoy some forms of minstrelsy or at least softened forms of it.[84] Yet the very nonelite J. Samuel Stemons also seemed to adopt and enforce some white stereotypes of African Americans in his writings.

As with African American participation in U.S. imperialism, dislocations of white supremacist discourse appear even as African Americans adopted and adapted the genres and discourses of white supremacy. Tucker's cartoon "Just Like White People" suggests as much. The cartoonist, consciously or not, brings attention not just to an economic system that encompasses all races but also to whiteness itself. Not just the bank, but presumably the figures in the cartoon are also, in a sense, just like white people. The cartoon exhibits several of the features scholar Monica Miller has identified with the history of black dandyism, which she defines as "the story of how and why black people became arbiters of style and how they use clothing and dress to define their identity in different and changing political and cultural contexts."[85] The "dandy's signature method," according to Miller, is "a pointed redeployment of clothing, gesture, and wit."[86] This produced not a small amount of derision and anxiety among whites, who during times of slavery passed sumptuary laws designed to curtail or forbid black extravagance.[87] African Americans, Miller writes, "understood intuitively that identity can be performed, that race is a fiction, and that both are culturally and historically based."[88]

Yet analyses that stress African American agency within minstrel aesthetics risk downplaying the consequences of working within the form. Whites finding enjoyment from dialect-speaking African Americans onstage or in fiction would likely miss veiled critiques of white supremacy and instead recognize only ignorance and deference, reinforcing their own racial biases. The *Freeman* editor's misgivings about Tucker's aesthetic style are clear in his introductory bio of the cartoonist. Charles Chesnutt, whose complex "story-within-a-story" plantation tales "play on the mutability of identity,"[89] deliberately abandoned writing in the black vernacular, only to be forced by Houghton Mifflin to return to his conjure tales in order to get a book of stories accepted.[90] African Americans would strongly protest minstrel cultural productions, including black entertainer Ernest Hogan's song

"All Coons Look Alike to Me." Black protest over racist caricatures would become particularly vehement a bit later in the twentieth century, with the 1915 release of the film *Birth of a Nation*.[91]

Chapter 1 examines drawn caricatures of the Irish and traces an evolution into more positive portrayals. Advertisers and advertising copy, too, began to associate the Irish with perseverance and charm. But the "productive fusion of ethnic identities and economic aspirations" that Susan L. Mizruchi describes advertisers creating did not extend to African Americans in the late nineteenth century. Because newspapers are a merger of interests and voices that may sit uncomfortably next to each other on the page, African American journalists and cartoonists made claims about African American strength and beauty that commerce might undo, through advertising's relentless appeal to mainstream (white) fears or vanities.

Ironically, the widespread white racism that limited black economic prospects created small economic niches that proved highly profitable for some African American entrepreneurs. Black undertakers could take advantage of social mores that dictated that only blacks could bury blacks; Pullman porters, likewise, came into being in part because of stereotypes of African American servility. Beauty products became another economic niche for African Americans in the late nineteenth century. But the links between appearance, identity, and self-worth within a white supremacist society placed the marketing of such products on treacherous ground. The juxtaposition of one black cartoonist's work with advertisements for African American hair products reveals how newspapers could sometimes be an inconsistent forum for advancing black equality.

Currently, little is known about the cartoonist "Hoffmann" beyond his cartoons themselves, which appear in the *Colored American* newspaper of Washington, D.C., around the turn of the century. Hoffmann typically depicts Uncle Sam, the American flag, or other symbols of democracy in ways that reveal the hypocrisy of a democratic discourse that was limited to one master race. Yet the advertisement "Black Skin Remover" consistently dogs Hoffmann's cartoons from nearby on the page, offering his black characters another way out, one that may not depend on resisting white racism and demanding enforcement of the Constitution. "Can the Leopard Change Its Spots?" Hoffmann asks of the Democratic Party donkey, draped in a sheet to disguise itself as a Republican elephant in a cartoon printed in the *Colored American* on June 22, 1901. "Could African Americans change theirs?" the nearby "Black Skin Remover" ad seems to inquire.

It is highly unlikely that such ironies were lost on Hoffmann. In "A Father's Blessing," from January 4, 1902, Hoffmann illustrates Uncle Sam holding a black and a white child in his lap. The children's hairstyles and physical placement seem to mimic the ever-present Crane and Co. hair tonic advertisement, visible just a few inches below Hoffmann's cartoon. The white child's hairstyle in particular resembles the African American woman after her transformation via the company's skin cream. Another cartoon, printed first on August 31, 1901, and titled "In the Land of the Free, etc." (Figure 4.3), is even more explicit about products that promise to ease the color line. The cartoon's caption begins, "A policeman studied a Negro's face, pronounced him a 'suspicious character,' and attempted his arrest." He winds up "dragged from the jail and hanged from a tree in the Court house yard." Uncle Sam studies a sign explaining that the man was "hanged because he was not good looking." In the background of the cartoon, next to the lynched man, hangs another, barely legible sign: "Use Dr. White's Face Bleach." If one assumes Dr. "White" is a "black" man selling skin products, yet another white-black binary is set up. Hoffmann, it seems, was only too aware of the advertisements that typically accompanied his political cartoons. In Hoffmann's cartoons, the mirror images, black-white binaries, and sheets removed to reveal something different underneath hint that racial identity, including whiteness itself, is a kind of veil or deception.

The black press as a whole vigorously debated hair straighteners and skin lighteners. Sol C. Johnson, editor of the *Savannah Tribune*, refused to run such ads, writing, "We look with pitying eyes upon the person who endeavors to undo nature by straightening his hair or bleaching his skin.... [T]hey are encouraged in it by a number of race journals, the pages of which are covered with these kinds of ads."[92] But the success of black commercial culture around cosmetics and the civil rights activism of black cosmetics entrepreneur Madam C. J. Walker, the first female self-made millionaire in U.S. history, complicates the picture. Furthermore, the Boston Chemical Co., Ozono, and the Richmond, Virginia–based Crane and Co. were white-owned firms that promised to turn dark skin lighter. Madam Walker, by contrast, whose empire was just beginning in 1900, spoke out against skin bleaching and denied that her hair product was a straightener; she called it a hair grower.[93] Scholar Kathy Peiss acknowledges a "contradictory rejection and embrace of Euro-American aesthetic standards" in the African American construction of the "New Negro" woman, who would claim the moral ground seen as the sole province of white womanhood.[94] "While many [African American women] fashioned their appearances by following in some measure the aesthetic of European beauty," Peiss writes, "they frequently understood their beauty rituals in ways that modified, undercut, and even challenged the charges of white emulation."[95] Visual culture would change slowly, however; by the 1920s, although text in Madam Walker's advertisements might praise the "matchless browns" and "glossy dark skin" of African American women, the accompanying illustrations still typically depicted women with decidedly European appearances.[96]

Figure 4.3 "In the Land of the Free, etc.," by Hoffmann, from *Colored American*, August 31, 1901, p. 16.

While Stemons's writings show an attraction to black caricature, his letters also show he and his sister considered the production of a black doll. Unlike Stemons's other inventions, however, there is no evidence that he ever received a patent for the doll.

Stemons's Individualism

Stemons never seemed to imagine mass black collective action or even a coalition with either Booker T. Washington or W.E.B. Du Bois after bringing them over to his way of thinking. Instead, he sought to carve out his own special take on the Negro Problem and promote that view through media, securing a living—via subscriptions or sales, advertising revenue, and probably speaker fees—as he helped his race advance. The newspaper and his other published writings were an assertion of his views; his individual success was simultaneously an example of achievement for his race. It becomes impossible to pull out Stemons's thinking from the print economy within which it resides. In Stemons's mind, as long as the Negro Problem was a top news story of the day, competing against other black newspapers would require distinguishing one's critique or platform from others'. Stemons was convinced that his particular strategy for black advancement would "revolutionize thought on the race question," telling Mary, "It follows a line of reasoning never before, so far as I know, taken up by any other person."[97] Stemons's specific political take on the Negro Problem was a part of providing a better product as much as attention to the quality of the newsprint, the creativity of the layout, or the amount and nature of paid advertisements.

Analyses of the black press that see its self-promotional aspects only in narrow business terms—say, how publishers might use their presses to promote their own personal enterprises—miss this relationship. Black individual success promoted black advancement and thus fought against racist views. Failure, likewise, reflected poorly on the race as a whole, adding even more stress to an already stressful occupation.[98]

An emphasis on individual achievement, of course, reflected the tenor of the times. Heather Cox Richardson interprets Washington's autobiography, *Up from Slavery*, as claiming for African Americans the nation's "free labor" ideology, which emphasized the opportunity of wage earners to rise to property-owning independence. According to Richardson, Reconstruction lost support with the broader society because African Americans began to be associated with labor interests that believed class conflict to be inevitable and who demanded government redistribution of wealth. Washington's well-received 1895 speech at the Cotton States and International Exposition in Atlanta, known as his "Atlanta Compromise" speech, served a purpose similar to *Up from Slavery*.[99] "Cast down your bucket where you are," Washington repeatedly implored African Americans, and asserted that "whatever other sins the South may be called upon to bear ... when it comes to business pure and simple, it is in the South that the Negro is given a man's chance in the commercial world."[100]

Stemons's marked individualism and entrepreneurialism is also reflected in his efforts as an inventor. In the first decades of the twentieth century, Stemons designed a street indicator for use on trolley cars, a noise-making toy, and possibly a black doll. He appears to have received patents for the indicator and the toy.[101] His letters suggest that the indicator was never constructed, partly because of lack of funds—his patent lawyer delicately discusses payment for his services in one letter in the Stemons collection—and because he struggled to find a suitable magnifying glass, presumably to enable passengers to read the street names.

New Thought's Influence on Stemons

Even Stemons's spiritual beliefs seem to stress personal achievement over collective worship. Of course, Stemons's intense ambition, self-promotion, and optimism should not be reduced to a simple product of its time—a Gilded Age outlook, say—any more than it should be seen as conforming to some overarching African American point of view in the nadir. But his letters do reveal his and Mary's avid interest and participation in New Thought, a late nineteenth-century health and spirituality-centered movement roughly akin to today's New Age philosophies. New Thought was a metaphysical belief system that peaked around the turn of the century; it could meld spiritual goals with material ones. The three figures most prominent in the movement were Phineas Quimby (1802–1866), Christian Science founder Mary Baker Eddy (1821–1910), and Emma Curtis Hopkins (1849–1925). New Thought practitioners believed in a unity of God and mind that could heal disease and bring about prosperity.

In the spring of 1906, Stemons wrote Mary, "I do not get as much New Thought as I should, because ... I am built [?] more in the intellectual than in the spiritual plane." Nevertheless, he had had great success with a new breathing technique outlined by Elizabeth Towne in her article "Just How to Wake the Solar Plexus."[102] (In a pamphlet of the same title published the following year, Towne describes how she kept asking the "Son of God" to grant her emotional health to no avail. Finally, she realized she was herself a "Sun" of God, built to radiate goodness outward from the body's core, the solar—or sun—plexus.) New Thought pamphlets were widely available on newsstands around the turn of the century.[103]

Though much of New Thought involved invoking positive thoughts to maintain good health and fight disease, many of its followers also linked economic prosperity to a mind trained to focus on success. Towne, for example, also wrote *How to Grow Success* (1903), in which she described the "law of attraction."[104] Stemons's sister appears to be the family's chief practitioner of New Thought. "You will understand that from now till June 1st I will need all of the help that you can possibly render me through New Thought methods," Stemons wrote his sister in the spring of 1909, hoping she would send positive thoughts his way so that he might secure a speaking position at an upcoming conference on the political and social status of African Americans in the nation.[105] Aside from such occasional, outright calls for her metaphysical expertise, Stemons may have more typically and deliberately crafted his letters with positive affirmations to evoke his and his sister's shared spiritual affinities and to attempt to conjure his professional aspirations. Viewed in this light, Stemons's frequent predictions of his imminent success are less pompous litany and more hopeful mantra.

New Thought itself was, of course, a product of its time. In fact, when Stemons admonished his sister, who had begun writing a column for the *Pilot*, not to express "surprise and chagrin" that no reader had responded to her Popular Opinion column, his reasoning may well have been influenced by New Thought—or it may simply reflect the market ideology of the early 1900s. The two overlap. "You of course know that it is a psychological fact that if you desire to draw support to yourself you must keep up an appearance of success in your undertaking," Stemons wrote Mary: "Just as soon as you complain and scold, that is notice to the public that you are failing in the particular of which you complain."[106] He added that many newspaper columnists simply respond to their own columns using pseudonyms, though he did not recommend this scheme to Mary.

The Stemons Brand

In the spring of 1907, after Graham left the *Pilot*, Stemons told his sister that the Reverend Tindley had said the *Pilot* was "too great a paper to let go down.... He said that he saw very plainly that I am to be to the Negro question what [William Lloyd] Garrison, and [Wendell] Phillips, and [Elijah] Lovejoy and [Charles] Sumner was to the slavery question, before the war. He said that the entire country will in a short time accept me as the true sentinel, to direct thought and action on this great question."[107] One wonders whether Tindley might be humoring Stemons, appealing to his vanity in order to appease or manipulate. And yet publication of the *Pilot* did bring Stemons, however briefly, local and even some national recognition. Letters and visits he received from prominent African Americans thrilled Stemons. "'The Big Boys' of the race have already begun to court my favor," he wrote Mary a few weeks after the *Pilot* began publishing in early 1907. William A. Sinclair, the author of *The Aftermath of Slavery*, one of the first books to push back against Redemption histories of emancipation and Reconstruction, called the office to congratulate Stemons on publication of the *Pilot*. Sutton E. Griggs, a Baptist minister, activist, and author of the utopian novel *Imperium in Imperio* also dropped by, missing Stemons but telling Graham "that he represented some association the object of which is to promote harmony between the races." Stemons said Griggs had planned to publish a newspaper but thought the *Pilot* might be better able to represent his cause.[108] The *Courant* had also given Stemons some clout; in the spring of 1906, with Stemons at the helm, he had a dust-up with R. A. Torrey, a well-known white American pastor and author who conducted revival meetings throughout the country in 1906–1907. Stemons had somehow torpedoed a plan of Torrey's for a special revival meeting for African Americans, apparently objecting that setting aside a race-based meeting would make African Americans think they were not welcome at regular ones. In a curt letter, Torrey called Stemons's view "altogether illogical. . . . We have had special meetings for men, but they did not think on account of that that they would be requested not to attend meetings where women were. We have had meetings in other places for working girls, but that did not make them think they would not be welcome at other meetings." Torrey repeated the same phraseology with university students, soldiers, cabmen, and policemen. "I did want some fruit among the colored people," Torrey wrote. "Their souls are as precious in God's sight as white people. . . . I noticed that they were not getting to the other meetings in any large numbers. . . . [N]ow such a meeting is impossible. It is too late."[109]

According to Stemons's letters, the nation's two most prominent race leaders also took note of the *Pilot*. Booker T. Washington wrote Stemons in the summer of 1908, "On many matters you and I do not agree, but I always read your paper, because when you do not agree with a person, you argue and do not abuse."[110] Washington wrote to praise a recent Stemons editorial, "Let Southern Representation Alone," about calls by some (more militant) African American leaders to reduce Southern states' representation in Congress should they continue to deny the vote to African Americans. Stemons mentions in 1908 at least one other letter from Washington, on an "insignificant matter," which Stemons took as a sign that the great leader was threatened by him: Stemons's book, Stemons surmised, had "already sent Booker T. 'up in the air.'"[111] Earlier, in February 1906, W.E.B. Du Bois apparently mentioned favorably a Stemons editorial in the *Courant* and reprinted it in his publication, the *Moon*.[112]

The constant percolation of new but soon-to-disappear media ventures during the long nineteenth century deserves scrutiny. This chapter attempts to describe this entrepreneurial landscape of newspaper start-ups and its impact on debates about race and citizenship. For a short time in the first decade of the twentieth century, J. Samuel Stemons could claim the title of race man. He attracted the attention of African American race leaders and black and white funders. Though little-known compared to T. Thomas Fortune, Stemons also helped to shape black thought in the nadir. Both men struggled continually to keep their papers afloat; Fortune's long-running *New York Age* would eventually be purchased, in part, by Booker T. Washington.[113] Debating race in a difficult publishing landscape could mean for African Americans casting one's arguments in ways attractive to white philanthropists or a broader white audience. But the desire to make a name for one's self also encouraged new thinking, even while it might encourage competition, not cooperation, with other race advocates engaged in their own print ventures. The so-called accommodationist black politics of the time may have emerged not exclusively from fears of white violence or from a grievous underestimation of the depth and durability of white supremacist ideologies and institutions. For activists and race leaders hoping to enter debate around the Negro Problem, an eye toward financial success pulled one toward crafting novel, marketable critiques and agendas. Stemons's experience in particular suggests that the terms "individualist" or "entrepreneurialist" could also help describe a trying, experimental era of black thought and resistance.

CONCLUSION

Wired for Connection—and Conflict

During T. Thomas Fortune's overseas journey, the transpacific cable reached Hawaii and, a few months later, the Philippines, connecting these new U.S. territories with San Francisco. American newspapers in both Hawaii and the Philippines announced the cable as the dawn of a new era of trade, expressing excitement at the prospect of immediate stock quotes and other news reports. One "Cable Day" speaker in Hawaii breathlessly announced that the cable had "close[d] one of the finest stanzas in the epic of action. Through the eternal harmonies, God has again spoken to His creatures. The invisible force, that is the nearest symbol of life, has once more struck the note of universal brotherhood, and everywhere the human soul responds to the electric appeal."[1]

African American journalists had long hoped for heightened solidarity and strength through media networks. The masthead of the *Richmond Planet* put such longing into graphic form, depicting an array of electric-like lines stretching out from a closed fist. The desire for African American networks of communication was particularly acute in part because the first domestic U.S. newswire, which started as a cooperative of New York City dailies in 1846 and later became the Associated Press (AP), did not strike a tone of "universal brotherhood," as the Cable Day speaker hoped. As Fortune's *New York Age* put it in 1891, the AP was frequently "an engine of misrepresentation and oftentimes libel" against African Americans. It distressed Fortune to see black newspapers reprint such material.[2] The AP depended on

Southern editors for news from the South—including Clark Howell, a director of the Associated Press, editor of the *Atlanta Constitution*, and ardent supporter of Jim Crow—and those editors frequently censored or distorted the news according to their racial animus. Republican journalists in the South often complained that telegraph operators "did their best to quash or color dispatches sent out." And the AP wire almost never quoted African American newspapers.[3]

Black and Irish Americans responded to discrimination by creating their own presses, with hopes of connecting, compelling, and channeling their readership into a unified force to secure full citizenship rights and American belonging. Could newspapers do this? Scholars must consider paradoxes to communications technologies when speculating about reading publics brought together through periodicals. On a national scale, in early America, one well-received study finds that "the more connected regions appeared to be (in print), the more regionalized (rather than nationalized) their identities became. . . . [M]aterial simultaneity across national space . . . produced an enhanced sense of regional difference. A growing sense of simultaneity, in other words, produced not nationalism but an ever more entrenched sectionalism . . . expressed through the phobic language of racism at the most local levels."[4] Menahem Blondheim found a similar process still at work in the summer of 1858, just a few years before the Civil War, as Jefferson Davis, future head of the Confederacy, visited the cooler New England climate on the advice of his doctors. Both Davis and his Yankee hosts were surprised and pleased at how much common ground they found despite heightened sectional tensions. But as Davis spoke congenially to Northerners on his way home, a press newly connected by telegraph wired dispatches of his words throughout the country, including the South, which became convinced that the Mississippi senator was compromising Southern interests. A new technology, Blondheim claims, impeded the political skill of massaging the message according to one's audience. Near-simultaneous communication required greater uniformity, and Davis had to reaffirm hard-line sectionalism to angry constituents immediately upon his return.[5]

Similar contradictions or ironies, if not paradoxes, have abounded in this book's examination of the generally smaller newspaper organs of nondominant groups. Black and Irish media were a site for Americanization, but they also forged, with varying degrees of success, a space for difference in American society—in fact, the immigrant press often embraced the diversity of "hyphenated Americans" as the very justification for these groups' inclusion in an American tapestry. Father Yorke did find the press a powerful engine to communicate ideas from "the Old Church that gave printing to the world,"[6] but publisher-priests like Yorke provoked resistance from the Vatican largely centered around its fear that Catholic publishing in the public sphere was changing the faith too much, too fast. Newspapers were important nodes of American power in the Pacific but also sites of resistance to that power; T. Thomas Fortune hoped to use newspapers to help bring about new Afro-Asian alliances but found racially charged resistance from both white and nonwhite editors and their presses.[7] And important, well-circulated discussions about minority-group politics appeared in journals that might disappear as quickly as they were born.

Because the relationship between medium and message is hard to pin down, historians can focus on what historical actors hoped or believed newspapers might do for their communities. This, too, is a way that newspapers influenced the race men and women of the nineteenth century, though here the newspaper is more of a black box or mirror reflecting media practitioners' desires. "There are fully 25,000,000 of Irish blood in the United States," Patrick Ford wrote a fellow Irish nationalist in 1899. "If our people ever understood themselves and would come together things would be as we could wish them to be."[8] T. Thomas Fortune's hope that a "newspaper organ" might help coalesce a cosmopolitan, mixed-race group of justice-minded Filipinos and foreigners in Manila is of a similar vein. In addition to being a place of power, newspapermen also imagined newspapers as sources of knowledge, as schools more closely connected to the real world than formal educational institutions. Newspapering provided, race editors thought, a privileged vantage point from which editors could gauge the varied characters newly gathered in American cities due to the exploitation and exile, attraction and opportunity of late nineteenth-century capitalism. The dude, the dandy, the corrupt preacher—the editor "knows them all, for he has dealings with them."[9]

But the newspaper medium itself came with expected conventions and styles, whether it was the need to court and display vendors' wares or the visual genres of advertising and cartooning, which, as in the minstrel form, might reflect dominant cultural attitudes and biases. Stemons's, Fortune's, and other editors' written descriptions of black or Jewish types seemed in dialogue with these visual typologies and sometimes with the labor needs of agriculturalists still desperate for field labor in the years following emancipation. Images in the black and ethnic press supported, contested, or more subtly "shadowed" dominant national iconographies of race and gender and the imagined international "burdens" of white men.[10] Black cartoonists who, like Moses Tucker, worked within the minstrel genre appear at first glance to be drawing the visual equivalent of the era's accommodationist black politics, and the endurance of such iconography in the black press attests, in part, to the financial and careerist needs of these cartoonists, who felt compelled to work within preexisting aesthetic worlds even while they critiqued them.[11] But a kind of ownership by African American illustrators of black images and black lifestyles may also be at work. The black dandy or dude, created in part in the minds of whites who saw African Americans as ridiculously putting on airs, might be embraced as stylish or hip or even countercultural by African Americans themselves. Stemons might have been correct about the harmfulness of Booker T. Washington's separatist economic vision for African American life. ("Cast down your bucket where you are," Washington told blacks up to the time of his death, on the eve of a very different African American action: exodus out of the South in the Great Migration.) But a kind of cultural separatism may be necessary to spark minority-group pride and artistic production. At least one scholar links Booker T. Washington's embrace of Ruskin's Arts and Crafts movement and patronage of black artists and photographers as a stepping-stone between Victorian aesthetics, with its belittling of black artistic production, and New Negro art. Near the end of his life, Washington began to embrace African art and culture and even implied that as a younger man he had distanced himself too much from African history and traditions. Tuskegee is certainly an "unexpected place" to find seeds of the Harlem Renaissance.[12]

Here, too, African Americans interested in cultural revival sometimes looked to the Irish. James Weldon Johnson, a major figure in the Harlem Renaissance, cited Irish playwright and collector of Irish folklore John Synge as an inspiration: "What the colored poet in the United States needs to do is something like what Synge did for the Irish; he needs to find a form that will express the racial spirit by symbols from within rather than by symbols from without."[13]

In fact, the Irish in this study keep appearing as models for other immigrant groups and for African Americans—in positive and negative ways. Some Irish American editors had been calling for a more multicultural, less assimilationist or "melting pot" conception of American citizenship well back into the nineteenth century. That many historians place the origins of American cultural pluralism or cosmopolitanism in the late nineteenth or early twentieth centuries (perhaps with pragmatists William James and John Dewey or with Randolph Bourne's 1916 essay "Trans-national America") requires revising. Irish activist-editors worked diligently and much earlier to expand American citizenship to include multiple loyalties and heritages. But simultaneously, the Irish trained other immigrant groups in the mores of city life, including its racial hierarchies—sometimes through their newspapers. African Americans reacted to this but could still be inspired by Irish independence and nationalist organizing, frequently described and sometimes orchestrated through Irish American presses.

Surprisingly, the Irish, not sub-Saharan Africans, may serve as the first racial foil for Western imperialism, the original, paradigmatic European image of the savage. Several historians locate the birth in the European mind of a wild and bestial "other" in twelfth-century British encounters with the Irishman, who then became the template through which Africans and American Indians were understood and described, in text and through circulated illustrations. In Shakespeare's *The Tempest*, for example, first performed as England was consolidating its rule over Ireland, the slave Caliban seems to have indeterminate heritage; his mother, Sycorax, comes from Algiers but is also described by Prospero as a "blue-eyed hag." Historian Nadja Durbach writes that it "was not . . . that Africanness was mapped onto Irish bodies, as historians have often suggested, but rather that the category of the 'Negro' was constructed in relationship to, and built upon, that of the 'Celt.'"[14] But via some combination of America's greater distance from most Fenian violence, its looser class structures, the efforts of Irish American activists and editors themselves, and advertisers' embrace of positive Irish images, the Irish in America slowly escaped their racialization as the nation moved to a more biracial scheme with overtones of white, European solidarity.

Though Americans may be familiar with Benjamin Franklin's publishing exploits or know that Mark Twain placed much of his fiction in serial form in newspapers, the full implications for U.S. history of so many artists, activists, and reformers being so closely associated with newspapers has not been explored. The birth of sociology as a profession, for example, is intimately tied to Robert E. Park, who himself was intimately tied to both newspapers and Booker T. Washington's Tuskegee Institute. Park began working for Washington in 1905, shortly after T. Thomas Fortune stopped his close association with the Wizard and after ten years of working as a reporter for various newspapers in the West, Midwest, and Northeast. Park had "a lifelong interest in communication as a force for integrating society and in the means of communication, especially the newspaper and the telephone."[15] Park worked for Washington for nearly a decade as a researcher and speechwriter before founding the so-called First Chicago School of sociology at the University of Chicago, whose sociologists were known, overall, for their curiosity and acceptance of, and sympathy for, black and immigrant cultures in the thriving Midwest metropolis. Their projects were "explicitly liberal and ameliorative, of a piece with the work of journalists like Jacob Riis and early social workers like Jane Addams," and sought to refute eugenics and social Darwinism.[16] Recent historians have argued for a much darker view, seeing Park's sociology and Washington's beliefs in an agricultural destiny for African Americans as key to a global economic restructuring of slave labor into liberal capitalist forms of imperialistic resource extraction.[17] This complex story, much of which draws on Tuskegee in Togo, West Africa, and not Washington's and Fortune's look toward the Pacific, needs further exploration—with newspapers, photography, and other communications media in mind.[18]

Irish nationalism sometimes contracted, at other times expanded to embrace social movements or express solidarity with victims of imperialism worldwide.[19] But Irish newspapers, as mentioned previously, could be sites for creating race conceptions that excluded others. Policing the borders of belonging was obvious on the West Coast, where Irish American editors such as Peter Yorke sought to "build up a wall" against Chinese immigration. In the process, Yorke tried to place white Christian laborers at the core of American belonging. The American Federation of Labor (AFL) practiced a similar tactic, warning in 1902 that capital and labor had not secured "a permanent industrial peace." Going forward, the AFL warned, employers and the employed needed "greater trust and confidence" than ever before, something that could "never be fulfilled between individuals of races so alien to one another as ourselves and the Chinese." The threat of labor discord was intimately linked to racially and religiously exclusionary legislation. Many Progressive reformers, whom Yorke did not trust, likewise supported anti-Asian efforts but from a different angle: like urban, ethnic political machines, big business also needed to be reined in and should not be allowed to amass power by importing "servile labor."[20] In the East and West, Progressive policy looked to quell disputes between capital and labor by supporting or at least not challenging segregation and/or exclusion policies. The defeat of Senator Charles Sumner's hopes for naturalization of the Chinese in 1870, around the time Ford first began publishing his *Irish World*, "predicted the abandoning of Reconstruction" for African Americans; the end of Reconstruction, in turn, "would seal the fate of the Chinese in the West."[21]

In fact, Yorke, Fortune, Stemons, and Ford all maintained tricky relationships to the era's Progressive reform efforts. All four were, in a very real way, reformers themselves. Newspapers were useful in their project to calibrate group identity within American norms and promote national belonging. Black and ethnic editors and publishers could bring their own facts to bear in newspaper-mediated debates that privileged evidentiary knowledge and muckraking exposés. But for the Irish, Progressive attacks on corruption might mean a campaign against Irish power in the nation's cities. Progressive educational reforms also struck Irish Catholics as at odds with their faith. Yet the gap between the nation's leading reform movement and African Americans was even larger. In this study, Elihu Root's speech on the "failure" of voting rights for African Americans, Robert Thompson's similar outlook in his columns in the *Irish World*, and Stemons's and other black Philadelphia reformers' difficulty in integrating industrial workforces—and perhaps Stemons's intimations that white publishers were freezing out black writers—demonstrate that much if not most Progressive reform stopped at the borders of African American communities and aspirations.

The risks and possible rewards to both Irish Americans and African Americans in their struggle for full citizenship were particularly heightened during the nation's imperial adventures at the turn of the century. Because the American majority conflated Christianity with Protestantism, Irish Americans could not afford to back out of debates about the fate of Catholic education in the Philippines—Christianizing Filipinos must not be equated with transforming them into Protestants.[22] The Irish American press, worried about Protestant evangelism in the islands, flexed its muscles and gained concessions from the Philippine Commission. Again, for African Americans, the stakes were higher. In fact, regimes of pedagogy and segregation were intimately linked, at home and abroad, in their deferral of full democratic rights for both African Americans and Filipinos.[23]

An excellent explication of such Jim Crow colonialism comes from reformer Charles Denby, who, in an 1899 article titled "What Shall We Do with the Philippines?" and published in a major Progressive forum, attempted to reassure Southern anti-imperialists regarding Progressives' plans in the new territory:

> We, who are a trifle progressive, are called "Imperialists," because we are not going to allow the poor Filipinos to vote ... but ... when the time comes that the Islanders are qualified to exercise the right of suffrage they will get it. In all human probability they will secure it sooner than some of the Negro population in some of the Southern States. Gentlemen of the South, gentlemen of Dixie—some of us Imperialists do not blame you at all for taking all possible legal measures to protect your cherished rights. Will you not forgive us, if we pursue the same policy with regard to a new and untried race?[24]

Many anti-imperialists of the time, particularly those from the South, came to their anti-interventionism in a different and more explicitly racialized way than the Irish. Many U.S. anti-imperialists opposed annexation of tropical territories on the presumption that the nonwhite inhabitants of those lands must be given American citizenship and the right to settle on the mainland United States—citizenship must follow the U.S. flag, according to this formulation. That, in turn, meant that the nation's new wards could travel to the metropole, where anti-imperialists feared they would corrupt American life and democracy with their innate inferiority. Denby, in the preceding passage, endorses citizenship restrictions until races suspected of being inferior prove themselves worthy of democracy. Denby's intellectual position as well as his political prominence matches John Cell's description of segregation as a modern urban movement—not one borne solely or even primarily out of the prejudices of "pre-modern," rural, or Southern America—and as "an ideological umbrella that enabled whites to agree while continuing to conflict."[25]

Emphasis on the territories and colonies as a testing ground for forms of segregation and control should not blind us to the complicated local manifestations of racial rule making in those new U.S. possessions, of which newspapers played a prominent part. Progressive journalist Stannard Baker visited Hawaii in 1911 and, like T. Thomas Fortune, detected the "New England conscience" of a planter class of missionary descent. (As a Progressive, however, he was horrified by the sugar companies' use of low-wage Asian labor, which he felt pushed out any possibility of the idealized, free white worker. "I have rarely visited any place where there was as much charity and as little democracy as in Hawaii," he wrote in *American Magazine*.)[26] Certainly, "Whites Only" barbershops, saloons, and brothels quickly sprang up in Manila after 1898;[27] Fortune's run-in with police, which some accounts placed in a bar, not on the street, could have involved an attempt on his part to defy segregation in Manila. But simultaneously, as Paul Kramer has shown, a more relaxed interaction could develop between Philippine elites and white Americans in Manila. When, at the 1904 World's Fair and Exposition in St. Louis, white women were seen fraternizing with Philippine Scouts (a Filipino army organized by the United States), the city's press exploded with rants against interracial mingling. New racial rules had developed in the colony that the metropole could not abide. Empire involved a "racial remaking of empire and the imperial remaking of race" on which Fortune and Booker T. Washington hoped to capitalize.[28]

Newspapers were key sites in these local battles over race, rights, and responsibilities. The "Lions of Manila"—Taft's words for the former U.S. soldiers staffing much of the American press in the city—practiced unvarnished white supremacy, using, for a time, lucrative advertising aimed at U.S. troops to fund newspapers that pushed back against the "Filipinization" of governance on the islands. Had U.S. troop levels remained high or if more white Americans had flocked to the nation's newest possession, perhaps a larger public centered around these newspapers might have more sharply threatened or shaped the American agenda in the Philippines. Similarly, though it may be hard to imagine today, if more African Americans had emigrated to the Philippines, as soldiers or as settlers, black newspapers might have gathered and amplified new voices for racial justice.

This book leaves its editors in the first or second decades of the twentieth century; the beginning of World War I is a common stopping point for historians of the "long nineteenth century." But all four editors profiled here lived beyond the war. Father Yorke's later years were marked by their quietude in comparison to his battles with the APA, his vocal support of the teamsters, or his caustic denunciations of the Chinese around the turn of the century. His tenure as a regent at the University of California was low-key; several letters between him and UC president Benjamin Wheeler show a priest seemingly resigned to doing little more than preventing a secular institution from endorsing Protestant forms of Christianity. Wheeler several times lamented that Yorke rarely attended regents meetings or spoke at campus functions; Yorke, who relocated to an East Bay parish after the great earthquake of 1906, responded that "between parishioners and refugees I have used up about all of my available vocabulary."[29]

Some of Yorke's last entries in a personal journal are wistful and match historians' descriptions of an Irish generation that perceived itself to be exiled in America. Seven months before his death, Yorke wrote in a journal entry, "Do you remember 1886 in Galway writing in the book you destroyed. The next day you left Ireland forever (1924 – 1886 = 38 years) and now you are 60 (completa)." Another (undated) entry reads, "The shadows are creeping in and if I am to do the work for the children that I ask health for I must this fall and winter do: 1) The book on Faith. 2) The book on Hope. 3) The book on Charity."[30] Yorke died on Palm Sunday in 1925. In a sense, his longtime rival Charles McClatchy became the more common model for Irish American belonging—proud of his heritage but more assimilated and less committed to ethnic militancy and Irish and Catholic superiority and separation.

T. Thomas Fortune returned from the Philippines and was reelected head of the Afro-American Council at its convention in July 1903 in Louisville, Kentucky. The gathering almost disbanded several times as resistance to Booker T. Washington's influence over the group reached a breaking point. Many of the leading critics and supporters of Washington stood at the helms of their own presses, including William Monroe Trotter and his Boston *Guardian*, and accusations and insults ricocheted in print. One letter writer to the *Colored American* was convinced that black leaders' colossal egos, their "cerebral elephantiasis," was the real culprit. He even penned a verse he thought the race leaders were effectively chanting: "Sing, oh my muse, the lofty theme / Sing I and Mine and Me! / We are lofty individuals now, / Way down in Tennessee."[31] Black and Irish weeklies were sites of bitter conflict as well as cooperation. In addition to the moral hazard of directing a press and seeing one's name in print,[32] activist-editors from marginalized groups surely felt the strain and stress of their precarious position in American society.

Just a few years later, partly in response to alcoholism, financial pressures, and Washington's moves to take ownership of his *New York Age*, Fortune suffered a nervous breakdown. He slowly recovered and toward the end of his life began again to write, edit, and agitate—eventually, and perhaps somewhat improbably, for Pan-Africanist Marcus Garvey. Starting in 1923, Fortune edited Garvey's publication, the *Negro World*, which, with a circulation that may have reached two hundred thousand, was the most widely read black weekly in the world, even printing special sections in Spanish and French. Colonial administrators worldwide banned its circulation. Jomo Kenyatta, the first president of an independent Kenya, spoke about how in 1921 "Kenya nationalists, unable to read, would gather round a reader of Garvey's newspaper . . . and listen to an article two or three times," then run "various ways through the forest" repeating the message of black nationalist pride to other Africans.[33] The account recalls the group of Fenian prisoners at the beginning of this book, huddled by candlelight in the hull of a British ship bound for Australia, poring over a handwritten nationalist weekly produced onboard.

James Samuel Stemons, after the *Pilot* shut its doors sometime in 1907 or 1908, briefly became an anticrime organizer in Philadelphia. He continued to write frequently to his sister, updating her on his campaigns. In this new activist role, Stemons still combined his militant call for equal economic opportunity for African Americans with a respectability politics that could turn attention away from economic and political injustices at crime's roots to stress perceived moral shortcomings in black communities. His efforts culminated in a joint conference he organized between groups working against crime and for industrial opportunities for African Americans. T. Thomas Fortune was a panelist at the conference, and he and Stemons surely crossed paths; Booker T. Washington heard of the event and wrote Stemons a letter inviting him to the annual Tuskegee conference. Stemons was disappointed with Philadelphia's response to his efforts, writing his sister that the mayor had taken his crime-fighting ideas and applied them only to white communities.[34] Stemons kept writing until his death, perhaps without the cocky confidence of his youth ("Already I can see in Caldwell a suspicion or enmity or rather jealousy over what he thinks I can do with the paper," he had written Mary in 1906, when he first started work on the church weekly the *Courant*).[35] He published a book on the Korean War in 1952. His semi-autobiographic novel, *Jay Ess*, was never published but is available in handwritten form at the Historical Society of Pennsylvania in Philadelphia.

Patrick Ford must have reflected on Irish progress in America toward the end of his life. The lessening of anti-Catholic bigotry and anti-English sentiment can make, from today's vantage point, Ford, Yorke, and their nineteenth-century Irish counterparts seem a bit sycophantic in their protestations of patriotism or paranoid in their dread of British or nativist plots. But progress in American belonging could be quickly reversed, even for the Irish, as federal response to immigrant communities during World War I shows. In January 1918, less than five years after Ford's death, Ford's son and other Irish editors found their newspapers censored by the U.S. government. The Wilson administration investigated the *Irish World* under the Espionage Act and would exclude from the U.S. mails five editions, despite the fact that the *World*, under the direction of Ford's son Robert, supported the U.S. war effort after April 1917. Ford's colleague and sometime critic John Devoy, editor of the *Gaelic-American*, was investigated in 1917 for alleged pro-German activities. An August 1917 edition of Father Peter Yorke's *Leader* was withheld from circulation. In fact, some Irish nationalists in Ireland and the United States actively sought arms from Germany for an attack on British forces in Ireland—any time Great Britain went to war, Irish America was prepared to strike. Yet it appears that U.S. censors argued, essentially, that simple support for Irish self-determination, not just dealings with Germany, was tantamount to disloyalty to the U.S. war effort.[36] Robert Bowen, a federal attorney charged with reviewing the Irish American press, questioned Robert Ford's patriotism in a letter to William H. Lamar, solicitor general of the post office: "There is no genuine Americanism on the right side of his Irish hyphen," Bowen claimed.[37] The comment would surely have made Robert's father fighting mad. Yet one imagines the elder Ford sitting down at his desk and coolly reaching for a pen.

In the years to come, Irish Americans and African Americans would continue to struggle over race and representation as motion pictures dramatically increased the power of images to reflect, blur, and perhaps refract society. As mobile communication systems proliferate and our society experiences new realms and vast increases of words and images, questions concerning how the media affect our social and political lives remain—and activists and reformers continue to respond to and employ mediated representations of our world in hopes of bringing forth a better one.

NOTES

INTRODUCTION

1. Walter McGrath, "Convict Ship Newspaper, *The Wild Goose*, Rediscovered," *Journal of the Cork Historical and Archaeological Society* 74 (1969): 20–31.

2. See, for example, Marshall McLuhan, *The Gutenberg Galaxy: The Making of Typographic Man* (Toronto: University of Toronto Press, 1962). Most media scholars today find McLuhan too technologically deterministic; Marshall T. Poe's thesis, following Harold Innis's work, that new technologies are "pulled" into existence by changing social, political, and economic forces and organized interests, is more common. See Marshall T. Poe, *A History of Communications: Media and Society from the Evolution of Speech to the Internet* (Cambridge: Cambridge University Press, 2011), 4.

3. Stanford M. Lyman, "Robert E. Park Reconsidered: The Early Writings," *American Sociologist* 21 (Winter 1990): 343.

4. See Shelley Fisher Fishkin, *From Fact to Fiction: Journalism and Imaginative Writing in America* (Cambridge, UK: Oxford University Press, 1985).

5. Walter L. Williams, "Black Journalism's Opinions about Africa during the Late Nineteenth Century," *Phylon* 34 (1973): 224.

6. Benedict Anderson, *Imagined Communities: Reflections on the Origin and Spread of Nationalism* (1983; repr., New York: Verso, 2006).

7. Jeremy D. Popkin, *Media and Revolution* (Lexington: University Press of Kentucky, 1995), 23.

8. Ibid. See also James W. Carey, *Communication as Culture: Essays on Media and Society*, rev. ed. (New York: Routledge, 2009), 17.

9. Popkin, *Media and Revolution*, 23–24 (emphasis in original).

10. "Catholic Newspapers," *Catholic Sentinel*, February 24, 1872, p. 1.

11. See Anderson, *Imagined Communities*.

12. Ibid., 7.

13. See Barbara Young Welke, *Law and the Borders of Belonging in the Long Nineteenth Century United States* (New York: Cambridge University Press, 2010), 11. Andreas Fahrmeir examines the evolution of citizenship in Great Britain, France, Germany, and the United States in *Citizenship: The Rise and Fall of a Modern Concept* (New Haven, CT: Yale University Press, 2007). Uday Mehta explores how a discourse of human rights evolved concurrently with slavery, colonialism, and other Western-orchestrated oppressions in "Liberal Strategies of Exclusion," *Politics and Society* 18 (December 1990): 427–454. T. H. Marshall's 1950 essay, "Citizenship and Social Class," is considered seminal and posits that civil, political, and social equality can exist within the economic inequalities of capitalism. See T. H. Marshall, "Citizenship and Social Class," in *Class, Citizenship, and Social Development* (Garden City, NY: Doubleday, 1964).

14. A note about newspaper attribution: Contemporary historians often consider the unsigned articles on the editorial pages of small nineteenth-century newsweeklies as the voice of the newspaper's editor. Readers of the time typically did, too. In the pages that follow, I usually attribute the words on these editorial pages to Ford, Yorke, or Fortune themselves. (Stemons's words come almost entirely from his signed letters to his sister, not from his newspapers.) Nevertheless, because activist-editors could sometimes employ small staffs, in the citations to this material I list an individual editor as author only if that editor's name was attached to the text as a signature or byline.

15. Frank Luther Mott, *American Journalism*, rev. ed. (New York: Macmillan, 1950), 441, 444–445.

16. See Robert E. Park, *The Immigrant Press and Its Control* (New York: Harper, 1922); and Sally M. Miller, *The Ethnic Press in the United States: A Historical Analysis and Handbook* (New York: Greenwood Press, 1987).

17. Emma Lou Thornbrough, *T. Thomas Fortune: Militant Journalist* (Chicago: University of Chicago Press, 1972); and Shawn Leigh Alexander, ed., *T. Thomas Fortune, the Afro-American Agitator: A Collection of Writings, 1880–1928* (Gainesville: University Press of Florida, 2008).

18. William Leonard Joyce, *Editors and Ethnicity: A History of the Irish-American Press, 1848–1883* (New York: Arno Press, 1976); and James Rodechko, *Patrick Ford and His Search for America: A Case Study of Irish-American Journalism, 1870–1913* (New York: Arno Press, 1976).

19. Oscar Handlin, *The Uprooted: The Epic Story of the Great Migrations That Made the American People* (New York: Grosset and Dunlap, 1951).

20. See Kathleen Neils Conzen et al., "The Invention of Ethnicity: A Perspective from the U.S.A.," *Journal of American Ethnic History* 12 (Fall 1992): 3–41.

21. See Matthew Frye Jacobson, *Whiteness of a Different Color: European Immigrants and the Alchemy of Race* (Cambridge, MA: Harvard University Press, 1999), 8; David R. Roediger, *The Wages of Whiteness: Race and the Making of the American Working Class* (New York: Verso, 1991); Eric L. Goldstein, *The Price of Whiteness: Jews, Race, and American Identity* (Princeton, NJ: Princeton University Press, 2006); and Noel Ignatiev, *How the Irish Became White* (New York: Routledge, 1995). Critiques of whiteness studies include Eric Arnesen, "Whiteness and the Historian's Imagination," *International Labor and Working-Class History* 60 (Fall 2001): 3–32; Peter Kolchin, "Whiteness Studies: The New History of Race in America," *Journal of American History* 89 (2002): 154–173; and Jack Niemonen, "Public Sociology or Partisan Sociology? The Curious Case of Whiteness Studies," *American Sociologist* 41 (2010): 48–81.

22. Jon Gjerde, *Catholicism and the Shaping of Nineteenth-Century America*, ed. S. Deborah Kang (New York: Cambridge University Press, 2012).

23. Joshua Paddison, *American Heathens: Religion, Race, and Reconstruction in California* (Berkeley: University of California Press, 2012), 9. Also see Stacey L. Smith, *Freedom's Frontier: California and the Struggle over Unfree Labor, Emancipation, and Reconstruction* (Chapel Hill: University of North Carolina Press, 2013).

24. Several scholars have found that, at least in congressional debate over annexation of the Philippines in 1899, white supremacist arguments were used primarily by anti-imperialists: in this view, because citizenship must follow the American flag, annexation would lead to the emigration of racially inferior peoples to American shores. See Christopher Lasch, "The Anti-imperialists, the Philippines, and the Inequality of Man," *Journal of Southern History* 24 (August 1958): 319–331; Eric T. L. Love, *Race over Empire: Racism and U.S. Imperialism, 1865–1900* (Chapel Hill: University of North Carolina Press, 2004); and Fabian Hilfrich, *Debating American Exceptionalism: Empire and Democracy in the Wake of the Spanish-American War* (New York: Palgrave Macmillan, 2012). Somewhat at odds with these works are studies that Paul Kramer calls "cultures of United States imperialism" scholarship, which describe a new, turn-of-the-century moment where social Darwinist philosophies and religiously inspired notions of Manifest Destiny and racial uplift worked together to push America outward toward the so-called uncivilized world. See Paul A. Kramer, "Power and Connection: Imperial Histories of the United States in the World," *American Historical Review* 116 (December 2011): 1348–1391. Though such scholarship may acknowledge that anti-imperialists played the race card with more vigor than the imperialists, the overall effect still can be to downplay many Americans' racially based, grave misgivings about expansion. A difference in sources may be at work here; Lasch, Love, and Hilfrich tend to favor diplomatic and congressional documents and may discount a pro-expansionist "white man's burden" atmosphere in the nation at large. Meanwhile, "cultures of imperialism" scholars draw on fiction, art, advertising, plays, and world's fairs but often exclude political or diplomatic sources. Susan Harris also examines the disparate viewpoints of the anti-imperialists in *God's Arbiters: Americans and the Philippines, 1891–1902* (New York: Oxford University Press, 2011).

25. Matthew Frye Jacobson, *Special Sorrows: The Diasporic Imagination of Irish, Polish, and Jewish Immigrants in the United States* (Cambridge, MA: Harvard University Press, 1995), 142.

26. Peter Schmidt calls "Jim Crow colonialism" a "new analytical frame . . . for understanding the paradoxical mix of citizen-building and subjection at the heart of Progressivist discourse at home and abroad." See Peter Schmidt, *Sitting in Darkness: New South Fiction, Education, and the Rise of Jim Crow Colonialism, 1865–1920* (Jackson: University Press of Mississippi, 2008), 14.

27. Allan Punzalan Isaac makes this point in *American Tropics: Articulating Filipino America* (Minneapolis: University of Minnesota Press, 2006), xxvi.

28. Martin Berger cautions that white scholars seeking to understand and expose racism by examining derogatory images of African Americans risk reproducing a white fascination with black bodies. Sustaining attention to the construction of white identity, he suggests, can partially mitigate this problem. Part of Berger's work involves uncovering ideologies of whiteness in images that do not depict nonwhites at all. See Martin Berger, *Sight Unseen: Whiteness and American Visual Culture* (Berkeley: University of California Press, 2005), 2–4.

29. Gerry Beegan, *The Mass Image: A Social History of Photomechanical Reproduction in Victorian London* (New York: Palgrave MacMillan, 2008), 18.

30. See Kevin K. Gaines, *Uplifting the Race: Black Leadership, Politics, and Culture in the Twentieth Century* (Chapel Hill: University of North Carolina Press, 1996), 197.

31. See M. Alison Kibler, *Censoring Racial Ridicule: Irish, Jewish, and African American Struggles over Race and Representation, 1890-1930* (Chapel Hill: University of North Carolina Press, 2015).

32. Booker T. Washington, speech to Brooklyn Institute of Arts and Sciences, February 22, 1903, in *The Booker T. Washington Papers*, ed. Louis R. Harlan and Raymond W. Smock (Chicago: University of Illinois Press, 1977), 7:87.

33. For an excellent look at imagery in the German-language press, see Peter Conolly-Smith, *Translating America: An Immigrant Press Visualizes American Popular Culture, 1895-1918* (Washington, DC: Smithsonian Books, 2004). Tony Michels explores New York's Jewish and socialist press in *A Fire in Their Hearts: Yiddish Socialists in New York* (Cambridge, MA: Harvard University Press, 2005).

34. The term was coined by African American historian Rayford W. Logan in *The Negro in American Life and Thought: The Nadir, 1877-1901* (New York: Dial Press, 1954).

35. Gaines notes a "brutal individualism" and "fierce, often covert competition" among black reformers in the early 1900s. In part because of a dearth of professional opportunities, leadership was "primarily a matter of dominance." See Gaines, *Uplifting the Race*, 201, 202.

36. See, for example, Cian McMahon, *The Global Dimensions of Irish Identity: Race, Nation, and the Popular Press, 1840-1880* (Chapel Hill: University of North Carolina Press, 2015).

37. David Brundage, *Irish Nationalists in America: The Politics of Exile, 1798-1998* (Oxford: Oxford University Press, 2016), 121. Irish American troops in the Philippines sometimes referred to Filipinos, sympathetically, as "smoked Irish." See James R. Barrett, *The Irish Way: Becoming American in the Multiethnic City* (New York: Penguin, 2012), 245.

38. Shawn Leigh Alexander, *An Army of Lions: The Civil Rights Struggle before the NAACP* (Philadelphia: University of Pennsylvania Press, 2011), 10-11.

39. Barrett, *The Irish Way*, 271.

40. Mott, *American Journalism*, 444-445, 589. Mott says that rural weeklies adapted to pressure from the dailies by becoming more local in nature, and editors found that "small items, using hundreds of names, increased circulation" (589).

41. Trish Loughran, *The Republic in Print: Print Culture in the Age of U.S. Nation Building* (New York: Columbia University Press, 2007).

42. Gary Gerstle, *American Crucible: Race and Nation in the Twentieth Century* (Princeton, NJ: Princeton University Press, 2001).

43. See Guy Emerson Mount, "The Last Reconstruction: Slavery Emancipation, and Empire in the Black Pacific" (Ph.D. diss., University of Chicago, 2018).

44. Eric Gardner sees the black periodical, not the slave narrative, as the center of African American literary production in the 1800s in *Unexpected Places: Relocating Nineteenth-Century African American Literature* (Jackson: University Press of Mississippi, 2009).

PART I

1. Joyce, *Editors and Ethnicity*, 49.

2. See Brundage, *Irish Nationalists in America*, 60; Joyce, *Editors and Ethnicity*, chap. 2; and Cian McMahon, "Ireland and the Birth of the Irish American Press, 1842-61," *American Periodicals: A Journal of History and Criticism* 19 (2009): 5.

3. McMahon, "Ireland and the Birth of the Irish-American Press," 7–9; Brundage, *Irish Nationalists in America*, 79–87.
4. Joyce, *Editors and Ethnicity*, 7.
5. Brundage, *Irish Nationalists in America*, 33.
6. Ibid, 88.
7. The best examination of this split is Angela Murphy's *American Slavery, Irish Freedom: Abolition, Immigrant Citizenship, and the Transatlantic Movement for Irish Repeal* (Baton Rouge: Louisiana State University Press, 2010).
8. Boston *Pilot*, March 21, 1898, quoted in Jacobson, *Special Sorrows*, 192.
9. Joyce, *Editors and Ethnicity*, 13.
10. McMahon, *The Global Dimensions of Irish Identity*, 181, 7.

CHAPTER 1

1. "Read—Reflect—Act," *Irish World*, March 25, 1871, p. 4. The first issue of the *Irish World* appeared on September 10, 1870; within a few months, Ford was printing his mission statement on the editorial page.
2. Ibid.
3. Ibid.
4. Ibid. (emphasis in original).
5. Ibid.
6. James McPherson, *Battle Cry of Freedom: The Civil War Era* (New York: Oxford University Press, 1988), 119–120.
7. The most complete biographical material on Ford and most detailed study of the content of the *Irish World* is Rodechko's *Patrick Ford*. Unusually with respect to most biographical sketches of Ford, Timothy J. Meagher reports that Ford was orphaned at an early age and that his guardians brought him to America. See Timothy J. Meagher, *The Columbia Guide to Irish American History* (New York: Columbia University Press, 2005), 255.
8. Rodechko suggests that John Boyle O'Reilly's *Pilot* rivaled Ford's paper in terms of influence, at least in the 1870s and possibly 1880s. Eric Foner calls the *Irish World* the "most important" Irish American newspaper by the early 1880s; Cian McMahon cites circulation figures that put the *World* at a hundred thousand by 1884, surpassing the *Pilot*, though all scholars agree that such figures are rough estimates. See Rodechko, *Patrick Ford*, 42; Eric Foner, *Politics and Ideology in the Age of the Civil War* (New York: Oxford University Press, 1980), 157; and McMahon, *Global Dimensions*, 170–171.
9. *Irish World*, January 28, 1871, quoted in McMahon, *Global Dimensions*, 171.
10. Roger Fischer, *Them Damned Pictures: Explorations in American Political Cartoon Art* (North Haven, CT: Archon Books, 1993), 41.
11. Though many advertising and trading cards in the collection are undated, enough dates and legible postmarks exist to outline changes in form over time.
12. For other cards, see http://www.arbycards.info/arbsat1.htm.
13. L. Perry Curtis, Jr., *Apes and Angels: The Irishman in Victorian Caricature*, rev. ed. (Washington, DC: Smithsonian Institution Press, 1997), 29, 102–108.
14. *Irish World*, May 23, 1903, and August 13, 1904, quoted in Kibler, *Censoring Racial Ridicule*, 76, 2.
15. The R. W. Bell Co. also circulated cards that depicted Jewish stereotypes. See Wendy A. Woloson, *In Hock: Pawning in America from Independence through the Great Depression* (Chicago: University of Chicago Press, 2009), 48.

16. Susan L. Mizruchi, *The Rise of Multicultural America: Economy and Print Culture, 1865–1915* (Chapel Hill: University of North Carolina Press, 2009), 2.
17. See, for example, Conzen et al., "The Invention of Ethnicity."
18. Mizruchi, *Rise of Multicultural America*, 2.
19. Richard Holt, "Ireland and the Birth of Modern Sport," in *The Gaelic Athletic Association, 1884–2009*, ed. Mike Cronin, William Murphy, and Paul Rouse (Portland, OR: Irish Academic Press, 2009), 44.
20. Joshua Brown, *Beyond the Lines: Pictorial Reporting, Everyday Life, and the Crisis of Gilded Age America* (Berkeley: University of California Press, 2002), 186.
21. Robin Bernstein, *Racial Innocence: Performing American Childhood from Slavery to Civil Rights* (New York: New York University Press, 2011), 77.
22. Ibid., 11.
23. Kevin Kenny, *The American Irish: A History* (New York: Pearson Education, 2000), 172.
24. Ibid., 173.
25. David Brundage, "'In Time of Peace, Prepare for War': Key Themes in the Social Thought of New York's Irish," in *The New York Irish*, ed. Ronald H. Baylor and Timothy J. Meagher (Baltimore: Johns Hopkins University Press, 1996), 323.
26. Davitt (1846–1906) was born during the Great Famine to a farming family in West Ireland. The family was eventually evicted and settled in East Lancashire. Davitt lost his right arm as a child while working at a spinning machine in an English factory. Imprisoned on weapons charges related to his membership in the Irish Republican Brotherhood, Davitt upon his release traveled to New York, where he met Henry George. See T. W. Moody, *Davitt and Irish Revolution, 1846–1882* (London: Oxford University Press, 1982); and Laurence Marley, *Michael Davitt: Freelance Radical and Frondeur* (Dublin: Four Courts Press, 2007).
27. "The Slaughter in Pennsylvania," *Irish World*, June 30, 1877, p. 4.
28. Rodechko discusses whether Ford embraced socialism in *Patrick Ford*, 74–76, and determines he did not.
29. "Disarming Workingmen," *Irish World*, October 4, 1879, p. 4.
30. "The Irish World's Sub-Head," *Irish World*, December 21, 1878, p. 4.
31. Kenny, *The American Irish*, 177.
32. "What the Land Movement Means," *Irish World*, January 8, 1881, p. 4. Fall River, a Massachusetts textile town that was the largest in America, saw several spinners' strikes in the 1870s.
33. Kenny, *The American Irish*, 178.
34. Kevin Kenny, "Diaspora and Comparison: The Global Irish as a Case Study," *Journal of American History* 90 (June 2013): 143.
35. For a discussion of Ford and the financial disputes over the Skirmishing Fund, see Joyce, *Editors and Ethnicity*, 167–168.
36. "Voice of the People," *Irish World*, March 3, 1877, p. 6. More recently, Niall Whelehan has pinpointed support for skirmishing and revolutionary violence in general as coming from first-generation working-class Irish Americans originally from Western and Southern Ireland, the areas hardest hit by the famine. See Niall Whelehan, *The Dynamiters: Irish Nationalism and Political Violence in the Wider World, 1867–1900* (Cambridge: Cambridge University Press, 2012).
37. See Foner, *Politics and Ideology*, 168–173. Alan O'Day believes that Irish American support for Irish independence campaigns has been exaggerated and suggests that monies sent to Ireland from America were instead mostly remittances, humanitarian aid for "rural distress," and religious donations for the construction of

churches. O'Day quotes Ford in letters to Michael Davitt expressing his discouragement about raising money for Ireland from his apolitical or preoccupied fellow countrymen. O'Day's arguments for a more nuanced and contingent discussion of Irish and Irish American connections and identity are strong; it should also be noted that his quotations from a discouraged Patrick Ford are from 1899, not the 1870s or 1880s. See Alan O'Day, "Imagined Irish Communities: Networks of Social Communication of the Irish Diaspora in the United States and Britain in the Late Nineteenth and Early Twentieth Centuries," *Immigrants and Minorities* 23 (2005): 399–424.

38. Discussion of Ford's break with George and his move to the center can be found in Rodechko, *Patrick Ford*, 92–93, 183–195; and Bruce Nelson, "Irish Americans, Irish Nationalism, and the 'Social Question,' 1916-1923," *boundary* 2 (Spring 2004): 155–156.

39. Rodechko, *Patrick Ford*, 38–39, 42.

40. Ibid., 41–42; McMahon, *Global Dimensions*, 171; Joyce, *Editors and Ethnicity*, 168.

41. Thomas Brown, *Irish-American Nationalism, 1870-1890* (Philadelphia: J. B. Lippincott, 1966), 136, 141.

42. Lawrence J. McCaffrey, "Forging Forward and Looking Back," cited in Baylor and Meagher, *New York Irish*, 217.

43. Ibid., 215.

44. Conolly-Smith, *Translating America*, 39–40.

45. McCaffrey, "Forging Forward," 229–230.

46. See *Irish World*, May 23, 1891, and May 30, 1891.

47. The most prominent exponent of the view of an exile sensibility among the Irish is Kerby A. Miller's seminal and much-debated *Emigrants and Exiles: Ireland and the Irish Exodus to North America* (Oxford: Oxford University Press, 1985).

48. Figures are from Timothy G. McMahon, *Grand Opportunity: The Gaelic Revival and Irish Society, 1893-1910* (Syracuse, NY: Syracuse University Press, 2008), 14–17.

49. Úna Ní Bhroiméil, *Building Irish Identity in America, 1870-1915: The Gaelic Revival* (Dublin: Four Courts Press, 2003), 32.

50. Ibid., 32–33.

51. Ibid., 41–44, 47.

52. "The Irish Language National Fund," *Irish World*, January 28, 1899, p. 5.

53. Thomas J. Shahan, "The Irish Language," *Irish World*, November 24, 1894, p. 1.

54. Bhroiméil, *Building Irish Identity*, 30.

55. La Vern J. Rippley, "Archbishop Ireland and the School Language Controversy," *U.S. Catholic Historian* 1 (Fall 1980): 3–5.

56. Ibid., 2.

57. Ibid., 10. Ireland told the German Catholic societies at the Minnesota gathering that whoever did not "thank God he is an American should . . . betake his foreign soul to foreign shores, and crouch in misery and abjection beneath tyranny's scepter." Rippley, "Archbishop Ireland," 5.

58. "Archbishop Ireland's Critics," *Irish World*, March 26, 1892, p. 4.

59. Ibid.

60. Steven M. Avella finds Catholic church leaders blocking in-language ethnic parishes on the West Coast, too, in *Sacramento and the Catholic Church: Shaping a Capital City* (Reno: University of Nevada Press, 2008), 114.

61. Harold A. Innis, *The Bias of Communication*, 2nd ed. (Toronto: University of Toronto Press, 2008), 33.

62. Paul Heyer, *Harold Innis* (New York: Rowman and Littlefield, 2003), 62.

63. See, for example, Charles R. Acland and William J. Buxton, eds., *Harold Innis in the New Century: Reflections and Refractions* (Montreal: McGill-Queen's University Press, 1999); Heyer, *Harold Innis*; and Poe, *A History of Communications*.

64. Menahem Blondheim, "Innis and His Bias of Communication," in *Canonic Texts in Media Research: Are There Any? Should There Be? How about These?* ed. Elihu Katz et al. (Cambridge, UK: Polity Press, 2003), 168.

65. Ibid., 168–169.

66. See Irish World Calendar, *Irish World*, January 11, 1890, p. 6.

67. Answers to Correspondents, *Irish World*, March 18, 1871.

68. John MacPhilpin, "Irish Type Fund," *Irish World*, July 19, 1890, p. 1.

69. Tidings from the Old Country, *Irish World*, September 6, 1890, p. 6.

70. David T. Z. Mindich finds the "application of an ethic of 'objectivity'" by the 1890s, with precursors of "fairness, detachment, nonpartisanship, and balance" valued from well before the 1830s; Hazel Dicken-Garcia is more cautious, situating "non-partisanship" in the era of its use and finding greater differences between its present-day and older connotations. Still, Dicken-Garcia finds a move toward formulating journalistic guidelines in the 1870s and 1880s that emphasized accuracy and impartiality. See David T. Z. Mindich, *Just the Facts: How "Objectivity" Came to Define American Journalism* (New York: New York University Press, 1998), 10–11; and Hazel Dicken-Garcia, *Journalistic Standards in Nineteenth-Century America* (Madison: University of Wisconsin Press, 1989), 219–222. Michael Schudson sees the press placing a particular emphasis on uncovering truths "realistically" during the 1890s as "part of the broader Progressive drive to found political reform on 'facts.'" Michael Schudson, *Discovering the News: A Social History of American Newspapers* (New York: Basic Books, 1978), 71.

71. "The 'Irish World' Confiscated in the British Post-Office," *Irish World*, January 11, 1890, p. 4.

72. Timothy J. Meagher, *Inventing Irish America: Generation, Class, and Ethnic Identity in a New England City, 1880–1928* (Notre Dame, IN: University of Notre Dame Press, 2001).

73. "A Riverside Parish," *Irish World*, June 15, 1895, p. 1.

74. Pope Leo XIII, "*Longinqua*: On Catholicism in the United States," January 6, 1895, para. 18, available at http://w2.vatican.va/content/leo-xiii/en/encyclicals/documents/hf_l-xiii_enc_06011895_longinqua.html.

75. Ibid., para. 6.

76. "Answering Possible Critics," *Irish World*, February 9, 1895, p. 4.

77. Ibid.

78. "MGR. Satolli on the Press," *Irish World*, February 2, 1895, p. 1.

79. Angela F. Murphy contends that the repeal movement could have survived the abolition controversy but collapsed because of O'Connell's defense of England. See Murphy, *American Slavery, Irish Freedom*.

80. Bruce Nelson, *Irish Nationalists and the Making of the Irish Race* (Princeton, NJ: Princeton University Press, 2012), 13.

81. Peter D. O'Neill and David Lloyd, *The Black and Green Atlantic: Cross-Currents of the African and Irish Diasporas* (New York: Palgrave Macmillan, 2007), 17 (emphasis in original).

82. See, for example, "They Love England," *Irish World*, December 28, 1895, p. 8; and "The Evils Imperialism Will Breed," *Irish World*, September 9, 1899, p. 1.

83. *Irish World*, June 24, 1871, quoted in McMahon, *Global Dimensions*, 172.

84. See Ford's long editorial, "The Southern Problem," *Irish World*, February 8, 1890, p. 4, in which he stated that "the wrong done to the negro at the South is not simply a local evil nor does it affect merely the black men of that section; but it is all-pervading and concerns us all" and suggested that Southern congressional representation be reduced by three-sevenths until African American suffrage was assured.

85. "Making a Governor Responsible for Lynching," *Irish World*, May 13, 1893, p. 4. Ford's first article on the Peterson case appeared in the May 6, 1893, edition.

86. "Disgraceful Lawlessness," *Irish World*, August 19, 1893, p. 4.

87. *Irish World*, April 19, 1879, quoted in McMahon, *Global Dimensions*, 173.

88. Matthew Frye Jacobson explores immigrants' responses to American imperialism, including in the Philippines, in *Special Sorrows*; Bruce Nelson explores Irish nationalism and the Boer War in *Irish Nationalists*, 121–147.

89. Stuart Anderson, *Race and Rapprochement: Anglo-Saxonism and Anglo-American Relations, 1895–1904* (Rutherford, NJ: Fairleigh Dickinson University Press, 1981), 12. For a more recent examination of the "intercolonial connections" between the United States and Great Britain, see Paul Kramer, "Empires, Exceptions, and Anglo-Saxons: Race and Rule between the British and United States Empires, 1880–1910," *Journal of American History* 88 (March 2002): 1315–1353.

90. J. D. O'Connell, "'Anglo-Saxon,' Humbug," *Irish World*, April 29, 1899, p. 1.

91. "Wanted—a Definition," *Irish World*, June 4, 1898, p. 4. Nearly thirty years earlier, Ford had similarly attacked the notion of America as an Anglo-Saxon nation, going as far as to declare in a headline, "The True American Type Celtic, not Anglo-Saxon." Indeed, Ford wrote, "we doubt whether there would have been any rebellion . . . of the colonies against the mother country, but for the Fenian spirit of the Irish element in the colonies. The Quaker and English sentiment was opposed to the Declaration, and the war. The American Revolution was the work of Irishmen." "The True American Type Celtic, Not Anglo-Saxon," *Irish World*, March 18, 1871.

92. "Good Man Devil," *Irish World*, November 4, 1899, p. 4.

93. "'Civilizing' the Filipinos," *Irish World*, May 27, 1899, p. 4.

94. McMahon, *Global Dimensions*, 163. Young Ireland was an Irish nationalist movement of the 1840s.

95. "The American-Irish Historical Society," *Irish World*, January 28, 1899, p. 6.

96. "Freedom's Fight Begun in Africa," *Irish World*, October 21, 1899, p. 12.

97. "Ho for the Transvaal!" *Irish World*, October 28, 1899.

98. "All Nationalities Help the Boers," *Irish World*, October 21, 1899, p. 12.

99. "Good Man Devil," 4.

100. "Americans and Boers," *Kentucky Irish American*, January 19, 1901.

101. Conzen et al., "The Invention of Ethnicity," 19–20.

102. "Good Man Devil," 4.

103. Editorial, Boston *Pilot*, February 24, 1900, p. 4. Editor John Boyle O'Reilly died in 1890.

104. "Maud Gonne," *Kentucky Irish American*, March 3, 1900, p. 1. Bruce Nelson examines how the global Irish responded to the Boer War and the "magnetic pull of a rights discourse grounded in white entitlement" in *Irish Nationalists*, 121–147.

105. Letter from William McKinley to the Secretary of War, December 21, 1898, quoted in Paul A. Kramer, *The Blood of Government: Race, Empire, the United States, and the Philippines* (Chapel Hill: University of North Carolina Press, 2006), 110.

106. See, for example, Louis Dalrymple's cartoon "School Begins," from *Puck*, January 25, 1899. William Allen Rogers had already drawn the same classroom theme

in "Uncle Sam's New Class in the Art of Self-Government," *Harpers Weekly*, August 27, 1898. According to Vicente Rafael, "Colonization as assimilation was deemed a moral imperative, as wayward native children cut off from their Spanish fathers and desired by other European powers would now be adopted and protected by the compassionate embrace of the United States." But Uncle Sam's wooden rod and the folklore about sadistic schoolmasters it evoked remained as allusions to the very real violence inherent in the imperial project. See Vicente L. Rafael, *White Love and Other Events in Filipino History* (Durham, NC: Duke University Press, 2000), 21.

107. Jacobson, *Special Sorrows*, 144–150.

108. Mortality figures, which for Filipino civilians include death from conditions created or exacerbated by war, such as disease, come from Michael H. Hunt and Steven I. Levine, *Arc of Empire: America's Wars in Asia from the Philippines to Vietnam* (Chapel Hill: University of North Carolina Press, 2012), 57–58.

109. "Outraging a People's Religion," *Irish World*, September 23, 1899, p. 1.

110. See David Noel Doyle, *Irish Americans: Native Rights and National Empires; The Structure, Divisions, and Attitudes of the Catholic Minority in the Decade of Expansion, 1890–1901* (New York: Arno Press, 1976), 271–273.

111. Father de Smet, "The Indian," *Irish World*, May 3, 1873, p. 1.

112. "Protestantism and Imperialism," *Irish World*, October 14, 1899, p. 4.

113. See, for example, "Revival of Moral Law the Only Sufficient Remedy for Lynching and Other Evils of the Day," *Irish World*, August 29, 1903; and "Our Moral Degeneracy," *Irish World*, July 27, 1901.

114. "The President on Lynching," *Irish World*, August 15, 1903, p. 4.

115. John Sampson, "Reaping What We Sowed—Does American Lawlessness and Barbarity Abroad Not Increase American Lawlessness and Barbarity at Home?" *Irish World*, September 12, 1903.

116. "Tortured and Burned," *Irish World*, April 29, 1899, p. 6.

117. Rodechko, *Patrick Ford*, 54.

118. Ibid., 153.

119. See James H. S. Bossard, "Robert Ellis Thompson—Pioneer Professor in Social Science," *American Journal of Sociology* 35 (September 1929): 239–249. Russell A. Kazal explores Thompson's ethnic cosmopolitan vision, in which different ethnicities contribute to a strong national whole, in "The Lost World of Pennsylvania Pluralism: Immigrants, Regions, and the Early Origins of Pluralist Ideologies in America," *Journal of American Ethnic History* 27 (Spring 2008): 7–42.

120. Bossard, "Robert Ellis Thompson," 241. Rodechko describes Thompson as Ford's leading columnist in Rodechko, *Patrick Ford*, 153.

121. Robert Ellis Thompson, "Nation and Empire," *Irish World*, January 4, 1900.

122. Robert Ellis Thompson, "The Cloud on the Southern Horizon," *Irish World*, August 19, 1899, p. 5.

123. Robert Ellis Thompson, "Our Brother in Black," *Irish World*, April 9, 1904. Quinn is likely Peter H. Quinn, a private in the Fourth Cavalry, who received the Medal of Honor on June 6, 1906, for bravery in battle in Luzon in 1899. See Center of Military History, "Medal of Honor Recipients: Philippine Insurrection," July 23, 2013, available at http://www.history.army.mil/html/moh/philippine.html.

124. Robert Ellis Thompson, "The Future of the South," *Irish World*, January 7, 1905.

125. Robert Ellis Thompson, *The Hand of God in American History* (New York: Thomas V. Crowell, 1902), 160–161.

126. Thomas Guglielmo, Matthew Frye Jacobson, and some other whiteness scholars distinguish between nineteenth-century conceptions of race as nation and race as color. See Thomas Guglielmo, *White on Arrival: Italians, Race, Color, and Power in Chicago, 1890–1945* (Oxford: Oxford University Press, 2003); and Jacobson, *Whiteness of a Different Color.*

127. David Brundage explores two hundred years of Irish American activism and nationalism in *Irish Nationalists in America.*

128. Brown, *Irish-American Nationalism,* 178–182.

129. Foner, *Politics and Ideology,* 195.

130. The concept of segregation as a shield supported by Progressives can be found in Michael McGerr, *A Fierce Discontent: The Rise and Fall of the Progressive Movement in America* (Oxford: Oxford University Press, 2003), 182–218.

131. David E. Nye, "Rewiring the 'Nation': The Place of Technology in American Studies," *American Quarterly* 58 (2006): 610–611.

CHAPTER 2

1. The address is quoted in James Jeffrey Roche, *Life of John Boyle O'Reilly* (New York: Cassell, 1891), 194–195.

2. The best in-depth examinations of Father Yorke are James P. Walsh, "Regent Peter C. Yorke and the University of California, 1900–1912" (Ph.D. diss., University of California, Berkeley, 1970); and James P. Walsh, *Ethnic Militancy: An Irish Catholic Prototype* (San Francisco: R and E Research Associates, 1972). Two important, if somewhat hagiographic, works are Bernard Cornelius Cronin, *Father Yorke and the Labor Movement in San Francisco, 1900–1910* (Washington, DC: Catholic University of America Press, 1943); and Joseph S. Brusher, *Consecrated Thunderbolt: A Life of Father Peter C. Yorke of San Francisco* (Hawthorn, NJ: F. J. Wagner, 1973). Important recent essays and chapters examining Yorke include Daniel J. Meissner, "California Clash: Irish and Chinese Labor in San Francisco, 1850–1870," in *The Irish in the San Francisco Bay Area: Essays on Good Fortune,* ed. Donald Jordan and Timothy J. O'Keefe (San Francisco: Executive Council of the Irish Literary and Historical Society, 2005), 54–86; David M. Emmons, *Beyond the American Pale: The Irish in the West, 1845–1910* (Norman: University of Oklahoma Press, 2010); and Barrett, *The Irish Way.*

3. For an excellent summation of contemporary scholarship on religion, see Randall J. Stephens, ed., "Introduction: American Religious History in Context," in *Recent Themes in American Religious History: Historians in Conversation* (Columbia: University of South Carolina Press, 2009), 2–10.

4. See, for example, Paddison, *American Heathens.* Jon Gjerde and John T. McGreevy see a struggle between Catholicism and Protestantism as stretching beyond antebellum America and shaping not just American notions of freedom but the state itself. See Gjerde, *Catholicism;* and John T. McGreevy, *Catholicism and American Freedom: A History* (New York: W. W. Norton, 2003).

5. See Walsh, *Ethnic Militancy;* and Walsh, "Regent Peter C. Yorke."

6. Walsh, *Ethnic Militancy,* 137.

7. Ibid., 134.

8. Michael V. Gannon, "Before and After Modernism: The Intellectual Isolation of the American Priest," in *The Catholic Priest in the United States: Historical Investigations,* ed. John Tracy Ellis (Collegeville, MN: Liturgical Press, 1971), 340–341; Jay P. Dolan, *The American Catholic Experience: A History from Colonial Times to*

the Present (Notre Dame, IN: University of Notre Dame Press, 1992), 315–319; James Hennesey, *American Catholics: A History of the Roman Catholic Community in the United States* (New York: Oxford University Press, 1981), 217. For a contrary view—that the late nineteenth and early twentieth centuries were intellectually productive times for American Catholicism—see Thomas E. Woods, Jr., *The Church Confronts Modernity: Catholic Intellectuals and the Progressive Era* (New York: Columbia University Press, 2004).

9. Biographical information on Father Yorke comes from Cronin, *Father Yorke*; Walsh, *Ethnic Militancy*; Brusher, *Consecrated Thunderbolt*; and the Reverend Peter C. Yorke Papers, Gleeson Library/Geschke Center, University of San Francisco.

10. Justin E. Nordstrom, *Danger on the Doorstep: Anti-Catholicism and American Print Culture in the Progressive Era* (Notre Dame, IN: University of Notre Dame Press, 2006), 110.

11. David H. Bennett, *The Party of Fear: From Nativist Movements to the New Right in American History* (Chapel Hill: University of North Carolina Press, 1988), 173.

12. Cronin, *Father Yorke*, 26–27.

13. Ibid., 30. In other U.S. cities, Anglo-Saxons typically dominated the corporate world, but the Irish and other European immigrant groups in San Francisco made inroads into the higher echelons of the economic structure, including publishing. The Spreckels family (Adolph, John, and Rudolph), sons of a German immigrant who made his fortune in Hawaiian sugar, owned the typically antilabor *Call*, one of the city's largest dailies. Though the *Chronicle* was Republican-aligned and the city's most conservative newspaper, it was tied by marriage to Irish San Francisco through the Tobin family, which was originally from County Tipperary and friendly with Father Yorke. William Randolph Hearst's *Examiner* captured the largest West Coast circulation and directed itself toward the common man. Father Yorke may have been popular and newsworthy enough in San Francisco to interest editors across the political spectrum with running his articles. See Michael Kazin, *Barons of Labor: The San Francisco Building Trades and Union Power in the Progressive Era* (Urbana: University of Illinois Press, 1987), 22, 27.

14. "Passing Events," *Irish World*, May 4, 1895, p. 8.

15. Joseph S. Brusher, "Peter C. Yorke and the A.P.A. in San Francisco," *Catholic Historical Review* 37 (July 1951): 129–130.

16. Ibid., 130.

17. Walsh, *Ethnic Militancy*, 14–17.

18. Nordstrom, *Danger on the Doorstep*, 10.

19. Peter C. Yorke, *The Ghosts of Bigotry: Six Lectures by Rev. P. C. Yorke, D. D.*, 2nd ed. (San Francisco: Text Book, 1913), 16.

20. Ibid., 16–17.

21. David M. Emmons has suggested that *Rerum Novarum* could be read alongside the nineteenth-century manifestos of Karl Marx and Henry George as a key work analyzing capital and labor in the nineteenth century. See Emmons, *Beyond the American Pale*, 327.

22. Pope Leo XIII, "*Rerum Novarum*: Rights and Duties of Capital and Labor," May 15, 1891, para. 1, available at http://www.vatican.va/holy_father/leo_xiii/encyclicals/documents/hf_l-xiii_enc_15051891_rerum-novarum_en.html.

23. Ibid., para. 2, 3.

24. Ibid., para. 8.

25. Ibid., para. 18.

26. Ibid., para. 27.

27. Ibid., para. 49.

28. Cronin, *Father Yorke*, 52–53.
29. Ibid., 56.
30. "Father Yorke's Series of Articles Dealing with the Existing Labor Trouble," *San Francisco Examiner*, September 27, 1901.
31. Peter Yorke, "On the Real Question at Issue," *San Francisco Examiner*, September 27, 1901.
32. Ibid.
33. Ibid.
34. Nordstrom, *Danger on the Doorstep*, 55. Michael McGerr similarly describes Progressivism as depending on the "notion of a verifiable, objective reality . . . a confrontation with facts." See McGerr, *A Fierce Discontent*, 247.
35. Nordstrom, *Danger on the Doorstep*, 55. Journalism historian Michael Schudson also identifies a "Progressive drive to found political reform on 'facts.'" See Schudson, *Discovering the News*, 71.
36. Progressives, according to Michael Kazin, "attacked party machines and party loyalty as fundamentally undemocratic methods of rule." Kazin, *Barons of Labor*, 285.
37. Steven M. Avella, "Irish Catholic Identity and California Public Life: Peter Yorke vs. C. K. McClatchy, 1890–1916," in Jordan and O'Keefe, *The Irish in San Francisco*.
38. Peter Yorke, "The Employers' Purpose Is to Destroy Unionism, Says the Rev. P. C. Yorke," *San Francisco Examiner*, September 27, 1901. James Walsh discusses Yorke and the graft trials in *Ethnic Militant*, 89–93.
39. Peter Yorke, "On the Mind of the Pope," *San Francisco Examiner*, September 28, 1901.
40. Ibid.
41. Cronin, *Father Yorke*, 85, 91.
42. *Oakland Enquirer*, October 9, 1901, quoted in Cronin, *Father Yorke*, 94–95. Like some other public figures and intellectuals explored briefly in Chapter 3, John P. Irish went against the grain of West Coast anti-Asian sentiment, at least with respect to the Japanese. He staunchly defended Japanese culture and Japanese Americans in California and would receive a reward for his efforts from Emperor Taishō. See Lon Kurashige, "Transpacific Accommodation and the Defense of Asian Immigrants," *Pacific Historical Review* 83 (May 2014): 294–313.
43. Emmons believes that American republicanism viewed the hierarchical Catholic Church as something akin to chattel slavery, making the Irish "unwanted strangers" in America, especially in the West. See Emmons, *Beyond the American Pale*, 13.
44. *The Monitor*, January 30, 1897, quoted in Avella, "Irish Catholic Identity," 38.
45. *Evening Bee*, November 2, 1898, quoted in Avella, "Irish Catholic Identity," 37.
46. "The 'Soggarth Aroon' [Dear priest] of Virginia City, and the 'Soggarth' [Priest] without the 'Aroon' [Dear] of San Francisco," *Saturday Bee*, September 28, 1901, quoted in Avella, "Irish Catholic Identity," 39.
47. "Gentlemen: An Eadh [The votes]?" *The Leader*, March 8, 1902, p. 5.
48. "Pope McClatchy," *The Leader*, April 12, 1902, p. 4.
49. *The Leader*, April 3, and May 27, 1916, quoted in Avella, "Irish Catholic Identity," 43–45.
50. David O'Brien, "Isaac Hecker," in *The Encyclopedia of American Catholic History*, ed. Michael Glazier and Thomas J. Shelley (Collegeville, MN: Liturgical Press, 1997), 624–626. Also see William L. Portier, "Isaac Hecker and *Testem Benevolentiae*: A Study in Theological Pluralism," in *Hecker Studies: Essays on the Thought of Isaac Hecker*, ed. John Farina (New York: Paulist Press, 1983), 11–48.

51. Pope Leo XIII, "*Testem Benevolentiae Nostrae*: Concerning New Opinions, Virtue, Nature and Grace, with Regard to Americanism," January 22, 1899, para. 14, 15, available at http://www.papalencyclicals.net/Leo13/l13teste.htm.

52. For an excellent summary of how Catholic historians have looked at the Americanism controversy, see Philip Gleason, "The New Americanism in Catholic Historiography," *U.S. Catholic Historian* 11 (Summer 1993): 1–18.

53. Michael Corrigan, "Archbishop Corrigan to the Pope," *San Francisco Call*, May 1, 1899, p. 1.

54. Gjerde, *Catholicism*, 12. Gjerde's "Protestant conundrum," in turn, stemmed from Protestants' own beliefs that their faith undergirded American liberty. "If Catholicism was to be abided in the United States, the Protestant puzzles were both how to integrate Catholicism into the nation and how to incorporate it without endangering religious liberty" (47).

55. Cronin, *Father Yorke*, 35–37.

56. "Father Yorke Received by His Holiness," *San Francisco Call*, May 29, 1899, p. 3.

57. "Our Gaelic World," *Irish World*, October 7, 1899, p. 8.

58. This was reported in an article titled "Church Desecration in the Philippines" in the *Irish World*, December 9, 1899, p. 7. Father Yorke was not at the helm of the *Monitor* at this time.

59. "The Philippine Question," *Irish-American*, November 22, 1902, p. 4. The New York City–based newspaper was edited by Patrick Meehan, who, until his death in 1906, "attempted to reconcile nationalism with Catholicism." "Additional Description: Biographical Note," Thomas F. Meehan Papers, Georgetown University Repository, available at https://findingaids.library.georgetown.edu/repositories/15/resources/10116.

60. Diary of A. J. Nicholson, July 3, 1898, pp. 71–73, Nicholson, A. J., Scrapbooks Relating to the Spanish-American War and the Philippine Insurrection, ca. 1893–1907, Bancroft Library, University of California, Berkeley. Little biographical information is available on Nicholson. He fought in the First Calvary Regiment, Company B.

61. Diary of A. J. Nicholson, February 18, 1899, pp. 33–34.

62. Ibid., 37. An entry on February 20, 1899, reveals soldiers' fears that "insurgents" were disguising themselves as priests: "'Priest' crossing the lines below Macati, ordered by sentry to halt, disobeyed, and was killed." A similar entry a few days later suggests a rapid change in the racialization of Filipinos after they began fighting U.S. troops: "Shortly after 6 a.m. Washington's left wing, assisted by Wyoming from accross [sic] the river, round out a hot-bed of Rebels, + score quite a killing. Lasted till after noon, 45 niggers piled up, + 36 Rifles captured." (Before this entry, Nicholson's descriptions of Filipinos tended to be neutral or more mildly patronizing, as when he discovered that many rebels wore amulets they believed would ward off bullets.) "Among the dead," Nicholson continued, "was a 'Priest' caught in the trenches, with a mouser rifle." Ibid., 37.

63. "Priest-Hunting in the Philippines," *The Leader*, January 1, 1902, p. 1. The newspaper's quotation of the order is accurate and comes from Bell's telegraphic circular no. 3, sent from Batangas on December 9, 1901. See *Hearings Before the Committee on the Philippines of the United States Senate* (Washington, DC: Government Printing Office, 1902), 1610, available at https://books.google.com/books?id=4lMTAAAAIAAJ.

64. Peter C. Yorke, "The Dragon's Teeth," April 23, 1896, Peter C. Yorke Papers, Gleeson Library/Geschke Center, University of San Francisco.

65. Letter from Peter Yorke to W. B. Crawley, February 4, 1897, Folder 3, Box 1, Peter C. Yorke Papers, Gleeson Library/Geschke Center, University of San Francisco. After Yorke's tenure at the *Monitor*, the paper would continue to stress the Catholic

Church's abilities to civilize more justly. When James "Jim" Smith was appointed governor-general of the Philippines in 1906, the *Monitor* claimed the Catholic graduate of Santa Clara University would treat Filipinos as "equals in a Christian sense and not as an 'inferior' brood of mere 'niggers.' In this way he gets closer to the native and inspires a higher degree of confidence and respect. . . . In brief, Governor Smith acts upon the enlightened and humane theory which has given the Spaniard unparalleled pre-eminence in the history of the civilization and Christianization of aboriginal savages." *The Monitor*, December 8, 1906.

66. "The Glorious Fourth," *The Leader*, July 5, 1902, p. 4.

67. "The Republic of Cuba," *The Leader*, May 24, 1902, p. 4. Yorke's misgivings about war in the Philippines had not stopped him from blessing troops leaving San Francisco Bay in 1898 for the islands; in a diary entry on May 22, 1898, Nicholson, who would set sail on the *City of Peking* for the Philippines, wrote that "Father Yorke holds forth at head-quarters, assisted by Father McKinnon (?) the Chaplain. Received orders at 9 p.m. that we would go in the morning. Boys cheering + all join in singing 'The Star Spangled Banner.'" Diary of A. J. Nicholson, May 22, 1898, p. 15.

68. Gjerde, *Catholicism*, 93.

69. Ibid., 144. For an account of the Eliot School rebellion in Boston in 1859, in which Catholic students refused to read the Ten Commandments, see McGreevy, *Catholicism and American Freedom*, 7–15.

70. See Benjamin Justice, "Thomas Nast and the Public School of the 1870s," *History of Education Quarterly* 45 (Summer 2005): 182–183.

71. Gjerde, *Catholicism*, 139.

72. Frank T. Reuter, "American Catholics and the Establishment of the Philippine Public School System," *Catholic Historical Review* 49 (October 1963): 367.

73. *The Monitor*, November 18, 1899, and *Catholic World*, August 1899, quoted in Reuter, "American Catholics," 368. Reuter incorrectly places Yorke at the head of the *Monitor* in November 1899; Yorke's tenure lasted from 1894 to 1898, though he returned from a year-long trip to Europe in November 1899 and may have written or helped to craft the editorial. It was more likely penned by Thomas A. Connelly, who edited the *Monitor* from 1899 to 1907.

74. Kramer, *Blood of Government*, 168–169.

75. Arthur Judson Brown, *The New Era in the Philippines* (New York: F. H. Revel, 1903), 168, available at http://babel.hathitrust.org/cgi/pt?id=ucl.b3142880;view=1up;seq=11. For biographical information on Brown, see R. Park Johnson, "The Legacy of Arthur Judson Brown," *International Bulletin of Missionary Research*, April 1986, pp. 71–75, available at http://www.bu.edu/missiology/missionary-biography/a-c/brown-arthur-judson-1856-1963/.

76. Quoted in Brown, *The New Era in the Philippines*, 174.

77. Reuter, "American Catholics," 366.

78. Philippine elites were certainly frustrated with secondary and tertiary education; they commonly sent their children to Europe for schooling, and these *ilustrados* had been key in the promotion of Filipino nationalism during Spanish rule. Filipinos also expressed widespread animosity toward several Catholic religious orders, which American occupiers initially mistook for frustration with Catholicism as a whole and readiness for conversion. See Kramer, *Blood of Government*, 42.

79. Reuter, "American Catholics," 371–373.

80. Ibid., 373–374.

81. *Freeman's Journal*, February 2, 1901, quoted in Reuter, "American Catholics," 374.

82. Boston *Pilot*, September 7, 1901, quoted in Reuter, "American Catholics," 374.
83. Oscar L. Evangelista, "Religious Problems in the Philippines and the American Catholic Church, 1898–1907," *Asian Studies* 6 (1968): 253.
84. "No Reason for Outcry: Archbishop Ireland Preaches on Negotiations Regarding Friars," *St. Paul Globe*, August 4, 1902, p. 1.
85. "Personal Opinion," *The Leader*, August 16, 1902, pp. 1, 4.
86. Ibid., 4.
87. Letter from William Howard Taft to Elihu Root, November 22, 1902, Box 1, William H. Taft Papers, 1784–1973, Library of Congress, Washington, DC.
88. Reuter, "American Catholics," 365.
89. William Howard Taft, foreword to *An Observer in the Philippines, or, Life in Our New Possessions*, by John Patrick Devins (New York: American Tract Society, 1905), 7.
90. Walsh, *Ethnic Militancy*, 3.
91. Ibid., 4–5.
92. *The Monitor*, December 1, 1906.
93. Walsh, "Regent Peter C. Yorke," 75–76.
94. Una M. Cadegan, "Running the Ancient Ark by Steam: Catholic Publishing," in *A History of the Book in America*, vol. 4, *Print in Motion: The Expansion of Publishing and Reading in the United States*, ed. Carl F. Kaestle and Janice E. Radway (Chapel Hill: University of North Carolina Press, 2014), 395.
95. John G. Deedy, Jr., "The Catholic Press: The Why and the Wherefore," in *The Religious Press in America*, ed. Martin E. Mary et al. (New York: Holt, Rinehart and Winston, 1963), 67.
96. See, for example, Deedy, "The Catholic Press," 68; and Cadegan, "Running the Ancient Ark," 397.
97. Deedy, "The Catholic Press," 72.
98. Ibid.
99. Donna J. Drucker, "An 'Aristocracy of Virtue': Cultural Development of the American Catholic Priesthood, 1884–1920s," *Religion and American Culture: A Journal of Interpretation* 21 (Summer 2011): 229–230.
100. Ibid., 227.
101. Ibid., 257–258.
102. Woods, *The Church Confronts Modernity*.
103. "As Others See Us," *The Leader*, February 15, 1902, p. 4.
104. "The Digger Indian," *The Leader*, January 25, 1902, p. 4.
105. "The Lay Editor, Again," *The Leader*, March 1, 1902, p. 4.
106. The *Catholic Sentinel* of Portland, Oregon, also addressed the press's power to do both good and evil. The "only way to neutralize the evil influence of the press is to . . . fill it with the spirit of goodness. To drive out bad newspapers, you introduce good ones; to counteract the influence of those that are anti-Catholic, you must support and circulate those that are Catholic." The paper, founded by a grocer and a printer, wrote of religious ministers, "What preacher ever reached as many minds as the newspaper can reach? The preacher's word, when once spoken, dies with the echo of his voice; but the printed word remains and men may read it again and again." *Catholic Sentinel*, February 24, 1872.
107. Evelyn G. Vernier, *A History of the Monitor* (unpublished manuscript, [1945?]), p. 2, Bancroft Library, University of California, Berkeley.
108. *The Monitor*, March 20, 1858, quoted in Vernier, *History of the Monitor*, 3–4.
109. Ibid., 4.

110. *Daily Evening Bulletin*, August 27 and 28, 1863, quoted in Vernier, *History of the Monitor*, 6–7.

111. *Daily Alta Californian*, April 16, 1865, quoted in Vernier, *History of the Monitor*, 9–10.

112. See Vernier, *History of the Monitor*, 12–14. A former employee of the *Monitor*, Bartley P. Oliver, described the paper in the 1870s as having editors who worked hard "to procure a fair living for their families. The paper was not an official organ as it was at present. Its circulation varied from year to year. It went some years as low as 2,000," which meant "just getting by," and other years as high as 4,000, which "meant comfort and more peaceful slumbers." From an article reprinted in the *Monitor*, December 16, 1933, quoted in Vernier, *History of the Monitor*, 14–15.

113. *The Monitor*, November 27, 1879, quoted in Vernier, *History of the Monitor*, 15.

114. Vernier, *History of the Monitor*, 16.

115. Cadegan, "Running the Ancient Ark," 398.

116. Ibid.

117. Ibid., 393.

118. Beegan, *The Mass Image*, 13.

119. Diana Walsh Pasulka examines how nineteenth-century Catholic periodicals countered stereotypes of Catholic "idol worship" by placing, through text and images, Catholic rituals within mainstream American practices of civil religion such as observance of the flag or national holidays. See Diana Walsh Pasulka, "The Eagle and the Dove: Constructing Catholic Identity through Word and Image in Nineteenth-Century United States," *Material Religion* 4 (November 2008): 306–325.

120. See Joshua Paddison, "Anti-Catholicism and Race in Post–Civil War San Francisco," *Pacific Historical Review* 78 (November 2009): 505–544.

121. Brundage, *Irish Nationalists in America*, 122; Ely M. Janis, *A Greater Ireland: The Land League and Transatlantic Nationalism in Gilded Age America* (Madison: University of Wisconsin Press, 2015), 132–133.

122. The meeting claimed an attendance of three thousand and included leading figures in labor and politics from around the state. See Elmer Clarence Sandmeyer, *The Anti-Chinese Movement in California* (Urbana: University of Illinois Press, 1991), 107.

123. The Chinese Exclusion Act of 1882 prohibited all Chinese laborers from entering the United States and regulated the passage of other exempt classes, such as merchants and teachers. See Erika Lee, *At America's Gates: Chinese Immigration during the Exclusion Era, 1882–1943* (Chapel Hill: University of North Carolina Press, 2003).

124. *California Chinese Exclusion Convention: Proceedings and List of Delegates* (San Francisco: Star Press, 1901), 104–105. Parenthetical references to "applause" or "laughter" appear in the Star Press printing.

125. Ibid., 105.

126. Castle Garden is now called Castle Clinton, a fortification in Battery Park, Manhattan, which was once an immigration center and is now part of the National Park Service.

127. *California Chinese Exclusion Convention*, 104–105.

128. Ibid., 105–106.

129. Ibid., 106.

130. Ibid.

131. Ibid., 106–107.

132. Ibid., 108. Yorke knew this was dehumanizing rhetoric and refused to back down: "Do not wonder that a Catholic priest should speak thus to you. It has oftentimes been charged that those who speak against the Chinese immigration are forgetful of the

brotherhood of man ... that their attitude is unchristian ... that they should welcome all these nations to their shores and to try to civilize them. Gentlemen, the grace of God is a very powerful thing, but the grace of God, it has been said, never gave any man common sense. (Laughter and applause.) And no doubt the people who urge these ... beautiful, high moral principles, are men who are filled with the grace of the Lord, and have nothing but high and holy aspirations; but we would wish that their aspirations would be a little lower, and that they would have a little more common sense. (Applause and laughter.)" Ibid., 108.

133. Isodore Jacoby, secretary of the cloak-makers' union, Local No. 8, of the International Ladies' Garment Workers' Union, claimed that "all that is necessary to beguile a San Francisco woman is to put some fancy label beneath the hanger of the garment, and it is sold by a smiling saleslady at prosperity prices as imported direct from Paris, London or New York, with all the germs of disease bred in a Chinatown filth thrown into the bargain." *California Chinese Exclusion Convention*, 115–116.

134. Meissner, "California Clash," 71.

135. Ibid., 72.

136. Ibid., 70. Alexander Saxton's seminal study is skeptical of the "cheap-labor argument" and puts anti-Chinese hostility on a continuum with other long-standing American race antagonisms: "The dominant society responded differently to Irish or Slavic than to Oriental cheap workers, not so much for economic as for ideological and psychological reasons." See Alexander Saxton, *The Indispensable Enemy: Labor and the Anti-Chinese Movement in California* (Berkeley: University of California Press, 1995), 2.

137. Kornel Chang, "Circulating Race and Empire: Transnational Labor Activism and the Politics of Anti-Asian Agitation in the Anglo-American Pacific World, 1880–1910," *Journal of American History* 96 (December 2008): 700.

138. Cole Harris, *The Resettlement of British Columbia: Essays on Colonialism and Geographic Change* (Vancouver: University of British Columbia Press, 1997), 160; Chang, "Circulating Race and Empire," 683.

139. Chang, "Circulating Race and Empire," 694–696.

140. Ibid., 697.

141. "The Merchants and the Chinese," *The Leader*, February 15, 1902, p. 4.

142. Letter from James D. Phelan to James H. Barry, September 26, 1914, Folder 17, Box 10, James H. Barry Papers, 1889–1957, Bancroft Library.

143. "Chinese Immigration," *The Monitor*, May 9, 1868, p. 1.

144. "Coolie Immigration," *The Monitor*, May 23, 1868, p. 4.

145. *The Monitor*, November 10, 1906. Paddison discusses similar East-West splits over Asian immigration among Protestant clergymen in *American Heathens*, 150. One month after this editorial, after President Roosevelt had strongly condemned discrimination against the Japanese in America, particularly an effort by San Francisco's board of education to segregate Japanese students into a Chinese school, the *Monitor* scolded Roosevelt for praising the Japanese. The president had "read the people of California a severe lecture on the iniquity of refusing to open welcoming arms to the incoming horde of Asiatic coolies from the militant island empire." *The Monitor*, December 8, 1906.

146. Gjerde writes, "We profit from viewing the development of an American nation as a process that triangulated race and religion so that Americans were superior racially (in the context of non-Europeans) and religiously (as Europeans but freed of the European papacy and the Old World)." Gjerde, *Catholicism*, 39.

147. Walsh, *Ethnic Militancy*, 109–110.

148. In a letter to University of California president Benjamin Ide Wheeler on May 10, 1909, for example, Yorke objected to a Protestant minister presiding over baccalaureate services at the university. Though nonsectarianism "in itself is nothing

desirable," Yorke wrote, still the university was bound by it. "Now the trouble about the Baccalaureate sermon is that it is a religious service and that it is a University religious service. Therefore especially when held in the University grounds it is impossible to make the public believe that the University *qua* University is not holding religious services." Letter from Peter C. Yorke to Benjamin Ide Wheeler, May 10, 1909, Folder 33, Box 66, CU-1, Records of the Regents of the University of California, Bancroft Library.

149. Peter C. Yorke, *Education in California: Three Letters by P. C. Yorke* (San Francisco: Text Book, 1900).

150. Terry Golway, "The Forgotten Virtues of Tammany Hall," *New York Times*, January 17, 2014, available at http://www.nytimes.com/2014/01/18/opinion/the-forgotten-virtues-of-tammany-hall.html. The quotation is from reformer Andrew D. White, president of Cornell University. See also Terry Golway, *Machine Made: Tammany Hall and the Creation of Modern American Politics* (New York: Liveright, 2014).

PART II

1. James P. Danky, ed. *African American Newspapers and Periodicals: A National Bibliography* (Cambridge, MA: Harvard University Press, 1998), xxxi.

2. Roland E. Wolseley, *The Black Press, U.S.A.*, 2nd ed. (Ames: Iowa State University Press, 1990), 24–61.

3. See Benjamin Fagan, *The Black Newspaper and the Chosen Nation* (Athens: University of Georgia Press, 2016).

4. Louis R. Harlan and Raymond W. Smock, eds., *The Booker T. Washington Papers* (Chicago: University of Illinois Press, 1977), 13:469.

5. William G. Jordan, *Black Newspapers and America's War for Democracy, 1914–1920* (Chapel Hill: University of North Carolina Press, 2001), 2.

6. Vishnu V. Oak, *The Negro Newspaper* (Yellow Springs, OH: Antioch Press, 1948), 30.

7. Gunnar Myrdal, *An American Dilemma: The Negro Problem and Modern Democracy* (New York: Harper and Row, 1944), 920.

8. Ibid., 923.

9. E. Franklin Frazier, *Black Bourgeoisie* (New York: Free Press, 1957), 191.

10. Ibid., 179.

11. Albert Lee Kreiling, "The Making of Racial Identities in the Black Press: A Cultural Analysis of Race Journalism in Chicago, 1878–1929" (Ph.D. diss., University of Illinois, Urbana-Champaign, 1973), iii.

12. Ibid., 3.

13. "Accustomed to the stable cultural world of a local traditional community, the southern migrant found in the northern city a fluid, impersonal world of modernity, in which status, identity, and culturally prescribed definitions of situations were no longer automatically conferred." Kreiling, "The Making of Racial Identities," 22.

14. Jordan, *Black Newspapers*, 5–6.

15. Ibid., 17–18.

CHAPTER 3

1. Quoted in "The Negro and the Filipino," *Washington Post*, June 27, 1903, p. 8.

2. The most comprehensive examination of Fortune's life remains Thornbrough's *T. Thomas Fortune*; for Fortune's overseas trip, see pp. 234–241. Shawn Leigh Alexander

skillfully analyzes and introduces Fortune's life and writings in *T. Thomas Fortune, the Afro-American Agitator*. Jinx Coleman Broussard examines Fortune's Pacific quest, emphasizing the racial affinities he expressed toward Filipinos, in *African American Foreign Correspondents: A History* (Baton Rouge: Louisiana State University Press, 2013), 32–39. Benjamin R. Justesen profiles Fortune, Booker T. Washington, Bishop Alexander Walters, and Congressman George Henry White in *Broken Brotherhood: The Rise and Fall of the National Afro-American Council* (Carbondale: Southern Illinois University Press, 2008). Michele Mitchell reprints Fortune's photographic self-portrait from Luzon in *Righteous Propagation: African Americans and the Politics of Racial Destiny after Reconstruction* (Chapel Hill: University of North Carolina Press, 2004), 65. Gretchen Murphy sees African American participation in empire as decentering the practices and discourses of U.S. imperialism in *Shadowing the White Man's Burden: U.S. Imperialism and the Problem of the Color Line* (New York: New York University Press, 2010), 8.

3. Broussard, *African American Foreign Correspondents*, 32–39.

4. W.E.B. Du Bois, "The Lash," *Horizon: A Journal of the Color Line*, May 1907, pp. 5–6.

5. Mitchell, *Righteous Propagation*, 65.

6. Louis R. Harlan, "Booker T. Washington and the White Man's Burden," *American Historical Review* 71 (January 1966): 441; Andrew Zimmerman, *Alabama in Africa: Booker T. Washington, the German Empire, and the Globalization of the New South* (Princeton, NJ: Princeton University Press, 2010), 237, 249. Also see Sven Beckert, "From Tuskegee to Togo: The Problem of Freedom in the Empire of Cotton," *Journal of American History* 92 (September 2005): 498–526; José-Manuel Navarro, *Creating Tropical Yankees: Social Science Textbooks and U.S. Ideological Control in Puerto Rico, 1898–1908* (New York: Routledge, 2002); and Anne Paulet, "To Change the World: The Use of American Indian Education in the Philippines," *History of Education Quarterly* 47 (May 2007): 173–202.

7. In several photographic portraits of Fortune, his skin tone appears quite pale; in others it is darker. One Associated Press cablegram reprinted in the Hawaiian press described the journalist as having the appearance of "a cultured Spaniard." "T. Thomas Fortune Deported From Philippines," *Hawaiian Gazette*, May 19, 1903, p. 3. On Hawaii and the Philippines, journalists rarely described Fortune as anything other than "black" or "Negro." Guy Emerson Mount considers Fortune's "white skinned African American male body" in "Building Multiracial Fortunes: Black Identity, Masculinity, and Authenticity through the Body of T. Thomas Fortune, 1883–1907" (MA thesis, San Diego State University, California, 2011), iv. Ingrid Dineen-Wimberly explores black leadership during this study's time period and finds that, counterintuitively, "for many mixed-race people, a Black identity . . . offered positions of power, upward mobility, and notoriety." See Ingrid Dineen-Wimberly, "Mixed-Race Leadership in African America: The Regalia of Race and National Identity in the U.S., 1862–1916" (Ph.D. diss., University of California, Santa Barbara, 2009).

8. Alexander, *T. Thomas Fortune*, xiii.

9. "News from All Parts of the United States," *Irish World*, March 22, 1890, p. 3.

10. Timothy Thomas Fortune, *Black and White: Land, Labor, and Politics in the South* (New York: Fords, Howard, and Hulbert, 1884), 29.

11. New York *Freeman*, February 27, 1886, quoted in Ely Janis, "Black and Green: Frederick Douglass, T. Thomas Fortune, Marcus Garvey, and the Irish," paper presented at the Organization of American Historians Annual Meeting, Seattle, Washington, March 26–29, 2009, p. 6.

12. Alexander, *T. Thomas Fortune*, 30.
13. Indianapolis *Freeman*, April 2, 1904, quoted in Arnold Shankman, "Black on Green: Afro-American Editors on Irish Independence, 1840–1921," *Phylon* 41 (1980): 284–299.
14. Quoted in Janis, "Black and Green," 3.
15. Shankman, "Black on Green," 290.
16. *New York Globe*, August 16, 1884, quoted in Shankman, "Black on Green," 293.
17. Brown, *Irish-American Nationalism*, 141.
18. Thornbrough, *T. Thomas Fortune*, 234–235.
19. Justesen, *Broken Brotherhood*, 112.
20. Thornbrough, *T. Thomas Fortune*, 234–235.
21. Ibid., 235. Clarkson was a Republican Party operative and a New York port surveyor who, during slavery, had "established and operated a twenty-eight mile section of the 'Underground Railway,' helping more than 500 slaves from Missouri, Arkansas and Texas flee into Canada." "Gen. J. S. Clarkson Dies in 77th Year," *New York Times*, June 1, 1918, p. 11.
22. Letter from T. Thomas Fortune to Booker T. Washington, November 3, 1902, in Louis R. Harlan and Raymond W. Smock, eds., *The Booker T. Washington Papers* (Chicago: University of Illinois Press, 1977), 6:571–572.
23. Letter from Booker T. Washington to Theodore Roosevelt, December 1, 1902, in Harlan and Smock, *Booker T. Washington Papers*, 6:600–601. After securing Fortune's appointment, Clarkson wrote Washington that, "for once," Fortune's "face has shown happiness." Letter from James Clarkson to Booker T. Washington, November 20, 1902, in Harlan and Smock, *Booker T. Washington Papers*, 6:588–589.
24. Morgan played a central role in the overthrow of Reconstruction in Alabama. See Joseph A. Fry, *John Tyler Morgan and the Search for Southern Autonomy* (Knoxville: University of Tennessee Press, 1992).
25. "Philippines for Negro," *Washington Post*, December 16, 1902, p. 3. Willard B. Gatewood concluded that Roosevelt and Root, by appointing Fortune, were attempting to mollify Morgan while providing a long-wanted patronage position for Fortune. See Willard B. Gatewood, *Black Americans and the White Man's Burden, 1898–1903* (Chicago: University of Illinois Press, 1975), 307.
26. For example, in 1890 Morgan had decried Fortune's push for the term "Afro-American" (to replace "Negro"), calling it a strategy by blacks to gain "incorporation, by marriage" into the nation's white families. Fortune shot back that only "Afro-American" could embrace "all the shades of color produced by the anxiety of the white men of the South to 'secure their incorporation' without marriage into the black families of the country!" Thornbrough, *T. Thomas Fortune*, 132.
27. See Fortune, "Race Absorption," *AME Church Review* 18, no. 1 (1901): 54–66, in Alexander, *T. Thomas Fortune*, 241–242.
28. "Why People Colonize," *New York Age*, October 31, 1891, p. 4.
29. T. Thomas Fortune, "Mob Violence in the South," *New York Sun*, May 2, 1899, p. 6.
30. Steven Hahn explores the politics of black-run emigrationist movements in the rural South and the real concessions from white planters these societies sometimes obtained in *A Nation under Our Feet: Black Political Struggles in the Rural South from Slavery to the Great Migration* (Cambridge, MA: Harvard University Press, 2003).
31. Helen Geracimos Chapin, *Shaping History: The Role of Newspapers in Hawai'i* (Honolulu: University of Hawaii Press, 1996). Hawaii became an incorporated territory of the United States in July 1898 and would achieve statehood in 1959.

32. "Looking After the Laborers," *Evening Bulletin*, December 18, 1902, p. 1.

33. "Fortune and the Homesteads," *Hawaiian Star*, December 30, 1902, p. 5.

34. Carroll D. Wright, *Report of the Commissioner of Labor on Hawaii, 1902* (Washington, D.C.: Government Printing Office, 1903), 22.

35. "Fortune Will Look After Local Labor," *Hawaiian Gazette*, December 19, 1902, p. 5.

36. "Labor Troubles on Maui," *Maui News*, January 26, 1901, p. 3.

37. According to the *Hawaiian Star*, a group of African American laborers on Maui apparently tired of charges that they were lawless or "undesirable" and "declared that they wanted fair play and did not want all to be judged by the actions of one ruffian." The paper continued: "The Japs of Spreckelsville threatened to do up the negroes and there is a good deal of feeling between the camps." The *Star* said the Japanese threatened to strike unless the African Americans were sent away, then "thought better of it" and, along with all but forty black laborers who left for Honolulu, "both races" returned to work. See "The Negroes Complain—Hold a Mass Meeting at Spreckelsville—Say They Are Not a Lawless Crowd—The Feeling between the Blacks and the Japanese," *Hawaiian Star*, June 12, 1901, p. 7.

38. Wright, *Report of the Commissioner*, 53.

39. Ibid., 33.

40. Ibid., 53.

41. "Negoes [sic] as Labor," Hawaiian *Star*, July 2, 1900, p. 4.

42. For an examination of how Progressives linked the so-called Negro Problem to labor and industrial management, see Paul R. D. Lawrie, *Forging a Laboring Race: The African American Worker in the Progressive Imagination* (New York: New York University Press, 2016).

43. "Fortune on Negro Labor," *Hawaiian Star*, December 19, 1902, p. 5. Fortune's quoted words here may include editorializing by the (presumably white) *Star* reporter, but his remarks about African American labor types are fairly consistent across newspaper coverage.

44. "He Will Investigate Our Labor Conditions," *Hawaiian Gazette*, December 19, 1902, p. 3. Fortune may be referring to the large number of Italian immigrants who worked in sugar plantations in Louisiana in the 1890s and the strained relations that occurred between them and the native-born. Following the 1890 assassination of a New Orleans police chief, eleven Italian immigrants who had been acquitted of the murder were lynched by a mob on March 14, 1891. See Vincent Scarpaci, "Italian Immigrants in Louisiana's Sugar Parishes" (Ph.D. diss., Rutgers University, New Jersey, 1972); and Barbara Botein, "The Hennessy Case: An Episode in Anti-Italian Nativism," *Louisiana History: The Journal of the Louisiana Historical Society* 20 (Summer 1979): 261–279.

45. Labor commissioner Wright included a description of stripping sugar cane: "Picture to yourself a 50 or 60 acre field of well-grown cane. It stands from 8 to 10 feet high . . . there is a deadly, muggy dampness everywhere, which renders the heat more oppressive . . . fine dust rises from the crackling leaves in clouds, which gets into the laborer's eyes and nostrils, covers his whole perspiring body with streaming dirt, and closes up his bronchial tubes as badly as if he were working a cotton gin in a closed room." Wright, *Report of the Commissioner*, 40–41.

46. "Fortune on Negro Labor," 5.

47. Indianapolis *Freeman*, May 25, 1889, quoted in James F. Brunson, *The Early Image of Black Baseball* (Jefferson, NC: McFarland, 2009), 74.

48. James W. Cook, "Seeing the Visual in U.S. History," *Journal of American History* 95 (September 2008), 432–441. On the *flâneur*, see Walter Benjamin, "Convolute

M [The Flâneur]," in *The Arcades Project*, trans. Howard Eiland and Kevin McLaughlin (Cambridge, MA: Harvard University Press, 1999); and Vanessa R. Schwartz, "Walter Benjamin for Historians," *American Historical Review* 106 (2001): 1721–1743.

49. Cook, "Seeing the Visual in U.S. History," 437. Fortune will describe a well-dressed Japanese "dude" a bit later.

50. "He Will Investigate Our Labor Conditions," 3. The *Gazette* identified Fortune as "editor of the N.Y. *Age*, president of the National Afro-American Council, of the Negro Business League," and "a co-worker of Booker T. Washington."

51. An editorial in the *Evening Bulletin* did express tentative support for the possibility of black labor on Hawaii. If Fortune could come up with a strong, practical plan, he would "find plenty of support from planter and the American population of the islands." The problem was the planters of the U.S. South, who, "notwithstanding racial prejudice and all the talk of negro domination," still hoped to keep the upright negro agriculturalist and jettison, possibly to the territories, the "rag tag and bobtail of the country with the riff raff of the city thrown in." "Labor from the South," *Evening Bulletin*, December 19, 1902, p. 4. The *Maui News*, January 3, 1903, p. 2, wrote in an editorial that Fortune's side-trip to Maui would surely profit his study, for negro labor from the Southern U.S. was tried, and failed, on Maui only. Fortune must note two "difficulties," however: low wages for labor and high food prices, and "the impossibility for such labor to secure and own their own homes on the Islands." If Fortune still saw land ownership as key to African American advancement, as he did as a younger man in *Black and White*, this assessment would have discouraged him.

52. "Fortune Will Look After Local Labor," *Hawaiian Gazette*, December 19, 1902, p. 8. The *Gazette* reported, possibly paraphrasing Fortune's own words, that Fortune's investigation of the possibility of negro labor on the island was "in no way connected to his mission, but it is rather in line with his work for the past quarter of a century, which has been looking to the uplifting of the race of which he is a representative." This differs from the *Washington Post* and American newspapers in Manila, which associated the emigration scheme with Senator Morgan's plan.

53. "Stewart and Fortune—Are Old Friends with Views That Differ," *Evening Bulletin*, December 19, 1902, p. 1.

54. Timothy Thomas Fortune, "Politics in the Philippine Islands," *Independent* 55 (September 1903): 2266–2268.

55. "He Will Investigate Our Labor Conditions," 3. The phrasing is peculiar, for "race distinctions" seem to be precisely what Fortune would support in limiting or excluding Chinese from the Philippines, in opposition to "Prof. Jenks."

56. Jenks is quoted in Brown, *The New Era in the Philippines*, 85. Arthur Judson Brown, secretary of the Board of Foreign Missions of the Presbyterian Church in the U.S.A., agreed that the Chinese could provide the "toning up of racial fibre" that Filipinos needed. Jenks is mentioned briefly in Kramer, *Blood of Government*, 295, in connection with his participation in the 1905 Lake Mohonk Conference of Friends of the Indian and Other Dependent Races.

57. Frederick Wells Williams, "The Chinese Immigrant in Further Asia," *American Historical Review* 5 (April 1900): 503–517. Williams's father was Samuel Wells Williams, an American missionary to China who defended the Chinese and wrote favorably about Chinese civilization even while hoping for their conversion to Christ. John Rodgers Haddad profiles the elder Williams in *The Romance of China: Excursions to China in U.S. Culture, 1778–1876* (New York: Columbia University Press, 2007). Lon Kurashige emphasizes the decades-long success of pro-Chinese intellectuals, religious leaders, and businessmen in staving off full Chinese exclusion in *Two Faces of Exclusion: The Untold*

History of Anti-Asian Racism in the United States (Chapel Hill: University of North Carolina Press, 2016). Paul Kramer suggests that Chinese exclusion can be regarded as more of a filter than a wall, for many U.S. politicians and merchants sought to let in some desired classes of Chinese. See Paul Kramer, "Imperial Openings: Civilization, Exemption, and the Geopolitics of Mobility in the History of Chinese Exclusion, 1868-1910," *Journal of the Gilded Age and Progressive Era* 14 (July 2015): 317-345.

58. See Moon-Ho Jung, *Coolies and Cane: Race, Labor and Sugar in the Age of Emancipation* (Baltimore: Johns Hopkins University Press, 2006).

59. The phrase is from April Merleaux, "The Political Culture of Sugar Tariffs: Immigration, Race, and Empire, 1898-1930," *International Labor and Working Class History* 81 (Spring 2012): 31.

60. "Topics of the Day," *The Independent*, January 2, 1903, p. 2. On the same page, Testa, who also edited the Hawaiian-language newspaper *Ka Makaainana* (The Commoner), warned that Hawaii's "Asiatics" were from the "lower classes" and implied that the newly constructed transpacific cable might facilitate politicians and planters in bringing in more, to Hawaii's detriment.

61. L. H., "The New President," *Home Rula Repubalika*, November 2, 1901, p. 7. Translated for the author by Kamalani Johnson, University of Hawaii at Hilo.

62. "While the Chinese Plantation Workers Were Once Again Declined, the American Negroes Are Soon to be Introduced to Hawaii," *Ke Aloha Aina*, December 27, 1902, p. 4. Translated for the author by Kamalani Johnson, University of Hawaii at Hilo, and Pomai Stone, Kawaihuelani Center for Hawaiian Languages.

63. "Fortune and the Homesteads," *Hawaiian Star*, December 30, 1902, p. 5.

64. Ibid.

65. Letter from Booker T. Washington to T. Thomas Fortune, February 3, 1903, in Harlan and Smock, *Booker T. Washington Papers*, 7:29.

66. See Willard B. Gatewood, "Theodore Roosevelt and the Indianola Affair," *Journal of Negro History* 53 (January 1968): 48-69. Black activists were thrilled with Roosevelt's refusal to back down on these two black political appointments, though they knew Roosevelt had appointed fewer African Americans to office than his predecessor, William McKinley. They would be hugely disappointed with the president four years later in the fall of 1906, after two events that Louis Harlan describes as shattering the "Washingtonian rhetoric of accommodation and progress": the Atlanta race riot and Roosevelt's dismissal, "without even the formality of a court martial" and on "weak" evidence, of three companies of black regular troops accused of involvement in a shootout in Brownsville, Texas. See Louis Harlan, *Booker T. Washington: The Wizard of Tuskegee, 1901-1915* (London: Oxford University Press, 1983), 2:295.

67. Letter from Booker T. Washington to T. Thomas Fortune, February 17, 1903, in Harlan and Smock, *Booker T. Washington Papers*, 7:80-81.

68. Eric Foner, *Reconstruction: America's Unfinished Revolution, 1863-1877* (New York: Francis Parkman Prize Edition, History Book Club, 2005), 283-285.

69. Elihu Root, "Address Delivered at a Meeting of the Union League Club," February 6, 1903, available at https://archive.org/stream/addressofhoneli00root#page/n1/mode/2up.

70. Washington to Fortune, February 17, 1903, in Harlan and Smock, *Booker T. Washington Papers*, 7:80-81.

71. Booker T. Washington, "The Educational and Industrial Emancipation of the Negro," in Harlan and Smock, *Booker T. Washington Papers*, 7:86.

72. Ibid., 7:86-87.

73. Ibid., 7:87.

74. Louis Harlan first explored Washington's interest in exporting Tuskegee farming methods and staff to Africa in "Booker T. Washington and the White Man's Burden," *American Historical Review* 71 (January 1966): 441–467.

75. "Fortune on Negro Labor," 5. According to the *Star*, Fortune explained that "the native labor on the Congo settlements does not work intelligently, being prone to cut down and destroy the rubber trees altogether at one sapping instead of so tapping them that they will be available the ensuing season." Washington was appointed head of the American branch of E. D. Morel's Congo Reform Association in 1904.

76. Letter from Booker T. Washington to T. Thomas Fortune, June 15, 1902, in Harlan and Smock, *Booker T. Washington Papers*, 6:481. Henry Francis Downing (1846–1928), an African American navy man, U.S. consul in West Africa, playwright, and novelist, wrote Washington on September 2, 1902, as manager of New Cotton Fields Ltd., a London company promoting cotton raising in West Africa. He told Washington that he sought "the services of an expert who would be able to locate areas suitable for the Company's operations." In the future, African Americans would settle on company lands. "It is my personal belief that the removing from the Southern States of even a small proportion of its skilled labour," Downing wrote, "will have a beneficial influence in the way of helping to bring about a better understanding between the various peoples in the Southern States." Harlan and Smock, *Booker T. Washington Papers*, 6:507.

77. Harlan, "Booker T. Washington and the White Man's Burden," 448.

78. Ibid.

79. Booker T. Washington, "Signs of Progress among the Negroes," *Century Magazine*, January 1900, pp. 472–478, available at http://www.unz.org/Pub/Century-1900jan-00472.

80. "Fortune to Speak," *Evening Bulletin*, December 27, 1902, p. 1.

81. "Fortune at Y.M.C.A.—Negro Publicist Talks about Character—General Armstrong Was His Friend—Links Lives of Lincoln, Armstrong, and Booker Washington in Clever Way," *Pacific Commercial Advertiser*, December 29, 1902, p. 3.

82. Edwin A. Start, "General Armstrong and the Hampton Institute," *New England Magazine* 6 (1892): 444, quoted in Gary Y. Okihiro, *Island World: A History of Hawaii and the United States* (Berkeley: University of California Press, 2008), 105–106.

83. Okihiro, *Island World*, 134.

84. Timothy Thomas Fortune, "The Filipino: A Social Study in Three Parts," *Voice of the Negro*, March 1904, p. 97.

85. T. Thomas Fortune, "The Kanaka Maiden," *Evening Bulletin*, December 27, 1902, p. 4.

86. Amy Ku'uleialoha Stillman, "Of the People Who Love the Land: Vernacular History in the Poetry of Modern Hawaiian Hula," *Amerasia Journal* 28 (2002): 85–108, cited in Noenoe K. Silva, *Aloha Betrayed: Native Hawaiian Resistance to American Colonialism* (Durham, NC: Duke University Press, 2004), 182. *Ka Makaainana* and *Independent* editor F. J. Testa printed a subversive book of traditional and nationalist songs, *Buke Mele Lahui*, in 1895; it is now a key source for the study of nineteenth-century Hawaii. See F. J. Testa, *Buke Mele Lahui* (1895; repr., Honolulu: Hawaiian Historical Society, 2003), available at http://www.ulukau.org/elib/collect/melelahui/index/assoc/D0.dir/doc3.pdf.

87. Letter from Booker T. Washington to T. Thomas Fortune, January 26, 1903, in Harlan and Smock, *Booker T. Washington Papers*, 7:14.

88. Gatewood, *Black Americans*, 204.

89. "The Eagle's Criticism," *Richmond Planet*, May 28, 1898, p. 2. The *Planet* also saw race affinities; it wrote about the Boer and the Philippine-American Wars, "England

has sent black men to fight for white men's rights in South Africa, and the United States has sent black men to take away black men's rights in the Philippine Islands. In both cases, the blacks get the worst end of the job." *Richmond Planet*, October 21, 1899, p. 4.

90. Sol Johnson, "Reflections," *Savannah Tribune*, March 18, 1899.

91. Ibid.

92. See Willard B. Gatewood's comprehensive look at letters from black soldiers in the Philippines, *Smoked Yankees and the Struggle for Empire: Letters from Negro Soldiers, 1898–1902* (Urbana: University of Illinois Press, 1971).

93. "Expansion or No Expansion," *The Freeman*, February 4, 1899, p. 4.

94. William C. Nell, "Danger in 'Patent Backs'—Southern Misrepresentation by the Associated Press," *New York Age*, January 3, 1891, p. 1.

95. Historian Bonnie M. Miller notes that *Freeman* editor George Knox often reproduced images originally printed elsewhere; the black press in particular faced financial constraints that led to their use of reprints and subscription services for illustrations. Bonnie Miller, e-mail communication with the author, February 15, 2012. See also Bonnie M. Miller, *From Liberation to Conquest: The Visual and Popular Cultures of the Spanish-American War of 1898* (Amherst: University of Massachusetts Press, 2011).

96. Kramer, *Blood of Government*, 98.

97. See Kristin L. Hoganson, *Fighting for American Manhood: How Gender Politics Provoked the Spanish-American and Philippine-American Wars* (New Haven, CT: Yale University Press, 1998). For an excellent collection of political cartoons from the Philippine-American War, see Abe Ignacio et al., *The Forbidden Book: The Philippine-American War in Political Cartoons* (San Francisco: T-Boli, 2004).

98. William R. Fulbright, "Horrors of War as Viewed by a Private in Manila," *The Freeman*, August 3, 1901, p. 1.

99. See, for example, editorial, *Savannah Tribune*, June 11, 1898.

100. See Paul W. Harris, "Racial Identity and the Civilizing Mission: Double-Consciousness at the 1895 Congress on Africa," *Religion and American Culture: A Journal of Interpretation* 18 (Summer 2008): 157–158.

101. Fortune, "Politics," 2266.

102. Anglo-American newspapers include the *Manila American*, the Manila *Freedom*, and the Manila *Cablenews*. By 1901 the Filipino press was split into three groups: pro-annexationists, a weak conservative Hispanic faction, and an original party of *Nacionalistas*. See Purisima Kalaw Katigbak, "The Press, Propaganda, and Twelve Years of American Sovereignty, 1898–1910: A Study of the Filipino and American Newspapers Published in the Philippines" (Ph.D. diss., Stanford University, California, 1962), 87.

103. "Chinese Are Wanted, but No Negroes," *Manila American*, February 10, 1903.

104. Ibid.

105. Ibid.

106. "Give Them a Chance," Manila *Freedom*, February 23, 1903.

107. Fortune, "Politics," 2268.

108. Letter from T. Thomas Fortune to Booker T. Washington, February 26, 1903, in Harlan and Smock, *Booker T. Washington Papers*, 7:100.

109. Fortune, "Politics," 2267.

110. Paddison, *American Heathens*, 175–184.

111. Orramel H. Gulick, "The Mission of Hawaii," *Missionary Review of the World* 13 (November 1900): 841.

112. See, for example, *Hawaiian Star*, July 2, 1900, p. 4, and "Queues Drop—Many Pigtails Shed in Honolulu," *Pacific Commercial Advertiser*, March 21, 1900, p. 10. Each

newspaper uses the spelling "Leung Chi-tso." In fact, Liang's tours of Australia, Hawaii, and the United States—where he met President Roosevelt in 1903—convinced him that the West was corrupt, practiced deadly discrimination against nonwhites, and was dominated by industrial trusts bent on imperialist expansion. See Hunt and Levine, *Arc of Empire*, 61–62.

113. Stephen H. Sumida, "Where in the World Is American Studies? Presidential Address to the American Studies Association, Houston, Texas, November 15, 2002," *American Quarterly* 55 (September 2003): 348–349. Sumida writes that before U.S. defeat of the Hawaiian kingdom, a Chinese merchant on the islands might have been considered a subject of the Hawaiian monarchy in an indigenous conception of nationhood—not an immigrant in an imperial one.

114. Letter from William Cameron Forbes to Brigadier General Frank McIntyre of the Bureau of Insular Affairs, in Larry Arden Lawcock, "Philippine Students in the United States and the Independence Movement, 1900–1935" (Ph.D. diss., University of California, Berkeley, 1975), 641n72.

115. In 1907 a bicameral Philippine Legislature was established, with the commission as the upper house and a popularly elected Philippine Assembly as the lower.

116. John W. Galloway (Twenty-Fourth Infantry, San Isidro, Philippines), December 30, 1899, quoted in Gatewood, *Smoked Yankees*, 252.

117. Amy Kaplan, "Black and Blue on San Juan Hill," in *Cultures of U.S. Imperialism*, ed. Donald Pease and Amy Kaplan (Durham, NC: Duke University Press, 1993), 235.

118. Michael C. Robinson and Frank N. Schubert, "David Fagen: An Afro-American Rebel in the Philippines, 1899–1901," *Pacific Historical Review* 44 (February 1975): 68–83.

119. Matthew Frye Jacobson, *Barbarian Virtues: The United States Encounters Foreign People at Home and Abroad, 1876–1917* (New York: Hill and Wang, 2001), 252. Also see Gatewood, *Smoked Yankees*, 259. Note that historians alternately describe this propaganda material as placards, flyers, or pamphlets and quote the passage referencing Sam Hose with a variety of wordings; see, for example, Cheryl Beredo, *Import of the Archive: U.S. Colonial Rule of the Philippines and the Making of American Archival History* (Sacramento, CA: Litwin Books, 2013), 46.

120. Daniel R. Williams, *The Odyssey of the Philippine Commission* (Chicago: A. C. McClurg, 1913), 287–288.

121. John Patrick Devins, *An Observer in the Philippines; or, Life in Our New Possessions* (New York: American Tract Society, 1905), 393.

122. Ibid., 393–395.

123. See William Crozier, "The Story of the Manila American—Written by William Crozier, Its Last Independent Editor," *Philippines Magazine*, October 1908, pp. 73–77; and William Crozier, "The American Press in Manila," *Cablenews-American Yearly Review Number*, August 28, 1911, pp. 100–101.

124. Katigbak, "The Press," 93.

125. Donna R. Gabaccia, *Foreign Relations: American Immigration in Global Perspective* (Princeton, NJ: Princeton University Press, 2012), 79.

126. In her work on Manifest Destiny and gender, Amy S. Greenberg finds among nineteenth-century white anti-annexationists in Hawaii a "restrained manhood," a "manly Christian" who had the upper hand, at least in the mid-1800s, over the more aggressive "martial manhood" style of filibusterers in Central America and the Caribbean. The press lions of Manila would certainly, in this formulation, resemble the martial manhood of Greenberg's filibusterers. See Amy S. Greenberg, *Manifest*

Manhood and the Antebellum American Empire (New York: Cambridge University Press, 2005), 232, 254–261.

127. See Richard Salmon, "Appealing to the Crowd: Henry James and the Science of Popularity," *Mosaic: An Interdisciplinary Critical Journal* 30 (June 1997): 57; and W. T. Stead, "Government by Journalism" (1886), in Richard Salmon, "'A Simulacrum of Power': Intimacy and Abstraction in the Rhetoric of the New Journalism," *Victorian Periodicals Review* 30 (Spring 1997): 44.

128. Katigbak characterizes *La Democracia* in "The Press," 87.

129. "La colonizacion negra—el cuestionario de Mr. Fortune," *La Democracia*, March 2, 1903, p. 1.

130. "El cuestionario de Mr. Fortune," *La Democracia*, March 4, 1903.

131. Thornbrough, *T. Thomas Fortune*, 237.

132. Fortune, "The Filipino: A Social Study," 93. The classic work on orientalism is Edward Said's *Orientalism* (1978; repr., New York: Vintage Books, 1994).

133. The poem is available at http://www.poetryfoundation.org/poem/174629.

134. Fortune, "The Filipino: A Social Study," 94. For a description of African American conceptions of Asia, see Helen H. Jun, "Black Orientalism: Nineteenth-Century Narratives of Race and U.S. Citizenship," *American Quarterly* 58 (December 2006): 1047–1066.

135. Fortune, "The Filipino: A Social Study," 94.

136. Timothy Thomas Fortune, "The Filipino: Some Incidents of a Trip through the Island of Luzon," *Voice of the Negro*, June 1904, p. 243.

137. Ibid., 240.

138. Ibid., 241.

139. See Neil Harris, "Iconography and Intellectual History: The Halftone Effect," in *New Directions in American Intellectual History*, ed. John Higham and Paul Conkin (Baltimore: John Hopkins University Press, 1979), 196–211.

140. Willard B. Gatewood, ed., *Slave and Freeman: The Autobiography of George L. Knox* (Lexington: University Press of Kentucky, 1979), 26–32.

141. Ibid., 31–40.

142. Miles Orvell, *The Real Thing: Imitation and Authenticity in American Culture, 1880–1940* (Chapel Hill: University of North Carolina Press, 1989), 48. Orvell sees in the late nineteenth century a mixture of Renaissance, Baroque, Classical, and invented styles imitative of aristocracy, "objects rich in narrative signs suggesting allegorical fantasy and far-off places—leaves, claw feet, embellished figures" (48). The description helps explain the tiny, toga-clad (white?) man pulling back the curtain on the portrait of the Reverend Jos. A. Booker (Figure 3.6).

143. Quoted in Nancy Martha West, "Men in the Age of Mechanical Reproduction: Masculinity, Photography, and the Death of Engraving in the Nineteenth Century," *Victorians Institute Journal* 27 (1999): 7.

144. West, "Men in the Age of Mechanical Reproduction," 8. Hazel V. Carby explores the relevance of gender to black intellectual production in *Race Men* (Cambridge, MA: Harvard University Press, 1998).

145. Ginger Hill, "'Rightly Viewed': Theorizations of Self in Frederick Douglass's Lectures on Pictures," in *Pictures and Progress: Early Photography and the Making of African American Identity*, ed. Maurice O. Wallace and Shawn Michelle Smith (Durham, NC: Duke University Press, 2012), 48.

146. Shawn Michelle Smith, *Photography on the Color Line: W.E.B. Du Bois, Race, and Visual Culture* (Durham, NC: Duke University Press, 2004).

147. Michael Scott Bieze and Marybeth Gasman, *Booker T. Washington Rediscovered* (Baltimore: Johns Hopkins University Press, 2012), 139–162; Michael Scott Bieze, "Ruskin in the Black Belt: Booker T. Washington, Arts and Crafts, and the New Negro," *Source: Notes in the History of Art* 24 (Summer 2005): 24–34.

148. Orvell, *The Real Thing*, 77. Jennifer Green-Lewis largely concurs with Orvell but stresses more tension between two modes of seeing in Victorian times: "positivist realism" and "metaphysical romance." Both schools embraced photography as a medium that, alternatively, validated empiricism "in its surface documentation of the world" or proved that visual accounts of that world were ultimately inadequate. Jennifer Green-Lewis, *Framing the Victorians: Photography and the Culture of Realism* (Ithaca, NY: Cornell University Press, 1996), 2.

149. Shawn Michelle Smith examines a retouched photo in Du Bois's compilation for the 1900 Paris Exposition, in which an image of two African Americans at a piano is superimposed with an elegant Victorian room. Smith, *Photography on the Color Line*, 111. Nancy West, however, thinks that a clear aesthetic preference for "exact reproduction" existed by the 1880s. West, "Men in the Age of Mechanical Reproduction," 19.

150. "Out in the Philippines," *Colored American*, January 16, 1904, p. 7.

151. "Opportunity for Young Men," *Colored American*, January 16, 1904, p. 7.

152. See Sven Beckert, "From Tuskegee to Togo," 498–526.

153. Lisa Gitelman and Geoffrey B. Pingree, eds., *New Media, 1740–1950* (Cambridge, MA: Harvard University Press, 2004), xxxiv.

154. The *Manila American* articles are reprinted in the *Evening Bulletin* (Honolulu) under the headline "T. Thomas Fortune Shocked Dignity of Americo-Filipino Dictatorship," June 5, 1903, p. 6.

155. Fortune, "The Filipino: Some Incidents," 246.

156. Thornbrough, *T. Thomas Fortune*, 240.

157. Fortune, "Politics," 2268. When thinking about newspapers and newspaper publics, journalism historians, in addition to Benedict Anderson's *Imagined Communities*, draw on Jürgen Habermas's *The Structural Transformation of the Public Sphere: An Inquiry into a Category of Bourgeois Society* (Cambridge, MA: Harvard University Press, 1991).

158. For an examination of a speech in which Lieutenant Gilmer attempts to reassure Filipinos that white American racism will not affect them, see Paul A. Kramer, "Race, Empire, and Transnational History," in *Colonial Crucible: Empire in the Making of the Modern American State*, ed. Alfred W. McCoy and Francisco A. Scarano (Madison: University of Wisconsin Press, 2009), 199–200.

159. *The Gazette* (Cleveland), April 21, 1900, quoted in Gatewood, *Smoked Yankees*, 263–264.

160. Charles H. Loeb, "Victim of Japs Has Given Life to Army: Capt. Robert G. Woods, 72, Was Key Man When Nips Entered Manila," *The Afro-American* (Chicago), May 12, 1945, p. 12, available at https://news.google.com/newspapers?nid=2211&dat=19450512&id=UB0mAAAAIBAJ&sjid=wP0FAAAAIBAJ&pg=3820,4860938&hl=en.

161. Gaines, *Uplifting the Race*, 34. For an excellent discussion of American colonizers' debates over which kind of education, industrial or academic, Filipinos should receive, see Meg Wesling, *Empire's Proxy: American Literature and U.S. Imperialism in the Philippines* (New York: New York University Press, 2011), 80–97.

162. Timothy Thomas Fortune, "The Filipino: The Filipinos Do Not Understand the Prejudice of White Americans against Black Americans," *Voice of the Negro*, May 1904, p. 199.

163. Untitled poem, *Filipino Students' Magazine*, April 1905, p. 25. Even the *Voice of the Negro* (June 4, 1903) printed a joke about black preachers in dialect at the bottom of Fortune's third installment on the Philippines.

164. Kahlil Gibran Muhammad traces the early racialization of crime in *The Condemnation of Blackness: Race, Crime, and the Making of Modern Urban America* (Cambridge, MA: Harvard University Press, 2010).

165. "Filipinos Benevolently Proscribed," *New York Age*, October 5, 1905, p. 2.

CHAPTER 4

1. Quoted in Joseph H. Lackner, "Dan A. Rudd, Editor of the *American Catholic Tribune*, from Bardstown to Cincinnati," *Catholic Historical Review* 80 (April 1994): 258.

2. Biographical material on Stemons comes from, in addition to what can be gleaned from his many letters to his sister, the biographical note in the James Samuel Stemons Papers at the Historical Society of Pennsylvania (HSP) in Philadelphia, and two of Stemons's published works: *The Key: A Tangible Solution of the Negro Problem* (New York: Neale, 1916) and *As Victim to Victims: An American Negro Laments with Jews* (New York: Fortuny's, 1941). The HSP also holds Stemons's 750-page, handwritten autobiographical novel, *Jay Ess*.

3. Letter from James Samuel Stemons (JSS) to Mary Stemons (MS), January 19, 1907, Folder 8, Box 1, James Samuel Stemons Papers (JSSP), HSP.

4. Stemons, *The Key*, 85.

5. Ibid., 91.

6. Ibid., 93.

7. Ibid., 94.

8. Ibid., 98–99.

9. Ibid., 98–100.

10. Ibid., 101.

11. William E. Montgomery, *Under Their Own Vine and Fig Tree: The African American Church in the South, 1865–1900* (Baton Rouge: Louisiana State University Press, 1993), 342.

12. Ibid., 339, 336.

13. Robert Gregg, *Sparks from the Anvil of Oppression: Philadelphia's African Methodists and Southern Migrants, 1890–1940* (Philadelphia: Temple University Press, 1993), 4–5. Gregg finds the black Methodist church in Philadelphia was almost exclusively composed of a "middling" class of African Americans—that is, a working class of laborers and servants of more means than the highly impoverished but below that of the city's black businessmen.

14. Muhammad, *Condemnation of Blackness*, 146, 148.

15. See R. R. Wright, Jr., *The Philadelphia Colored Directory: A Handbook of the Religious, Social, Political, Professional, Business and Other Activities of the Negroes of Philadelphia* (Philadelphia: Philadelphia Colored Directory Co., 1907), 24.

16. W.E.B. Du Bois, *The Philadelphia Negro: A Social Study* (1899; repr., New York: Schocken Books, 1967).

17. JSS to MS, January 18, 1906, Folder 6, Box 1, JSSP, HSP.

18. Mott, *American Journalism*, 589, 444–445.

19. Thomas D. Clark, *The Southern Country Editor* (Indianapolis, IN: Bobbs-Merrill, 1948), 35.

20. Lois Brown, ed., *The Encyclopedia of the Harlem Literary Renaissance* (New York: Facts on File, 2006), 350. Hopkins would be ousted by September 1904; see Alisha

R. Knight, "Furnace Blasts for the Tuskegee Wizard: Revisiting Pauline Elizabeth Hopkins, Booker T. Washington, and the *Colored American Magazine*," *American Periodicals* 17 (2007): 41–64.

21. Letter from Booker T. Washington to Robert Ogden, August 9, 1904, in Harlan and Smock, *Booker T. Washington Papers*, 8:42–43.

22. Letter from Charles Chesnutt to W.E.B. Du Bois, July 27, 1903, quoted in Paul G. Partington, "The Moon Illustrated Weekly: The Precursor of the Crisis," *Journal of Negro History* 48 (July 1963): 207.

23. Partington, "The Moon Illustrated Weekly," 209–210.

24. Du Bois, in an article for *The Voice of the Negro*, claimed that $3,000 of Tuskegee "hush money" was subsidizing the black press. See Mark Bauerlein, "Washington, Du Bois, and the Black Future," *Wilson Quarterly*, Fall 2004, available at http://archive.wilsonquarterly.com/essays/washington-du-bois-and-black-future. Fortune wrote critically about Du Bois's own funding efforts in the *New York Age* of February 1, 1906. See Partington, "The Moon Illustrated Weekly," 211.

25. JSS to MS, January 18, 1906, Folder 6, Box 1, JSSP, HSP.

26. JSS to MS, February 21, 1906, Folder 6, Box 1, JSSP, HSP.

27. JSS to MS, March 26, 1906, Folder 6, Box 1, JSSP, HSP.

28. Alfreda M. Duster, ed., *Crusade for Justice: The Autobiography of Ida B. Wells* (Chicago: University of Chicago Press, 1970), 31.

29. Barbara Diggs-Brown, "Ida B. Wells-Barnett: About the Business of Agitation," in *A Living of Words: American Women in Print Culture*, ed. Susan Albertine (Knoxville: University of Tennessee Press, 1995), 146.

30. Duster, *Crusade for Justice*, 39.

31. Diggs-Brown, "Ida B. Wells-Barnett," 143–144.

32. JSS to MS, April 12, 1906, Folder 6, Box 1, JSSP, HSP.

33. JSS to MS, January 2, 1907, Folder 8, Box 1, JSSP, HSP.

34. JSS to MS, February 7, 1907, Folder 8, Box 1, JSSP, HSP. The elder Graham, a Republican and professor of criminal law and procedure at the University of Pennsylvania, was a delegate in 1923 to Denmark as part of the Twenty-First Conference of the Inter-Parliamentary Union, founded in 1889. The organization today describes itself as a collection of national parliaments working to "protect and build global democracy through political dialogue and concrete action." Inter-Parliamentary Union, "About Us," available at https://www.ipu.org/about-us (accessed August 6, 2018).

35. JSS to MS, January 17, 1907, Folder 8, Box 1, JSSP, HSP.

36. JSS to MS, January 19, 1907, Folder 8, Box 1, JSSP, HSP.

37. Ibid.

38. JSS to MS, February 7, 1907, Folder 8, Box 1, JSSP, HSP.

39. JSS to MS, February 14, 1907, Folder 9, Box 1, JSSP, HSP.

40. Ibid.

41. JSS to MS, February 23, 1907, Folder 9, Box 1, JSSP, HSP.

42. JSS to MS, March 3, 1907, Folder 9, Box 1, JSSP, HSP.

43. JSS to MS, March 4, 1907, Folder 9, Box 1, JSSP, HSP.

44. George L. Knox, for example, publisher of the Indianapolis *Freeman*, made its job-printing department profitable, helping to grow the newspaper. See Gatewood, *Slave and Freeman*, 31.

45. Lisa Gitelman, *Paper Knowledge: Toward a Media History of Documents* (Durham, NC: Duke University Press, 2014), 25–26. Gitelman calls the lack of scholarship on job printing a major lacuna within print culture studies and media history.

46. JSS to MS, June 5, 1907, Folder 10, Box 1, JSSP, HSP.

47. JSS to MS, June 16, 1907, Folder 10, Box 1, JSSP, HSP.
48. JSS to MS, October 21, 1907, Folder 11, Box 1, JSSP, HSP.
49. JSS to MS, May 24, 1907, Folder 10, Box 1, JSSP, HSP. "Dr. Tindley" is the Reverend Charles Albert Tindley, pastor of East Calvary Methodist Episcopal church and known today as the father of gospel music. Stemons and Tindley were involved in a number of anticrime organizations from 1909 through 1912. Muhammad explores Tindley and Stemons's crime-fighting efforts in *Condemnation of Blackness*, 174–187.
50. JSS to MS, June 16, 1907, Folder 10, Box 1, JSSP, HSP.
51. JSS to MS, July 27, 1907, Folder 10, Box 1, JSSP, HSP.
52. See Logan, *The Negro in American Life and Thought*.
53. See Harlan, *Booker T. Washington*, 2:295.
54. For two studies that use the Ngram Viewer, see Patricia M. Greenfield, "The Changing Psychology of Culture from 1800 to 2000," *Psychological Science* 24 (2013): 1722–1731; and Jean-Baptiste Michel et al., "Quantitative Analysis of Culture Using Millions of Digitized Books," *Science* 331 (2011): 176–182. For critiques of "digital humanities," see Ryan Heuser and Long Le-Khac, "Learning to Read Data: Bringing Out the Humanistic in the Digital Humanities," *Victorian Studies* 54 (Autumn 2011): 79–86; and Adam Kirsch, "Technology Is Taking Over English Departments: The False Promise of the Digital Humanities," *New Republic*, May 2, 2014, available at https://newrepublic.com/article/117428/limits-digital-humanities-adam-kirsch.
55. JSS to MS, April 22, 1906, Folder 7, Box 1, JSSP, HSP.
56. James Samuel Stemons, "The Negro's Only Hope Is for Equal Opportunities for Work," Chicago *Broad Ax*, January 2, 1909, p. 5.
57. Ibid.
58. Stemons, *The Key*, 13. Though published in 1915, the book reprints Stemons's essay of 1907. One contemporary scholar observes that nineteenth-century debates over the proper type of education for African Americans "often dead-ended on the liberal arts question precisely because a black future in the professions or in thriving private enterprise or in expanding corporate management was completely unimaginable for the majority of thinkers and writers." See Carla Willard, "Timing Impossible Subjects: The Marketing Style of Booker T. Washington," *American Quarterly* 53 (December 2001): 627.
59. Clipping of "Boys Are Alert to Learn a Trade," *Philadelphia Public Ledger*, 1907, Folder 10, Box 1, JSSP, HSP.
60. Letter from "Overseer of Apprentices" [signature illegible] to JSS, Folder 10, Box 1, JSSP, HSP.
61. Stemons, *The Key*, 152–155.
62. One of the most influential studies of the Negro Problem was Frederick L. Hoffman's *Race Traits and Tendencies of the American Negro*, published in 1896, which consistently pushed against environmental or societal explanations for health and crime disparities between blacks and whites and toward biological causes. Muhammad examines Hoffman's enduring influence in *Condemnation of Blackness*.
63. Stemons, *The Key*, 155–156.
64. Evelyn Brooks Higginbotham, *Righteous Discontent: The Women's Movement in the Black Baptist Church, 1880–1920* (Cambridge, MA: Harvard University Press, 1994).
65. Muhammad, *Condemnation of Blackness*, 179–180.
66. Ibid., 180.
67. Du Bois, *The Philadelphia Negro*, 97. See also Mia Bay, "'The World Was Thinking Wrong about Race': *The Philadelphia Negro* and Nineteenth-Century Science," in *W.E.B. Du Bois, Race, and the City: "The Philadelphia Negro" and Its Legacy*,

ed. Michael B. Katz and Thomas J. Sugrue (Philadelphia: University of Pennsylvania Press, 1998), 41–59. Du Bois's biographer David Levering Lewis writes that Du Bois at this time measured African American morality with "a rigid Calvinist ruler." See David Levering Lewis, *W.E.B. Du Bois: A Biography, 1868–1963* (New York: Henry Holt, 1993), 196.

68. Muhammad's important study is not ultimately an in-depth look at Stemons's life or politics. "This book asks," he writes, "how did European immigrants—the Irish and the Italians and the Polish, for example—gradually shed their criminal identities while blacks did not? In other words, how did criminality go from plural to singular?" Muhammad, *Condemnation of Blackness*, 5. Muhammad traces how "ideas of racial inferiority and crime" became attached to African Americans while "ideas of class and crime"—notions more productive of state-based anticrime efforts—became associated with European immigrants and the white working class (6).

69. Stemons, *As Victim to Victims*, n.p. (introduction).
70. Ibid., 15.
71. Ibid., n.p.
72. Ibid., 144.
73. Ibid., 227.
74. Ibid.
75. Ibid., 228.
76. Ibid.
77. Ibid., 247.
78. Richard Dewey, "Book Review," *American Sociological Review* 6 (October 1941): 756.
79. Monique Bourque, "Register of the Papers of James Samuel Stemons, 1894–1922," August 1990, available at http://www2.hsp.org/collections/Balch%20manuscript_guide/html/stemons.html.
80. Editorial, *The Freeman*, June 8, 1889.
81. From the exhibition *Drawing the Line: The Emergence of Editorial Cartoons by African American Artists in the Indianapolis Freeman and the Richmond Planet*, O'Kane Gallery, University of Houston, January 18–February 24, 2005.
82. Eric Lott, *Love and Theft: Blackface Minstrelsy and the American Working Class* (New York: Oxford University Press, 1993), 19.
83. Kevin Gaines describes the genre as "pliable" in *Uplifting the Race*, 197.
84. Editors at *Voice of the Negro*, for example, filled space at the bottom of T. Thomas Fortune's last article on the Philippines with a negro dialect joke about black preachers, borrowed from the *Atlanta Constitution*. See Fortune, "The Filipino: Some Incidents," 246.
85. Monica Miller, *Slaves to Fashion: Black Dandyism and the Styling of Black Diasporic Identity* (Durham, NC: Duke University Press, 2009), 1.
86. Ibid., 5.
87. Ibid., 92.
88. Ibid., 90.
89. Charles Duncan, "The Black and the White: Charles W. Chesnutt's Narrator-Protagonists and the Limits of Authorship," *Journal of Narrative Technique* 28 (Spring 1998): 115.
90. Richard Ohmann, *Selling Culture: Magazines, Markets, and Class at the Turn of the Century* (London: Verso, 1996), 258–259.
91. See Kibler, *Censoring Racial Ridicule*, 28–30.
92. Sol C. Johnson, editorial, *Savannah Tribune*, July 7, 1900.

93. A'Lelia Bundles, *On Her Own Ground: The Life and Times of Madam C. J. Walker* (New York: Scribner, 2001), 66.

94. Kathy Peiss, *Hope in a Jar: The Making of America's Beauty Culture* (New York: Henry Holt, 1998), 206.

95. Ibid., 204.

96. Ibid., 218.

97. JSS to MS, May 24, 1907, Folder 10, Box 1, JSSP, HSP.

98. Scott A. Sandage has looked at "losing" in America. "Failure," whose antebellum definition was "breaking in business," became, according to Sandage, more of an identity in the nineteenth century, a marker not of circumstances largely out of one's control but rather of an inner lack: "I feel like a failure." Ambition, by contrast, was "the holy host in the religion of American enterprise." Scott A. Sandage, *Born Losers: A History of Failure in America* (Cambridge, MA: Harvard University Press, 2005), 5, 11, 14.

99. Heather Cox Richardson, *The Death of Reconstruction: Race, Labor, and Politics in the Post-Civil War North, 1865-1901* (Cambridge, MA: Harvard University Press, 2001).

100. Booker T. Washington, "Address Delivered at the Opening of the Cotton States and International Exposition," September 18, 1895, available at https://babel.hathitrust.org/cgi/pt?id=nnc2.ark:/13960/t5dc20642;view=1up;seq=1.

101. The patents for Stemons's street indicator and toy can be found in the *Official Gazette of the United States Patent Office* 123, no. 3 (1906): 927–928, available at http://books.google.com/books?id=z9V8AAAAMAAJ&pg=PA927, and 283, no. 3 (1921): 491, available at http://books.google.com/books?id=R_G10dfQgXQC&pg=PA491.

102. JSS to MS, April 22, 1906, Folder 7, Box 1, JSSP, HSP. See also Elizabeth Towne, "Just How to Wake the Solar Plexus," available at http://newthoughtlibrary.com/towneElizabeth/solarPlexus/.

103. Dawn Hutchinson, "New Thought's Prosperity Theology and Its Influence on American Ideas of Success," *Nova Religio: The Journal of Alternative and Emergent Religions* 18 (November 2014): 28–44.

104. Ibid., 36.

105. JSS to MS, May 9, 1909, Folder 13, Box 1, JSSP, HSP.

106. JSS to MS, April 26, 1907, Folder 10, Box 1, JSSP, HSP.

107. JSS to MS, May 24, 1907, Folder 10, Box 1, JSSP, HSP.

108. JSS to MS, January 31, 1907, Folder 8, Box 1, JSSP, HSP. Griggs's *Imperium in Imperio* (state within a state), originally published in 1899, has been reprinted with an introduction by Cornel West. See Sutton Griggs, *Imperium in Imperio* (New York: Modern Library, 2003).

109. Letter from R. A. Torrey to JSS, April 2, 1906, Folder 6, Box 1, JSSP, HSP.

110. Letter from Booker T. Washington to JSS, June 6, 1908, Folder 12, Box 1, JSSP, HSP.

111. JSS to MS, October 13, 1908, Folder 12, Box 1, JSSP, HSP.

112. JSS to MS, February 23, 1906, Folder 6, Box 1, JSSP, HSP.

113. For a detailed look at Washington's financial and editorial interests in the *Age*, see Emma Lou Thornbrough, "More Light on Booker T. Washington and the *New York Age*," *Journal of Negro History* 43 (January 1958): 34–49.

CONCLUSION

1. "Cable Day," *The Independent* (Honolulu), January 2, 1903, p. 2. The Manila *Cablenews* was similarly romantic, writing, "The Children of Israel never had greater

cause for rejoicing at sight of the Promised Land than have the people of the Philippines at the completion of the American Pacific cable." "The Pacific Cable," *The Cablenews* (Manila), July 6, 1903.

2. Nell, "Danger in 'Patent Backs,'" 1.

3. Mark Wahlgren Summers, *The Press Gang: Newspapers and Politics, 1865–1878* (Chapel Hill: University of North Carolina Press, 1994), 218–222. Summers believes Reconstruction could have turned out differently had the AP wire been less biased. His examples are primarily from the 1870s, but the *Age*'s interest in race and patent backs suggests that the bias continued at least into the 1890s.

4. Loughran, *The Republic in Print*, 345.

5. Menahem Blondheim, *News over the Wires: The Telegraph and the Flow of Public Information in America, 1844–1897* (Cambridge, MA: Harvard University Press, 1994), 192–194.

6. Yorke, *Ghosts of Bigotry*, 16.

7. Helen H. Jun recommends that, instead of debating levels of cross-racial bigotries among nonwhite groups, historians should focus on how "the institution of citizenship constitutes a narrow discursive field within which differently racialized groups are forced to negotiate their exclusion in relationship to others." Jun, "Black Orientalism," 1049.

8. O'Day, "Imagined Irish Communities," 402.

9. *Freeman* (Indianapolis), May 25, 1889, quoted in Brunson, *The Early Image of Black Baseball*, 74.

10. See Murphy, *Shadowing the White Man's Burden*, 2–3.

11. Black and Irish cartoonists' labor within discriminatory systems of meaning closely matches, of course, the experience of black and Irish entertainers performing in plays and vaudeville acts in the nineteenth and twentieth centuries. See Kibler, *Censoring Racial Ridicule*, especially pp. 21–50.

12. See Bieze, "Ruskin in the Black Belt," 24–34; and Bieze and Gasman, *Booker T. Washington Rediscovered*, 139–162.

13. James Weldon Johnson, "Preface to *The Book of American Negro Poetry*," in *James Weldon Johnson: Writings* (New York: Literary Classics of the United States, 2004), 713.

14. Nadja Durbach, *Spectacles of Deformity: Freak Shows and Modern British Culture* (Berkeley: University of California Press, 2009), 160.

15. Martin Bulmer, "Robert Park's Journey into Sociology," in *The Anthem Companion to Robert Park*, ed. Peter Kivisto (New York: Anthem Press, 2017), 38.

16. Gideon Lewis-Kraus, "The Trials of Alice Goffman," *New York Times Magazine*, January 12, 2016, available at https://www.nytimes.com/2016/01/17/magazine/the-trials-of-alice-goffman.html.

17. See Zimmerman, *Alabama in Africa*.

18. The optimism of African Americans and immigrants in the late nineteenth century about photography's ability to present their groups more realistically must be tempered by its use by authorities to regulate, classify, and restrict. See Anna Pegler-Gordon, *In Sight of America: Photography and the Development of U.S. Immigration Policy* (Berkeley: University of California Press, 2009).

19. The insight is David Brundage's, in *Irish Nationalists in America*.

20. Kurashige, "Transpacific Accommodation," 307–308.

21. Saxton, *Indispensable Enemy*, 105. For California's debate around the 1870 act and ratification of the Fourteenth and Fifteenth Amendments, which revolved tightly around race, religion, and "heathenism," see Joshua Paddison, "Race, Religion,

and Naturalization: How the West Shaped Citizenship Debates in the Reconstruction Congress," in *Civil War Wests: Testing the Limits of the United States*, ed. Aron Arenson and Andrew R. Graybill (Berkeley: University of California Press, 2015), 192–195; Paddison, *American Heathens*, chap. 1; and Jun, "Black Orientalism," 1047–1066.

22. See Harris, *God's Arbiters*, 14–15. To Barbara Young Welke, religion had less power than race, gender, or mental and physical ableness to exclude persons from citizenship in nineteenth-century America. The U.S. Census, Welke writes, "never inquired as to religious identity"; the First Amendment protected the free exercise of religion; and the Constitution forbade religious tests for office holding. "Protestantism . . . was not fundamental to individual legal capacity, to legal personhood, in the way that ability, race, and gender were." Welke, *Law and the Borders of Belonging*, 11. Welke focuses on a narrower, legal definition of citizenship than this book's approach. But scholars who explore a broader social and cultural view of citizenship and who see religion as partly constitutive of race must still grapple with these points.

23. As early as 1951, C. Vann Woodward drew connections between U.S. colonial policies in the Caribbean and the Philippines and the beginnings of Jim Crow in the U.S. South. See C. Vann Woodward, *Origins of the New South, 1877–1913* (Baton Rouge: Louisiana State University Press, 1951).

24. Charles Denby, "What Shall We Do with the Philippines?" *Forum* 27 (March 1899): 48. Peter Schmidt discusses Denby's article in *Sitting in Darkness*, 104.

25. See John W. Cell, *The Highest Stage of White Supremacy: The Origins of Segregation in South Africa and the American South* (New York: Cambridge University Press, 1982), xii.

26. Stannard Baker, "Wonderful Hawaii—a World Experiment Station, II: The Land and the Landless," *American Magazine* 73 (December 1911): 204–206, quoted in John S. Whitehead, "Western Progressives, Old South Planters, or Colonial Oppressors: The Enigma of Hawai'i's 'Big Five,' 1898–1940," *Western Historical Quarterly* 30 (Autumn 1999): 304.

27. For a description of black soldiers' lives in Manila, see Gatewood, *Black Americans*, 261–292.

28. Kramer, *Blood of Government*, 3; see also 229–284 for Kramer's discussion of the Philippine exhibit at the Louisiana Purchase Exposition in St. Louis.

29. Letter from Peter C. Yorke to Benjamin Wheeler, September 12, 1906, Folder 33, Box 66, CU-1, Records of the Regents of the University of California, Bancroft Library.

30. Peter Yorke journal, August 14, 1924, Folder 97, Box 2, Peter C. Yorke Papers, Gleeson Library/Geschke Center, University of San Francisco. Notes in the collection suggest that the handwritten journal material is not original and was copied by another priest from a journal of Peter Yorke.

31. *The Colored American*, July 11, 1903, quoted in Alexander, *Army of Lions*, 210–211.

32. Christopher Lasch explores the flattery inherent in much modern media and communications technologies in *The Culture of Narcissism: American Life in an Age of Diminishing Expectations* (New York: W. W. Norton, 1979) and *The Minimal Self: Psychic Survival in Troubled Times* (New York: W. W. Norton, 1984). A unique and more recent examination is Thomas de Zengotita, *Mediated: How the Media Shapes Your World and the Way You Live in It* (New York: Bloomsbury, 2005).

33. John Hope Franklin and August Meier, eds., *Black Leaders of the Twentieth Century* (Urbana: University of Illinois Press, 1982), 120.

34. Khalil Gibran Muhammad details Stemons's anticrime organizing in *Condemnation of Blackness*, 146-191.

35. Letter from James Samuel Stemons to Mary Stemons, January 18, 1906, Folder 6, Box 1, James Samuel Stemons Papers, Historical Society of Pennsylvania, Philadelphia.

36. Mick Mulcrone, "'Those Miserable Little Hounds': World War I Postal Censorship of the *Irish World*," *Journalism History* 20 (Spring 1994): 15-24.

37. Ibid., 22.

BIBLIOGRAPHY

ARCHIVAL SOURCES

Bancroft Library, University of California, Berkeley
    James H. Barry Papers, 1889–1957
    Nicholson, A. J., Scrapbooks Relating to the Spanish-American War and the Philippine Insurrection, ca. 1893–1907
    Records of the Regents of the University of California
Gleeson Library/Geschke Center, University of San Francisco
    Peter C. Yorke Papers
Historical Society of Pennsylvania, Philadelphia
    James Samuel Stemons Papers
Library of Congress, Washington, DC
    William H. Taft Papers, 1784–1973
Tamiment Library and Robert F. Wagner Labor Archives, New York University
    Mick Moloney Irish-American Music and Popular Culture Irish Americana Collection

NEWSPAPERS

Mainstream, United States
New York Sun
New York Times
San Francisco Call
San Francisco Examiner
St. Paul Globe
Washington Post

Irish American
Catholic Sentinel
Catholic World
Freeman's Journal
Irish-American
Irish World and American Industrial Liberator
Kentucky Irish American
The Leader
The Monitor
The Pilot

African American
The Afro-American (Chicago)
The Broad Ax (Chicago)
The Colored American
The Freeman (Indianapolis)
New York Age
Richmond Planet
Savannah Tribune

Hawaii
Evening Bulletin
Hawaiian Gazette
Hawaiian Star
The Independent (Honolulu)
Ka Makaainana
Ke Aloha Aina
Maui News
Pacific Commercial Advertiser

Philippines
The Cablenews (Manila)
Freedom (Manila)
La Democracia
Manila American

PUBLISHED PRIMARY SOURCES

Brown, Arthur Judson. *The New Era in the Philippines*. New York: F. H. Revell, 1903. Available at http://babel.hathitrust.org/cgi/pt?id=ucl.b3142880;view=1up;seq=11.

California Chinese Exclusion Convention: Proceedings and List of Delegates. San Francisco: Star Press, 1901.

Crozier, William. "The American Press in Manila." *Cablenews-American Yearly Review Number*, August 28, 1911, pp. 100–101.

———. "The Story of the Manila American—Written by William Crozier, Its Last Independent Editor." *Philippines Magazine*, October 1908, pp. 73–77.

Denby, Charles. "What Shall We Do with the Philippines?" *Forum* 27 (March 1899): 47–51.

Devins, John Patrick. *An Observer in the Philippines; or, Life in Our New Possessions*. New York: American Tract Society, 1905.

Du Bois, W.E.B. "The Lash." *Horizon: A Journal of the Color Line*, May 1907, pp. 5–6.
Fortune, Timothy Thomas. *Black and White: Land, Labor and Politics in the South*. New York: Fords, Howard, and Hulbert, 1884.
———. "The Filipino: A Social Study in Three Parts." *Voice of the Negro*, March 1904, pp. 93–99.
———. "The Filipino: Some Incidents of a Trip through the Island of Luzon." *Voice of the Negro*, June 1904, pp. 240–246.
———. "The Filipinos Do Not Understand the Prejudice of White Americans against Black Americans." *Voice of the Negro*, May 1904, pp. 199–203.
———. "Politics in the Philippine Islands." *The Independent* 55 (September 24, 1903): 2266–2268.
Gulick, Orramel H. "The Mission of Hawaii." *Missionary Review of the World* 13 (November 1900): 829–892.
Hearings Before the Committee on the Philippines of the United States Senate. Washington, DC: Government Printing Office, 1902. Available at https://books.google.com/books?id=4lMTAAAAIAAJ.
Le Caron, Henri [Thomas Beach]. *Twenty-Five Years in the Secret Service: The Recollections of a Spy*. London: William Heinemann, 1893. Available at http://catalog.hathitrust.org/Record/000195617.
O'Brien, William. *Recollections*. London: MacMillan, 1905. Available at https://archive.org/stream/recollections1905obri#page/n9/mode/2up.
Pope Leo XIII. "*Longinqua*: On Catholicism in the United States." January 6, 1895. Available at http://w2.vatican.va/content/leo-xiii/en/encyclicals/documents/hf_l-xiii_enc_06011895_longinqua.html.
———. "*Rerum Novarum*: Rights and Duties of Capital and Labor." May 15, 1891. Available at http://www.vatican.va/holy_father/leo_xiii/encyclicals/documents/hf_l-xiii_enc_15051891_rerum-novarum_en.html.
———. "*Testem Benevolentiae Nostrae*: Concerning New Opinions, Virtue, Nature and Grace, with Regard to Americanism." January 22, 1899. Available at http://www.papalencyclicals.net/Leo13/l13teste.htm.
Roche, James Jeffrey. *Life of John Boyle O'Reilly*. New York: Cassell, 1891.
Root, Elihu. "Address Delivered at a Meeting of the Union League Club." February 6, 1903. Available at https://archive.org/stream/addressofhoneli00root#page/n1/mode/2up.
Stemons, James Samuel. *The Key: A Tangible Solution of the Negro Problem*. New York: Neale, 1916.
———. *As Victim to Victims: An American Negro Laments with Jews*. New York: Fortuny's, 1941.
Taft, William Howard. Foreword to *An Observer in the Philippines; or, Life in Our New Possessions*, by John Patrick Devins, 7–8. New York: American Tract Society, 1905.
Testa, F. J. *Buke Mele Lahui*. 1895. Reprint, Honolulu: Hawaiian Historical Society, 2003. Available at http://www.ulukau.org/elib/collect/melelahui/index/assoc/D0.dir/doc3.pdf.
Thompson, Robert Ellis. *The Hand of God in American History*. New York: Thomas V. Crowell, 1902.
Washington, Booker T. "Address Delivered at the Opening of the Cotton States and International Exposition." September 18, 1895. Available at https://babel.hathitrust.org/cgi/pt?id=nnc2.ark:/13960/t5dc20642;view=1up;seq=1.
———. "Signs of Progress among the Negroes." *Century Magazine*, January 1900, pp. 472–478. Available at available at http://www.unz.org/Pub/Century-1900jan-00472.

Williams, Daniel R. *The Odyssey of the Philippine Commission*. Chicago: A. C. McClurg, 1913.
Williams, Frederick Wells. "The Chinese Immigrant in Further Asia." *American Historical Review* 5 (April 1900): 503–517.
Wright, Carroll D. *Report of the Commissioner of Labor on Hawaii, 1902*. Washington, DC: Government Printing Office, 1903.
Wright, R. R., Jr. *The Philadelphia Colored Directory: A Handbook of the Religious, Social, Political, Professional, Business and Other Activities of the Negroes of Philadelphia*. Philadelphia: Philadelphia Colored Directory Co., 1907.
Yorke, Peter C. *Education in California: Three Letters by P. C. Yorke*. San Francisco: Text Book, 1900.
———. *The Ghosts of Bigotry: Six Lectures by Rev. P. C. Yorke, D. D.* 2nd ed. San Francisco: Text Book, 1913.

SECONDARY SOURCES

Acland, Charles R., and William J. Buxton, eds. *Harold Innis in the New Century: Reflections and Refractions*. Montreal: McGill-Queen's University Press, 1999.
Alexander, Shawn Leigh. *An Army of Lions: The Civil Rights Struggle before the NAACP*. Philadelphia: University of Pennsylvania Press, 2011.
———, ed. *T. Thomas Fortune, the Afro-American Agitator: A Collection of Writings, 1880–1928*. Gainesville: University Press of Florida, 2008.
Anderson, Benedict. *Imagined Communities: Reflections on the Origin and Spread of Nationalism*. 1983. Reprint, New York: Verso, 2006.
Anderson, Stuart. *Race and Rapprochement: Anglo-Saxonism and Anglo-American Relations, 1895–1904*. Rutherford, NJ: Fairleigh Dickinson University Press, 1981.
Arnesen, Eric. "Whiteness and the Historian's Imagination." *International Labor and Working-Class History* 60 (Fall 2001): 3–32.
Avella, Steven M. "Irish Catholic Identity and California Public Life: Peter Yorke vs. C. K. McClatchy, 1890–1916." In *The Irish in San Francisco: Essays on Good Fortune*, edited by Donald Jordan and Timothy J. O'Keefe, 28–50. San Francisco: Executive Council of the Irish Literary and Historical Society, 2005.
———. *Sacramento and the Catholic Church: Shaping a Capital City*. Reno: University of Nevada Press, 2008.
Barrett, James R. *The Irish Way: Becoming American in the Multiethnic City*. New York: Penguin, 2012.
Bauerlein, Mark. "Washington, Du Bois, and the Black Future." *Wilson Quarterly*, Fall 2004. Available at http://archive.wilsonquarterly.com/essays/washington-du-bois-and-black-future.
Bay, Mia. "'The World Was Thinking Wrong about Race': *The Philadelphia Negro* and Nineteenth-Century Science." In *W.E.B. Du Bois, Race, and the City: "The Philadelphia Negro" and Its Legacy*, edited by Michael B. Katz and Thomas J. Sugrue, 41–60. Philadelphia: University of Pennsylvania Press, 1998.
Beckert, Sven. "From Tuskegee to Togo: The Problem of Freedom in the Empire of Cotton." *Journal of American History* 92 (September 2005): 498–526.
Beegan, Gerry. *The Mass Image: A Social History of Photomechanical Reproduction in Victorian London*. New York: Palgrave Macmillan, 2008.
Benjamin, Walter. "Convolute M [The Flâneur]." In *The Arcades Project*, translated by Howard Eiland and Kevin McLaughlin, 416–455. Cambridge, MA: Harvard University Press, 1999.

Bennett, David H. *The Party of Fear: From Nativist Movements to the New Right in American History*. Chapel Hill: University of North Carolina Press, 1988.

Beredo, Cheryl. *Import of the Archive: U.S. Colonial Rule of the Philippines and the Making of American Archival History*. Sacramento, CA: Litwin Books, 2013.

Berger, Martin. *Sight Unseen: Whiteness and American Visual Culture*. Berkeley: University of California Press, 2005.

Bernstein, Robin. *Racial Innocence: Performing American Childhood from Slavery to Civil Rights*. New York: New York University Press, 2011.

Bhroiméil, Úna Ní. *Building Irish Identity in America, 1870–1915: The Gaelic Revival*. Dublin: Four Courts Press, 2003.

Bieze, Michael Scott. "Ruskin in the Black Belt: Booker T. Washington, Arts and Crafts, and the New Negro." *Notes in the History of Art* 24 (Summer 2005): 24–34.

Bieze, Michael Scott, and Marybeth Gasman. *Booker T. Washington Rediscovered*. Baltimore: Johns Hopkins University Press, 2012.

Blondheim. Menahem. "Innis and His Bias of Communication." In *Canonic Texts in Media Research: Are There Any? Should There Be? How about These?* edited by Elihu Katz, John Durham Peters, Tamar Liebes, and Avril Orloff, 156–190. Cambridge, UK: Polity Press, 2003.

———. *News over the Wires: The Telegraph and the Flow of Public Information in America, 1844–1897*. Cambridge, MA: Harvard University Press, 1994.

Bossard, James H. S. "Robert Ellis Thompson—Pioneer Professor in Social Science." *American Journal of Sociology* 35 (September 1929): 239–249.

Botein, Barbara. "The Hennessy Case: An Episode in Anti-Italian Nativism." *Louisiana History: The Journal of the Louisiana Historical Society* 20 (Summer 1979): 261–279.

Broussard, Jinx Coleman. *African American Foreign Correspondents: A History*. Baton Rouge: Louisiana State University Press, 2013.

Brown, Joshua. *Beyond the Lines: Pictorial Reporting, Everyday Life, and the Crisis of Gilded Age America*. Berkeley: University of California Press, 2002.

Brown, Lois, ed. *The Encyclopedia of the Harlem Literary Renaissance*. New York: Facts on File, 2006.

Brown, Thomas. *Irish-American Nationalism, 1870–1890*. Philadelphia: J. B. Lippincott, 1966.

Brundage, David. *Irish Nationalists in America: The Politics of Exile, 1798–1998*. Oxford: Oxford University Press, 2016.

———. "'In Time of Peace, Prepare for War': Key Themes in the Social Thought of New York's Irish." In *The New York Irish*, edited by Ronald H. Baylor and Timothy J. Meagher, 321–334. Baltimore: Johns Hopkins University Press, 1996.

Brunson, James F. *The Early Image of Black Baseball*. Jefferson, NC: McFarland, 2009.

Brusher, Joseph S. *Consecrated Thunderbolt: A Life of Father Peter C. Yorke of San Francisco*. Hawthorn, NJ: J. F. Wagner, 1973.

———. "Peter C. Yorke and the A.P.A. in San Francisco." *Catholic Historical Review* 37 (July 1951): 129–150.

Bulmer, Martin. "Robert Park's Journey into Sociology." In *The Anthem Companion to Robert Park*, edited by Peter Kivisto. New York: Anthem Press, 2017.

Bundles, A'Lelia. *On Her Own Ground: The Life and Times of Madam C. J. Walker*. New York: Scribner, 2001.

Cadegan, Una M. "Running the Ancient Ark by Steam: Catholic Publishing." In *A History of the Book in America*, vol. 4, *Print in Motion: The Expansion of Publishing and*

Reading in the United States, edited by Carl F. Kaestle and Janice A. Radway, 392–410. Chapel Hill: University of North Carolina Press, 2014.

Carby, Hazel V. *Race Men*. Cambridge, MA: Harvard University Press, 1998.

Carey, James W. *Communication as Culture: Essays on Media and Society*. Rev. ed. New York: Routledge, 2009.

Cell, John W. *The Highest Stage of White Supremacy: The Origins of Segregation in South Africa and the American South*. New York: Cambridge University Press, 1982.

Center of Military History. "Medal of Honor Recipients: Philippine Insurrection." July 23, 2013. Available at http://www.history.army.mil/html/moh/philippine.html.

Chang, Kornel. "Circulating Race and Empire: Transnational Labor Activism and the Politics of Anti-Asian Agitation in the Anglo-American Pacific World, 1880–1910." *Journal of American History* 96 (December 2008): 678–701.

Chapin, Helen Geracimos. *Shaping History: The Role of Newspapers in Hawai'i*. Honolulu: University of Hawaii Press, 1996.

Clark, Thomas D. *The Southern Country Editor*. Indianapolis, IN: Bobbs-Merrill, 1948.

Conolly-Smith, Peter. *Translating America: An Immigrant Press Visualizes American Popular Culture, 1895–1918*. Washington, DC: Smithsonian Books, 2004.

Conzen, Kathleen Neils, David A. Gerber, Ewa Morawska, George E. Pozzetta, and Rudolph J. Vecoli. "The Invention of Ethnicity: A Perspective from the U.S.A." *Journal of American Ethnic History* 12 (Fall 1992): 3–41.

Cook, James W. "Seeing the Visual in U.S. History." *Journal of American History* 95 (September 2008): 432–441.

Cronin, Bernard Cornelius. *Father Yorke and the Labor Movement in San Francisco, 1900–1910*. Washington, DC: Catholic University of America Press, 1943.

Curtis, L. Perry, Jr. *Apes and Angels: The Irishman in Victorian Caricature*. Rev. ed. Washington, DC: Smithsonian Institution Press, 1997.

Danky, James P., ed. *African American Newspapers and Periodicals: A National Bibliography*. Cambridge, MA: Harvard University Press, 1998.

Deedy, John G., Jr. "The Catholic Press: The Why and the Wherefore." In *The Religious Press in America*, edited by Martin E. Mary, John G. Deedy, David Wolf Silverman, and Robert Lekachman, 65–121. New York: Holt, Rinehart and Winston, 1963.

Dewey, Richard. "Book Review." *American Sociological Review* 6 (October 1941): 756.

de Zengotita, Thomas. *Mediated: How the Media Shapes Your World and the Way You Live in It*. New York: Bloomsbury, 2005.

Dicken-Garcia, Hazel. *Journalistic Standards in Nineteenth-Century America*. Madison: University of Wisconsin Press, 1989.

Diggs-Brown, Barbara. "Ida B. Wells-Barnett: About the Business of Agitation." In *A Living of Words: American Women in Print Culture*, edited by Susan Albertine, 132–150. Knoxville: University of Tennessee Press, 1995.

Dineen-Wimberly, Ingrid. "Mixed-Race Leadership in African America: The Regalia of Race and National Identity in the U.S., 1862–1916." Ph.D. diss., University of California, Santa Barbara, 2009.

Dolan, Jay P. *The American Catholic Experience: A History from Colonial Times to the Present*. Notre Dame, IN: University of Notre Dame Press, 1992.

Doyle, David Noel. *Irish Americans: Native Rights and National Empires; The Structure, Divisions, and Attitudes of the Catholic Minority in the Decade of Expansion, 1890–1901*. New York: Arno Press, 1976.

Drucker, Donna J. "An 'Aristocracy of Virtue': Cultural Development of the American Catholic Priesthood, 1884–1920s." *Religion and American Culture: A Journal of Interpretation* 21 (Summer 2011): 227–258.

Du Bois, W.E.B. *The Philadelphia Negro: A Social Study.* 1899. Reprint, New York: Shocken Books, 1967.
Duncan, Charles. "The Black and the White: Charles W. Chesnutt's Narrator-Protagonists and the Limits of Authorship." *Journal of Narrative Technique* 28 (Spring 1998): 111–133.
Durbach, Nadja. *Spectacles of Deformity: Freak Shows and Modern British Culture.* Berkeley: University of California Press, 2009.
Duster, Alfreda M., ed. *Crusade for Justice: The Autobiography of Ida B. Wells.* Chicago: University of Chicago Press, 1970.
Emmons, David M. *Beyond the American Pale: The Irish in the West, 1845–1910.* Norman: University of Oklahoma Press, 2010.
Evangelista, Oscar L. "Religious Problems in the Philippines and the American Catholic Church, 1898–1907." *Asian Studies* 6 (1968): 248–262.
Fagan, Benjamin. *The Black Newspaper and the Chosen Nation.* Athens: University of Georgia Press, 2016.
Fahrmeir, Andreas. *Citizenship: The Rise and Fall of a Modern Concept.* New Haven, CT: Yale University Press, 2007.
Fischer, Roger. *Them Damned Pictures: Explorations in American Political Cartoon Art.* North Haven, CT: Archon Books, 1993.
Fishkin, Shelley Fisher. *From Fact to Fiction: Journalism and Imaginative Writing in America.* Cambridge, UK: Oxford University Press, 1985.
Foner, Eric. *Politics and Ideology in the Age of the Civil War.* New York: Oxford University Press, 1980.
———. *Reconstruction: America's Unfinished Revolution, 1863–1877.* New York: History Book Club, 2005.
Franklin, John Hope, and August Meier, eds. *Black Leaders of the Twentieth Century.* Urbana: University of Illinois Press, 1982.
Frazier, E. Franklin. *Black Bourgeoisie.* New York: Free Press, 1957.
Fry, Joseph A. *John Tyler Morgan and the Search for Southern Autonomy.* Knoxville: University of Tennessee Press, 1992.
Gabaccia, Donna R. *Foreign Relations: American Immigration in Global Perspective.* Princeton, NJ: Princeton University Press, 2012.
Gaines, Kevin K. *Uplifting the Race: Black Leadership, Politics, and Culture in the Twentieth Century.* Chapel Hill: University of North Carolina Press, 1996.
Gannon, Michael V. "Before and After Modernism: The Intellectual Isolation of the American Priest." In *The Catholic Priest in the United States: Historical Investigations*, edited by John Tracy Ellis, 293–383. Collegeville, MN: Liturgical Press, 1971.
Gardner, Eric. *Unexpected Places: Relocating Nineteenth-Century African American Literature.* Jackson: University Press of Mississippi, 2009.
Gatewood, Willard B. *Black Americans and the White Man's Burden, 1898–1903.* Urbana: University of Illinois Press, 1975.
———, ed. *Slave and Freeman: The Autobiography of George L. Knox.* Lexington: University Press of Kentucky, 1979.
———. *Smoked Yankees and the Struggle for Empire: Letters from Negro Soldiers, 1898–1902.* Urbana: University of Illinois Press, 1971.
———. "Theodore Roosevelt and the Indianola Affair." *Journal of Negro History* 53 (January 1968): 48–69.
Gerstle, Gary. *American Crucible: Race and Nation in the Twentieth Century.* Princeton, NJ: Princeton University Press, 2001.

Gitelman, Lisa. *Paper Knowledge: Toward a Media History of Documents*. Durham, NC: Duke University Press, 2014.

Gitelman, Lisa, and Geoffrey B. Pingree, eds. *New Media, 1740–1950*. Cambridge, MA: Harvard University Press, 2004.

Gjerde, Jon. *Catholicism and the Shaping of Nineteenth-Century America*. Edited by S. Deborah Kang. New York: Cambridge University Press, 2012.

Gleason, Philip. "The New Americanism in Catholic Historiography." *U.S. Catholic Historian* 11 (Summer 1993): 1–18.

Goldstein, Eric L. *The Price of Whiteness: Jews, Race, and American Identity*. Princeton, NJ: Princeton University Press, 2006.

Golway, Terry. "The Forgotten Virtues of Tammany Hall." *New York Times*, January 17, 2014. Available at http://www.nytimes.com/2014/01/18/opinion/the-forgotten-virtues-of-tammany-hall.html.

———. *Machine Made: Tammany Hall and the Creation of Modern American Politics*. New York: Liveright, 2014.

Greenberg, Amy S. *Manifest Manhood and the Antebellum American Empire*. New York: Cambridge University Press, 2005.

Greenfield, Patricia M. "The Changing Psychology of Culture from 1800 to 2000." *Psychological Science* 24 (2013): 1722–1731.

Green-Lewis, Jennifer. *Framing the Victorians: Photography and the Culture of Realism*. Ithaca, NY: Cornell University Press, 1996.

Gregg, Robert. *Sparks from the Anvil of Oppression: Philadelphia's African Methodists and Southern Migrants, 1890–1940*. Philadelphia: Temple University Press, 1993.

Guglielmo, Thomas. *White on Arrival: Italians, Race, Color, and Power in Chicago, 1890–1945*. Oxford: Oxford University Press, 2003.

Habermas, Jürgen. *The Structural Transformation of the Public Sphere: An Inquiry into a Category of Bourgeois Society*. Cambridge, MA: Harvard University Press, 1991.

Haddad, John Rodgers. *The Romance of China: Excursions to China in U.S. Culture, 1778–1876*. New York: Columbia University Press, 2007.

Hahn, Steven. *A Nation under Our Feet: Black Political Struggles in the Rural South from Slavery to the Great Migration*. Cambridge, MA: Harvard University Press, 2003.

Handlin, Oscar. *The Uprooted: The Epic Story of the Great Migrations That Made the American People*. New York: Grosset and Dunlap, 1951.

Harlan, Louis R. *Booker T. Washington*. Vol. 2, *The Wizard of Tuskegee, 1901–1915*. London: Oxford University Press, 1983.

———. "Booker T. Washington and the White Man's Burden." *American Historical Review* 71 (January 1966): 441–467.

Harlan, Louis R., and Raymond W. Smock, eds. *The Booker T. Washington Papers*. 14 vols. Chicago: University of Illinois Press, 1977.

Harris, Cole. *The Resettlement of British Columbia: Essays on Colonialism and Geographic Change*. Vancouver: University of British Columbia Press, 1997.

Harris, Neil. "Iconography and Intellectual History: The Halftone Effect." In *New Directions in American Intellectual History*, edited by John Higham and Paul Conkin, 196–211. Baltimore: Johns Hopkins University Press, 1979.

Harris, Paul W. "Racial Identity and the Civilizing Mission: Double-Consciousness at the 1895 Congress on Africa." *Religion and American Culture: A Journal of Interpretation* 18 (Summer 2008): 145–176.

Harris, Susan K. *God's Arbiters: Americans and the Philippines, 1891–1902*. New York: Oxford University Press, 2011.

Hennesey, James. *American Catholics: A History of the Roman Catholic Community in the United States.* New York: Oxford University Press, 1981.

Heuser, Ryan, and Long Le-Khac. "Learning to Read Data: Bringing Out the Humanistic in the Digital Humanities." *Victorian Studies* 54 (Autumn 2011): 79–86.

Heyer, Paul. *Harold Innis.* Lanham, MD: Rowman and Littlefield, 2003.

Higginbotham, Evelyn Brooks. *Righteous Discontent: The Women's Movement in the Black Baptist Church, 1880–1920.* Cambridge, MA: Harvard University Press, 1994.

Hilfrich, Fabian. *Debating American Exceptionalism: Empire and Democracy in the Wake of the Spanish-American War.* New York: Palgrave Macmillan, 2012.

Hill, Ginger. "'Rightly Viewed': Theorizations of Self in Frederick Douglass's Lectures on Pictures." In *Pictures and Progress: Early Photography and the Making of African American Identity,* edited by Maurice O. Wallace and Shawn Michelle Smith, 41–82. Durham, NC: Duke University Press, 2012.

Hoganson, Kristin L. *Fighting for American Manhood: How Gender Politics Provoked the Spanish-American and Philippine-American Wars.* New Haven, CT: Yale University Press, 1998.

Holt, Richard. "Ireland and the Birth of Modern Sport." In *The Gaelic Athletic Association, 1884–2009,* edited by Mike Cronin, William Murphy, and Paul Rouse, 33–46. Portland, OR: Irish Academic Press, 2009.

Hunt, Michael H., and Steven I. Levine. *Arc of Empire: America's Wars in Asia from the Philippines to Vietnam.* Chapel Hill: University of North Carolina Press, 2012.

Hutchinson, Dawn. "New Thought's Prosperity Theology and Its Influence on American Ideas of Success." *Nova Religio: The Journal of Alternative and Emergent Religions* 18 (November 2014): 28–44.

Ignacio, Abe, Enrique de la Cruz, Jorge Emmanuel, and Helen Toribio. *The Forbidden Book: The Philippine-American War in Political Cartoons.* San Francisco: T-Boli, 2004.

Ignatiev, Noel. *How the Irish Became White.* New York: Routledge, 1995.

Innis, Harold A. *The Bias of Communication.* 2nd ed. Toronto: University of Toronto Press, 2008.

Inter-Parliamentary Union. "About Us." Available at https://www.ipu.org/about-us (accessed August 6, 2018).

Isaac, Allan Punzalan. *American Tropics: Articulating Filipino America.* Minneapolis: University of Minnesota Press, 2006.

Jacobson, Matthew Frye. *Barbarian Virtues: The United States Encounters Foreign People at Home and Abroad, 1876–1917.* New York: Hill and Wang, 2001.

———. *Special Sorrows: The Diasporic Imagination of Irish, Polish, and Jewish Immigrants in the United States.* Cambridge, MA: Harvard University Press, 1995.

———. *Whiteness of a Different Color: European Immigrants and the Alchemy of Race.* Cambridge, MA: Harvard University Press, 1999.

Janis, Ely M. "Black and Green: Frederick Douglass, T. Thomas Fortune, Marcus Garvey, and the Irish." Paper presented at the Organization of American Historians Annual Meeting, Seattle, Washington, March 26–29, 2009.

———. *A Greater Ireland: The Land League and Transatlantic Nationalism in Gilded Age America.* Madison: University of Wisconsin Press, 2015.

Johnson, James Weldon. "Preface to *The Book of American Negro Poetry.*" In *James Weldon Johnson: Writings,* edited by William L. Andrews, 688–719. New York: Literary Classics of the United States, 2004.

Johnson, R. Park. "The Legacy of Arthur Judson Brown." *International Bulletin of Missionary Research*, April 1986, pp. 71–75. Available at http://www.bu.edu/missiology/missionary-biography/a-c/brown-arthur-judson-1856-1963.

Jordan, William G. *Black Newspapers and America's War for Democracy, 1914–1920.* Chapel Hill: University of North Carolina Press, 2001.

Joyce, William Leonard. *Editors and Ethnicity: A History of the Irish-American Press, 1848–1883.* New York: Arno Press, 1976.

Jun, Helen H. "Black Orientalism: Nineteenth-Century Narratives of Race and U.S. Citizenship." *American Quarterly* 58 (December 2006): 1047–1066.

Jung, Moon-Ho. *Coolies and Cane: Race, Labor, and Sugar in the Age of Emancipation.* Baltimore: Johns Hopkins University Press, 2006.

Justesen, Benjamin R. *Broken Brotherhood: The Rise and Fall of the National Afro-American Council.* Carbondale: Southern Illinois University Press, 2008.

Justice, Benjamin. "Thomas Nast and the Public School of the 1870s." *History of Education Quarterly* 45 (Summer 2005): 171–206.

Kaestle, Carl F., and Janice Radway, eds. *A History of the Book in America.* Vol. 4, *Print in Motion: The Expansion of Publishing and Reading in the United States.* Chapel Hill: University of North Carolina Press, 2014.

Kaplan, Amy. "Black and Blue on San Juan Hill." In *Cultures of U.S. Imperialism*, edited by Donald Pease and Amy Kaplan, 219–236. Durham, NC: Duke University Press, 1993.

Katigbak, Purisima Kalaw. "The Press, Propaganda, and Twelve Years of American Sovereignty, 1898–1910: A Study of the Filipino and American Newspapers Published in the Philippines." Ph.D. diss., Stanford University, Stanford, California, 1962.

Kazal, Russell A. "The Lost World of Pennsylvania Pluralism: Immigrants, Regions, and the Early Origins of Pluralist Ideologies in America." *Journal of American Ethnic History* 27 (Spring 2008): 7–42.

Kazin, Michael. *Barons of Labor: The San Francisco Building Trades and Union Power in the Progressive Era.* Urbana: University of Illinois Press, 1987.

Kenny, Kevin. *The American Irish: A History.* New York: Pearson Education, 2000.

———. "Diaspora and Comparison: The Global Irish as a Case Study." *Journal of American History* 90 (June 2013): 134–162.

Kibler, M. Alison. *Censoring Racial Ridicule: Irish, Jewish, and African American Struggles over Race and Representation, 1890–1930.* Chapel Hill: University of North Carolina Press, 2015.

Kirsch, Adam. "Technology Is Taking Over English Departments: The False Promise of the Digital Humanities." *New Republic*, May 2, 2014. Available at https://newrepublic.com/article/117428/limits-digital-humanities-adam-kirsch.

Knight, Alisha R. "Furnace Blasts for the Tuskegee Wizard: Revisiting Pauline Elizabeth Hopkins, Booker T. Washington, and the *Colored American Magazine*." *American Periodicals* 17 (2007): 41–64.

Kolchin, Peter. "Whiteness Studies: The New History of Race in America." *Journal of American History* 89 (June 2002): 154–173.

Kramer, Paul A. *The Blood of Government: Race, Empire, the United States, and the Philippines.* Chapel Hill: University of North Carolina Press, 2006.

———. "Empires, Exceptions, and Anglo-Saxons: Race and Rule between the British and United States Empires, 1880–1910." *Journal of American History* 88 (March 2002): 1315–1353.

———. "Imperial Openings: Civilization, Exemption, and the Geopolitics of Mobility in the History of Chinese Exclusion, 1868–1910." *Journal of the Gilded Age and Progressive Era* 14 (July 2015): 317–345.

———. "Power and Connection: Imperial Histories of the United States in the World." *American Historical Review* 116 (December 2011): 1348–1391.

———. "Race, Empire, and Transnational History." In *Colonial Crucible: Empire in the Making of the Modern American State*, edited by Alfred W. McCoy and Francisco A. Scarano, 199–209. Madison: University of Wisconsin Press, 2009.

Kreiling, Albert Lee. "The Making of Racial Identities in the Black Press: A Cultural Analysis of Race Journalism in Chicago, 1878–1929." Ph.D. diss., University of Illinois, Urbana-Champaign, 1973.

Kurashige, Lon. "Transpacific Accommodation and the Defense of Asian Immigrants." *Pacific Historical Review* 83 (May 2014): 294–313.

———. *Two Faces of Exclusion: The Untold History of Anti-Asian Racism in the United States*. Chapel Hill: University of North Carolina Press, 2016.

Lackner, Joseph H. "Dan A. Rudd, Editor of the *American Catholic Tribune*, from Bardstown to Cincinnati." *Catholic Historical Review* 80 (April 1994): 258–281.

Lasch, Christopher. "The Anti-Imperialists, the Philippines, and the Inequality of Man." *Journal of Southern History* 24 (August 1958): 319–331.

———. *The Culture of Narcissism: American Life in an Age of Diminishing Expectations*. New York: W. W. Norton, 1979.

———. *The Minimal Self: Psychic Survival in Troubled Times*. New York: W. W. Norton, 1984.

Lawcock, Larry Arden. "Philippine Students in the United States and the Independence Movement, 1900–1935." Ph.D. diss., University of California, Berkeley, 1975.

Lawrie, Paul R. D. *Forging a Laboring Race: The African American Worker in the Progressive Imagination*. New York: New York University Press, 2016.

Lee, Erika. *At America's Gates: Chinese Immigration during the Exclusion Era, 1882–1943*. Chapel Hill: University of North Carolina Press, 2003.

Lewis, David Levering. *W.E.B. Du Bois: A Biography, 1868–1963*. New York: Henry Holt, 1993.

Lewis-Kraus, Gideon. "The Trials of Alice Goffman." *New York Times Magazine*, January 12, 2016. Available at https://www.nytimes.com/2016/01/17/magazine/the-trials-of-alice-goffman.html.

Logan, Rayford W. *The Negro in American Life and Thought: The Nadir, 1877–1901*. New York: Dial Press, 1954.

Lott, Eric. *Love and Theft: Blackface Minstrelsy and the American Working Class*. New York: Oxford University Press, 1993.

Loughran, Trish. *The Republic in Print: Print Culture in the Age of U.S. Nation Building*. New York: Columbia University Press, 2007.

Love, Eric T. L. *Race over Empire: Racism and U.S. Imperialism, 1865–1900*. Chapel Hill: University of North Carolina Press, 2004.

Lyman, Stanford M. "Robert E. Park Reconsidered: The Early Writings." *American Sociologist* 21 (Winter 1990): 342–351.

Marley, Laurence. *Michael Davitt: Freelance Radical and Frondeur*. Dublin: Four Courts Press, 2007.

Marshall, T. H. "Citizenship and Social Class." In *Class, Citizenship, and Social Development*. Garden City, NY: Doubleday, 1964.

McCaffrey, Lawrence J. "Forging Forward and Looking Back." In *The New York Irish*, edited by Ronald H. Baylor and Timothy J. Meagher, 213–233. Baltimore: Johns Hopkins University Press, 1996.

McGerr, Michael. *A Fierce Discontent: The Rise and Fall of the Progressive Movement in America*. Oxford: Oxford University Press, 2003.

McGrath, Walter. "Convict Ship Newspaper, *The Wild Goose*, Rediscovered." *Journal of the Cork Historical and Archaeological Society* 74 (1969): 20–31.

McGreevy, John T. *Catholicism and American Freedom: A History*. New York: W. W. Norton, 2003.

McLuhan, Marshall. *The Gutenberg Galaxy: The Making of Typographic Man*. Toronto: University of Toronto Press, 1962.

McMahon, Cian. *The Global Dimensions of Irish Identity: Race, Nation, and the Popular Press, 1840–1880*. Chapel Hill: University of North Carolina Press, 2015.

———. "Ireland and the Birth of the Irish-American Press, 1842–61." *American Periodicals: A Journal of History and Criticism* 19 (2009): 5–20.

McMahon, Timothy G. *Grand Opportunity: The Gaelic Revival and Irish Society, 1893–1910*. Syracuse, NY: Syracuse University Press, 2008.

McPherson, James. *Battle Cry of Freedom: The Civil War Era*. New York: Oxford University Press, 1988.

Meagher, Timothy J. *The Columbia Guide to Irish American History*. New York: Columbia University Press, 2005.

———. *Inventing Irish America: Generation, Class, and Ethnic Identity in a New England City, 1880–1928*. Notre Dame, IN: University of Notre Dame Press, 2001.

Mehta, Uday. "Liberal Strategies of Exclusion." *Politics and Society* 18 (December 1990): 427–454.

Meissner, Daniel J. "California Clash: Irish and Chinese Labor in San Francisco, 1850–1870." In *The Irish in the San Francisco Bay Area: Essays on Good Fortune*, edited by Donald Jordan and Timothy J. O'Keefe, 54–86. San Francisco: Executive Council of the Irish Literary and Historical Society, 2005.

Merleaux, April. "The Political Culture of Sugar Tariffs: Immigration, Race, and Empire, 1898–1930." *International Labor and Working Class History* 81 (Spring 2012): 28–48.

Michel, Jean-Baptiste, Yuan Kui Shen, Aviva Presser Aiden, Adrian Veres, Matthew K. Gray, Joseph P. Pickett, and Dale Hoiberg. "Quantitative Analysis of Culture Using Millions of Digitized Books." *Science* 331 (2011): 176–182.

Michels, Tony. *A Fire in Their Hearts: Yiddish Socialists in New York*. Cambridge, MA: Harvard University Press, 2005.

Miller, Bonnie M. *From Liberation to Conquest: The Visual and Popular Cultures of the Spanish-American War of 1898*. Amherst: University of Massachusetts Press, 2011.

Miller, Kerby A. *Emigrants and Exiles: Ireland and the Irish Exodus to North America*. Oxford: Oxford University Press, 1985.

Miller, Monica. *Slaves to Fashion: Black Dandyism and the Styling of Black Diasporic Identity*. Durham, NC: Duke University Press, 2009.

Miller, Sally M. *The Ethnic Press in the United States: A Historical Analysis and Handbook*. New York: Greenwood Press, 1987.

Mindich, David T. Z. *Just the Facts: How "Objectivity" Came to Define American Journalism*. New York: New York University Press, 1998.

Mitchell, Michele. *Righteous Propagation: African Americans and the Politics of Racial Destiny after Reconstruction*. Chapel Hill: University of North Carolina Press, 2004.

Mizruchi, Susan L. *The Rise of Multicultural America: Economy and Print Culture, 1865–1915*. Chapel Hill: University of North Carolina Press, 2009.

Montgomery, William E. *Under Their Own Vine and Fig Tree: The African American Church in the South, 1865–1900*. Baton Rouge: Louisiana State University Press, 1993.

Moody, T. W. *Davitt and Irish Revolution, 1846–1882*. London: Oxford University Press, 1982.

Mott, Frank Luther. *American Journalism*. Rev. ed. New York: Macmillan, 1950.
Mount, Guy Emerson. "Building Multiracial Fortunes: Black Identity, Masculinity, and Authenticity through the Body of T. Thomas Fortune, 1883–1907." Master's thesis, San Diego State University, San Diego, California, 2011.
———. "The Last Reconstruction: Slavery Emancipation, and Empire in the Black Pacific." Ph.D. diss., University of Chicago, 2018.
Muhammad, Khalil Gibran. *The Condemnation of Blackness: Race, Crime, and the Making of Modern Urban America*. Cambridge, MA: Harvard University Press, 2010.
Mulcrone, Mick. "'Those Miserable Little Hounds': World War I Postal Censorship of the *Irish World*." *Journalism History* 20 (Spring 1994): 15–24.
Murphy, Angela F. *American Slavery, Irish Freedom: Abolition, Immigrant Citizenship, and the Transatlantic Movement for Irish Repeal*. Baton Rouge: Louisiana State University Press, 2010.
Murphy, Gretchen. *Shadowing the White Man's Burden: U.S. Imperialism and the Problem of the Color Line*. New York: New York University Press, 2010.
Myrdal, Gunnar. *An American Dilemma: The Negro Problem and Modern Democracy*. New York: Harper and Row, 1944.
Navarro, José-Manuel. *Creating Tropical Yankees: Social Science Textbooks and U.S. Ideological Control in Puerto Rico, 1898–1908*. New York: Routledge, 2002.
Nelson, Bruce. "Irish Americans, Irish Nationalism, and the 'Social Question,' 1916–1923." *boundary 2* (Spring 2004): 147–178.
———. *Irish Nationalists and the Making of the Irish Race*. Princeton, NJ: Princeton University Press, 2012.
Niemonen, Jack. "Public Sociology or Partisan Sociology? The Curious Case of Whiteness Studies." *American Sociologist* 41 (March 2010): 48–81.
Nordstrom, Justin E. *Danger on the Doorstep: Anti-Catholicism and American Print Culture in the Progressive Era*. Notre Dame, IN: University of Notre Dame Press, 2006.
Nye, David E. "Rewiring the 'Nation': The Place of Technology in American Studies." *American Quarterly* 58 (2006): 597–618.
Oak, Vishnu V. *The Negro Newspaper*. Yellow Springs, OH: Antioch Press, 1948.
O'Brien, David. "Isaac Hecker." In *The Encyclopedia of American Catholic History*, edited by Michael Glazier and Thomas J. Shelley, 624–626. Collegeville, MN: Liturgical Press, 1997.
O'Day, Alan. "Imagined Irish Communities: Networks of Social Communication of the Irish Diaspora in the United States and Britain in the Late Nineteenth and Early Twentieth Centuries." *Immigrants and Minorities* 23 (2005): 399–424.
Ohmann, Richard. *Selling Culture: Magazines, Markets, and Class at the Turn of the Century*. London: Verso, 1996.
Okihiro, Gary Y. *Island World: A History of Hawaii and the United States*. Berkeley: University of California Press, 2008.
O'Neill, Peter D., and David Lloyd. *The Black and Green Atlantic: Cross-Currents of the African and Irish Diasporas*. New York: Palgrave Macmillan, 2007.
Orvell, Miles. *The Real Thing: Imitation and Authenticity in American Culture, 1880–1940*. Chapel Hill: University of North Carolina Press, 1989.
Paddison, Joshua. *American Heathens: Religion, Race, and Reconstruction in California*. Berkeley: University of California Press, 2012.
———. "Anti-Catholicism and Race in Post–Civil War San Francisco." *Pacific Historical Review* 78 (November 2009): 505–544.

———. "Race, Religion, and Naturalization: How the West Shaped Citizenship Debates in the Reconstruction Congress." In *Civil War Wests: Testing the Limits of the United States*, edited by Aron Arenson and Andrew R. Graybill, 181–200. Berkeley: University of California Press, 2015.

Park, Robert E. *The Immigrant Press and Its Control*. New York: Harper, 1922.

Partington, Paul G. "The Moon Illustrated Weekly—the Precursor of the Crisis." *Journal of Negro History* 48 (July 1963): 206–216.

Pasulka, Diana Walsh. "The Eagle and the Dove: Constructing Catholic Identity through Word and Image in Nineteenth-Century United States." *Material Religion* 4 (November 2008): 306–325.

Paulet, Anne. "To Change the World: The Use of American Indian Education in the Philippines." *History of Education Quarterly* 47 (May 2007): 173–202.

Pegler-Gordon, Anna. *In Sight of America: Photography and the Development of U.S. Immigration Policy*. Berkeley: University of California Press, 2009.

Peiss, Kathy. *Hope in a Jar: The Making of America's Beauty Culture*. New York: Henry Holt, 1998.

Poe, Marshall T. *A History of Communications: Media and Society from the Evolution of Speech to the Internet*. Cambridge: Cambridge University Press, 2011.

Popkin, Jeremy D. *Media and Revolution*. Lexington: University Press of Kentucky, 1995.

Portier, William L. "Isaac Hecker and *Testem Benevolentiae*: A Study in Theological Pluralism." In *Hecker Studies: Essays on the Thought of Isaac Hecker*, edited by John Farina, 11–48. New York: Paulist Press, 1983.

Rafael, Vicente L. *White Love and Other Events in Filipino History*. Durham, NC: Duke University Press, 2000.

Reuter, Frank T. "American Catholics and the Establishment of the Philippine Public School System." *Catholic Historical Review* 49 (October 1963): 365–381.

Richardson, Heather Cox. *The Death of Reconstruction: Race, Labor, and Politics in the Post–Civil War North, 1865–1901*. Cambridge, MA: Harvard University Press, 2001.

Rippley, La Vern J. "Archbishop Ireland and the School Language Controversy." *U.S. Catholic Historian* 1 (Fall 1980): 1–16.

Robinson, Michael C., and Frank N. Schubert. "David Fagen: An Afro-American Rebel in the Philippines, 1899–1901." *Pacific Historical Review* 44 (February 1975): 68–83.

Rodechko, James. *Patrick Ford and His Search for America: A Case Study of Irish-American Journalism, 1870–1913*. New York: Arno Press, 1976.

Roediger, David R. *The Wages of Whiteness: Race and the Making of the American Working Class*. New York: Verso, 1991.

Said, Edward. *Orientalism*. 1978. Reprint, New York: Vintage Books, 1994.

Salmon, Richard. "Appealing to the Crowd: Henry James and the Science of Popularity." *Mosaic: An Interdisciplinary Critical Journal* 30 (June 1997): 57.

———. "'A Simulacrum of Power': Intimacy and Abstraction in the Rhetoric of the New Journalism." *Victorian Periodicals Review* 30 (Spring 1997): 44.

Sandage, Scott A. *Born Losers: A History of Failure in America*. Cambridge, MA: Harvard University Press, 2005.

Sandmeyer, Elmer Clarence. *The Anti-Chinese Movement in California*. Urbana: University of Illinois Press, 1991.

Saxton, Alexander. *The Indispensable Enemy: Labor and the Anti-Chinese Movement in California*. Berkeley: University of California Press, 1995.

Scarpaci, Vincent. "Italian Immigrants in Louisiana's Sugar Parishes." Ph.D. diss., Rutgers University, New Brunswick, NJ, 1972.

Schmidt, Peter. *Sitting in Darkness: New South Fiction, Education, and the Rise of Jim Crow Colonialism, 1865-1920*. Jackson: University Press of Mississippi, 2008.

Schudson, Michael. *Discovering the News: A Social History of American Newspapers*. New York: Basic Books, 1978.

Schwartz, Vanessa R. "Walter Benjamin for Historians." *American Historical Review* 106 (December 2001): 1721-1743.

Shankman, Arnold. "Black on Green: Afro-American Editors on Irish Independence, 1840-1921." *Phylon* 41 (1980): 284-299.

Silva, Noenoe K. *Aloha Betrayed: Native Hawaiian Resistance to American Colonialism*. Durham, NC: Duke University Press, 2004.

Smith, Shawn Michelle. *Photography on the Color Line: W.E.B. Du Bois, Race, and Visual Culture*. Durham, NC: Duke University Press, 2004.

Smith, Stacey L. *Freedom's Frontier: California and the Struggle over Unfree Labor, Emancipation, and Reconstruction*. Chapel Hill: University of North Carolina Press, 2013.

Stephens, Randall J. "Introduction: American Religious History in Context." In *Recent Themes in American Religious History: Historians in Conversation*, edited by Randall J. Stephens, 1-10. Columbia: University of South Carolina Press, 2009.

Stillman, Amy Ku'uleialoha. "Of the People Who Love the Land: Vernacular History in the Poetry of Modern Hawaiian Hula." *Amerasia Journal* 28 (2002): 88-108.

Sumida, Stephen H. "Where in the World Is American Studies? Presidential Address to the American Studies Association, Houston, Texas, November 15, 2002." *American Quarterly* 55 (September 2003): 348-349.

Summers, Mark Wahlgren. *The Press Gang: Newspapers and Politics, 1865-1878*. Chapel Hill: University of North Carolina Press, 1994.

Thornbrough, Emma Lou. "More Light on Booker T. Washington and the *New York Age*." *Journal of Negro History* 43 (January 1958): 34-49.

———. *T. Thomas Fortune: Militant Journalist*. Chicago: University of Chicago Press, 1972.

Vernier, Evelyn G. *A History of the Monitor*. Unpublished manuscript, [1945?]. Bancroft Library, University of California, Berkeley.

Wallace, Maurice O., and Shawn Michelle Smith, eds. *Pictures and Progress: Early Photography and the Making of African American Identity*. Durham, NC: Duke University Press, 2012.

Walsh, James P. *Ethnic Militancy: An Irish Catholic Prototype*. San Francisco: R and E Research Associates, 1972.

———. "Regent Peter C. Yorke and the University of California, 1900-1912." Ph.D. diss., University of California, Berkeley, 1970.

Washington, Booker T. "The Educational and Industrial Emancipation of the Negro." In *The Booker T. Washington Papers*, vol. 7, *1903-4*, edited by Louis R. Harlan and Raymond W. Smock, 85-97. Chicago: University of Illinois Press, 1977.

Welke, Barbara Young. *Law and the Borders of Belonging in the Long Nineteenth Century United States*. New York: Cambridge University Press, 2010.

Wesling, Meg. *Empire's Proxy: American Literature and U.S. Imperialism in the Philippines*. New York: New York University Press, 2011.

West, Nancy Martha. "Men in the Age of Mechanical Reproduction: Masculinity, Photography, and the Death of Engraving in the Nineteenth Century." *Victorians Institute Journal* 27 (1999): 7-31.

Whelehan, Niall. *The Dynamiters: Irish Nationalism and Political Violence in the Wider World, 1867-1900*. Cambridge: Cambridge University Press, 2012.

Whitehead, John S. "Western Progressives, Old South Planters, or Colonial Oppressors: The Enigma of Hawai'i's 'Big Five,' 1898–1940." *Western Historical Quarterly* 30 (Autumn 1999): 295–326.

Willard, Carla. "Timing Impossible Subjects: The Marketing Style of Booker T. Washington." *American Quarterly* 53 (December 2001): 624–669.

Williams, Walter L. "Black Journalism's Opinions about Africa during the Late Nineteenth Century." *Phylon* 34 (1973): 224–235.

Woloson, Wendy A. *In Hock: Pawning in America from Independence through the Great Depression*. Chicago: University of Chicago Press, 2009.

Wolseley, Roland E. *The Black Press, U.S.A.* 2nd ed. Ames: Iowa State University Press, 1990.

Woods, Thomas E., Jr. *The Church Confronts Modernity: Catholic Intellectuals and the Progressive Era*. New York: Columbia University Press, 2004.

Woodward, C. Vann. *Origins of the New South, 1877–1913*. Baton Rouge: Louisiana State University Press, 1951.

Zimmerman, Andrew. *Alabama in Africa: Booker T. Washington, the German Empire, and the Globalization of the New South*. Princeton, NJ: Princeton University Press, 2010.

INDEX

Page numbers in italics refer to illustrations.

Abbot, Lyman, 60
abolitionist movement, 23, 44, 54
accommodationist black politics, 158
Act of Union, 17–18, 19
Addams, Jane, 163
advice literature, priestly, 75–76
Africa: Congo, 107, 195n75; Garvey's *The Negro World* and, 168; West African cotton plantations, 125, 195n76
African American editors. *See specific editors and newspapers*
African American laborers: and colonization and labor exportation schemes, 98–99, 107, 195n76; Hawaii and, 99–103, 192n37, 193n51; types of, 101
African Americans: affinity and resentment toward Irish Americans by, 9–10; beauty products for, 151–152, *153*; black churches, 134; black dandyism, 150, 162; and colonization and labor exportation schemes, 98–99, 107, 195n76; economic entrepreneurship among, 151; racist caricatures of, 148–154, *149*; Roosevelt's black political appointments, 105, 106, 194n66; social trajectory of, 9; Thompson on, 53. *See also specific publications and persons*

The Afro-American (Chicago), 128
Afro-American Council, 167
Aguinaldo, Emilio, 46, 51, 112
Alemany, Joseph S., 77–78
Alexander, Shawn Leigh, 189–190n2
Aliened American, 89
American Celt, 18
American Federation of Labor (AFL), 164
American Historical Review, 103
"Americanism" controversy, 67–68
American Magazine, 166
American Protective Association (APA), 20, 58, 59–60, 65, 85
Ancient Order of Hibernians, 32
Anderson, Benedict, 3, 4, 13
Anglo-Saxonism, 45–46, 54, 111, 179n91
Armstrong, Samuel C., 109
assimilation, "benevolent," 49–50
Associated Press (AP), 111–112, 159–160, 205n3
Atlanta Constitution, 160
Avella, Steven M., 177n60

Baker, Stannard, 166
Balfour, A. J., 49
Barrows, David P., 73
Barry, James H., 83

Beach, Thomas (Henri Le Caron), 21
Bedou, A. P., 124
Bee (Washington, D.C.), 89
Bell, J. K., 70
belonging, 4, 164
Benjamin, Walter, 101
Berger, Martin, 173n28
Bernstein, Robin, 31
Bethlehem Steel Company, 144
Bhroiméil, Úna Ní, 38
Bieze, Michael Scott, 124
blackface minstrelsy, 148–150, *149*, 161
black press, historiography of, 89–92
"Black Skin Remover" advertisement, 151, *153*
Blaine, James G., 35, 96–97
Blondheim, Menahem, 40, 160
Boer (South African) War, 46–49, 111
Bourne, Randolph, 162
Bowen, Robert, 169
Bowers, Henry, 59
Brady, Thomas A., 77
Britain and the Boer War, 46–49
Broad Ax (Chicago), 143
Broussard, Jinx Coleman, 189–190n2
Brown, Arthur Judson, 72, 193n56
Brown, J. E., 96
Brown, Joshua, 30
Brown, Thomas N., 54
Brusher, Joseph S., 60
Buffalo *Express*, 132
Burchard, Samuel, 35
Burke, Thomas Nicolas, 60
Burns, Anthony, 23
Byron, Lord, 119

Cable Day, 159
The Cablenews (Manila), 117, 196n102
Cadegan, Una, 79
Cahan, Abraham, 147
Cahensly, Peter Paul, 38–39
Caldwell, A. P., 134–135, 137, 168
Carey, James W., 3, 90
Carlyle, Thomas, 53
cartoons, caricatures, and visual culture: African Americans in, 148–152, *149*, *153*; on Boer War, 47–49, *48*; exclusionary and inclusionary racial viewpoints in, 7–8; Filipinos in, 50, *112*, 112–113; Irish Americans in, 25–31, *26–28*, *30*; simian images, *26*, 26–28, *27*
Casey, Bernard, 34

Catholic Citizen, 50
Catholicism: "Americanization" of, 73–74; Cahenslyism (German language) and, 38–39; as foreign religion, 65; Gjerde and McGreevy on struggle between Protestantism and, 181n4; immigration patterns and, 19; intellectual production of, 58, 67, 75–76, 85–86, 181–182n8; *Leader* and Catholic Church, 74–76; Philippine public education debate, 71–74, 108; Philippines and, 50; print capitalism and, 78; Progressivism and, 64; sacramentality and newsprint, 78–79; uneasy truce of, with Protestantism, 42. *See also Irish World and American Industrial Liberator*; *The Leader*; *Monitor*
Catholic newspapers, growth of, 75
Catholic Sentinel, 186n106
Catholic World, 67, 72
Cell, John, 165–166
Century Magazine, 108
Chamberlain, Joseph, 49
Chang, Kornel, 83
Chase, William Calvin, 89
Chesnutt, Charles, 136, 150
Chinese exclusion: Chinese Exclusion Act (1882), 80, 187n123; end of Reconstruction and, 164; Ford on, 45; Geary Act (1892), 80; Hawaiian exemption sought for, 99, 105; labor movement and, 83; numbers of Chinese immigrants, 82; Yorke at Chinese Exclusion Convention (1901), 80–84; Yorke on, 69
Chinese laborers: abatement campaign, 80; Fortune on, 103; Hawaii and, 99, 100, 103–105; numbers of, in California, 82; Philippines and, 114; Yorke on, 81–82
churches, black, 134
citizenship, 4; African American rights and, 2, 24, 142; Boer War and, 46; British citizenship and the Irish, 44; Chinese exclusion and, 13; Denby on, 165; and fears of empire's reach, 165, 173n24; Fortune and, 95, 101; the Irish and broadened conceptions of, 54; Irish commitment to African American citizenship, 46, 52, 162; Jun on, 205n7; "melting pot" conception of, 162; Morgan's colonization scheme and, 98; Philippines and, 71, 113; race and religion as mutually constitutive of, 6, 80; race-labor-religion interplay and, 10; religion, race, and class

in, 57; Root on Reconstruction and, 106; Stemons and, 143; Thompson and, 53; Yorke and, 59, 81
civilizing discourses: black, toward Filipinos, 113; Catholic, 51, 184–185n65; Hampton Institute and, 109, 129; Hawaii and, 109; *Judge* cartoon on, 108; Thompson and, 54
Clan na Gael, 31–32
Clark, Thomas, 135
Clarkson, James S., 97, 191n21, 191n23
Cleveland, Grover, 35
Collins, Tom, 30
colonization schemes, 97–98
Colored American, 89, 120–121, 125, *126*, 128, 135, 151–152, *153*, 167
Columbus, Christopher, 51
Congo, 107, 195n75
Congress, Southern states' representation in, 157
Connelly, Thomas A., 84, 185n73
Cook, James W., 101
Cooper, Edward, 101
Cornish, Samuel Eli, 89
Corrigan, Michael, 67–68
The Courant, 134–137, 168
Cox, Minnie M., 105
Crawley, W. B., 70
The Crisis, 136
Crozier, William, 117
Crum, William D., 105
Cuba, 50, 108, 111

Dabney, Wendell P., 130
Daily Alta California, 77
Daily Evening Press, 77
dandyism, black, 150, 162
Darwin, Charles, 53
Davis, Jefferson, 160
Davitt, Michael, 32, 33, 176n26, 176–177n37
Deedy, John G., Jr., 75
Denby, Charles, 165
de Smet, Father, 51
Devoy, John, 31, 34, 169
Dewey, George, 49, 72, 112
Dewey, John, 2, 162
Dewey, Richard, 147
Dicken-Garcia, Hazel, 178n70
Diggs-Brown, Barbara, 138
Dineen-Wimberly, Ingrid, 190n7
Douglass, Frederick: fundraising and, 138; Ireland trip by, 10, 96; on Irish Americans, 96; *North Star* and, 2, 89; on photography, 124
Downing, Henry Francis, 195n76
Draymen's Association, 63
Dreiser, Theodore, 2
Drucker, Donna J., 75–76
Du Bois, W.E.B.: Calvinist morality and, 202–203n67; and financing of periodicals, 136; on Fortune, 94; Paris Exposition photographic exhibit by, 124, 199n149; *The Philadelphia Negro*, 134, 146; Stemons and, 142, 154, 157; "talented tenth," 143; Washington–Du Bois dichotomy, 91
Duffy, Charles Gavan, 18
Durbach, Nadja, 163

Easter Rising (April 1916), 66
economics of the black press, 135–41
Eddy, Mary Baker, 155
editorial page attributions, 172n14
education: anti-Catholicism and, 59, 60; Fortune on, 96; German language and, 38; Hawaii and, 109; industrial, for African Americans, 120, 129; for Irish Americans, 85; *Judge* cartoon on, 108; in Philippines, 71–74, 108, 185n78; Protestant reform movement and, 58; Stemons on, 143; Washington and, 11; Yorke as University of California regent, 56, 66, 85, 188–189n148; Yorke on, 56, 58, 60, 74, 76, 85
Emmons, David M., 182n21, 183n43
empire. *See* imperialism
Employers' Association of San Francisco, 63, 65
engravers, 123–124
entertainers, black and Irish, 205n11
Espionage Act, 169
Evening Bulletin, 110, 193n51

Fagen, David, 116
Fahrmeir, Andreas, 172n13
fairness in early journalism, 41–42
famine in Ireland, 19, 33
Fenians, 31
Fifteenth Amendment, 53
Filipinos: American press in Manila on, 114–115; Washington on bodily examination of, 8, 107, 108. *See also* Philippines during U.S. occupation
filler cartoons, 25. *See also* cartoons, caricatures, and visual culture

Fischer, Roger, 25
flâneurs, 101
Foner, Eric, 34, 54, 175n8 (chap. 1)
Forbes, William Cameron, 116
Ford, James W., 147
Ford, Patrick, 22–24, *23*; on Anglo-Saxonism, 179n91; on Boer War, 46–49; Burns fugitive slave case and, 23; in 1890s and beyond, 34–36; fund-raising by, 33–34; Gaelic and, 36–37; Garrison and, 23, 44; Irish caricatures and, 25–31; on Irish solidarity, 21–22, 161; later years of, 168; on *Longinqua* encyclical, 43; on lynching, 44–45; mission statement by, 21–22; news columns and, 40–42; racial egalitarianism and, 9, 43–46, 80; radicalism and growing conservatism of, 24; Republican Party and, 96; Skirmishing Fund and, 18–19; "The Southern Problem," 179n84; space-biased and time-biased media and, 40; Thompson versus, 52; on Yorke, 60; Yorke compared to, 43, 57. *See also Irish World and American Industrial Liberator*
Fortune, T. Thomas, 95–96; advocacy of "Afro-American" term by, 191n26; appointment of, as special immigrant agent, 97; arrest of, in Manila, 127, 166; Associated Press and, 159; *Black and White*, 96, 98; black female employees of, 89–90; black labor exportation schemes and, 107; Booker T. Washington and, 93, 94, 95, 97, 105, 107, 115, 136; colonization schemes and, 97–98; concern about legacy by, 91; in Hawaii, 98–105, 109; hostility toward, in Manila, 114–115; on imperialism, 114; Irish Americans and, 9–10; "The Kanaka Maiden," 110; labor movement and, 30; later years of, 167–168; Luzon travel and *Voice of the Negro* articles by, 113, 118–120, 127; photographic self-portrait by, 93, *94*, 120; and poll of Filipinos on black emigration, 118; recommendations for the Philippines by, 127; "Self-Respect and Its Basis" lecture by, 109; speech in Washington, D.C., by (1903), 93; on types of black laborers, 101; Washington–Du Bois dichotomy and, 91; Wells and, 138
fourth estate, press as, 13, 43
Franklin, Benjamin, 163
Frazier, E. Franklin, 90

Frederick Douglass' Paper, 89. *See also North Star*
Freedom (Manila), 114–115, 196n102
Freedom's Journal, 2, 89
The Freeman (Indianapolis), 120; on Filipinos, 111; on Irish Americans, 96; masthead and halftone photography in, 120–125, *121*, *122*, *123*; "Native Insurgent Soldiers" illustration in, *112*, 112–113; "patent back" material in, 111–112; profitability of, 201n44; reproduced images in, 196n95; "Specimens of Afro-American Statesmen" illustration in, 101, *102*; Tucker cartoons and blackface minstrelsy in, 148–151, *149*
The Freeman (New York), 95, 96. *See also New York Age; New York Globe*
Freeman's Journal, 18, 73
Free Speech, 137–138
Froude, James, 60–61
funding of newspapers, 5, 135–137, 138
Funston, Frederick, 69

Gabaccia, Donna, 117–18
Gaelic-American, 169
Gaelic language, 36–38
Gaelic League, 37, 68–69
Gaelic societies, 37
Gage, Henry T., 66
Gaines, Kevin K., 174n35
Gardiner, George, 30
Gardner, Eric, 174n44
Garrison, William Lloyd, 2, 23, 44
Garvey, Marcus, 10, 168
Gasman, Marybeth, 124
Gatewood, Willard B., 191n25
Geary Act (1892), 80
George, Henry, 2; Ford and, 24, 33, 34, 42, 52; Irish American identification with, 54; Maguire and, 66; Powderly and, 80; *Progress and Poverty*, 35
German Americans, 35
German colonialists in West Africa, 125
Gibbons, James Cardinal, 42, 67
Giffard, W. M., 102–103
Gilman, J. A., 102
Gilmer, David J., 125, *126*, 128
Gitelman, Lisa, 125, 201n45
Gjerde, Jon, 68, 71, 181n4, 184n54
Gladden, Washington, 60
Goldstein, Eric L., 6
Gonne, Maud, 49

Graham, George S., 138, 201n34
Graham, Warren C., 138–141, 157
Greenberg, Amy S., 197–198n126
Green Lantern, 17
Green-Lewis, Jennifer, 199n148
greeting cards, 25
Gregg, Robert, 134, 200n13
Griggs, Sutton E., 157
Guardian (Boston), 167
Guglielmo, Thomas, 181n126

Hahn, Steven, 191n30
Hamill, James, 77
Hampton Institute, 108, 109, 129
Handlin, Oscar, 6
The Hand of God in American History (Thompson), 53
Hardy, Thomas, 124
Harlan, Louis, 94, 194n66, 195n74
Harlem Renaissance, 124, 162
Harpers Weekly, 25, 121
Harrington, John, 78
Harris, Susan, 173n24
Hawaii, 98–105, 109, 159, 166, 191n31, 193nn51–52
Hawaiian Gazette, 102–103, 193n52
Hawaiian Star, 104, 105, 107, 192n37
Haymarket Affair, 34
Hearst, William Randolph, 63, 85, 182n13
Hecker, Isaac Thomas, 42, 67
Heyer, Paul, 39
Hiberian Chronicle (*Shamrock*), 17
Higginbotham, Evelyn Brooks, 145
Hilfrich, Fabian, 173n24
Hill, Ginger, 124
Hoag, John T., 24
Hoffman, Frederick L., 202n62
Hogan, Ernest, 150–151
Home Rula Repubalika, 104
Hopkins, Emma Curtis, 155, 200–201n20
Hopkins, Pauline, 135
Hose, Sam, 52, 116, 197n119
Hougoumont (British convict ship), 1
Howell, Clark, 160
Hubbard, Elbert, 60
Hughes, John, 18
"hyphenated Americans," issue of, 66, 160

identity formation, gradual versus sudden processes of, 3
images. *See* cartoons, caricatures, and visual culture
Impartial Citizen, 89
imperialism: Anglo-Saxonism, 45–46, 54, 111, 179n91; Denby and, 165; Ford's *Irish World* and, 45–46; Fortune on, 114; Irish as first racial foil for, 162–163; "Jim Crow colonialism," 7, 165, 173n26; lynching and, 51–52; and remaking of race, 166; Thompson on, 52–53; transnational, multiracial identities and, 46; visual tropes and, 8; white supremacism and anti-interventionism, 165; Yorke on, 70–71. *See also* Philippine-American War; Philippines during U.S. occupation; Spanish-American War
The Independent (Honolulu), 103–104, 127–128
industrial jobs, African Americans and, 143–144
Innis, Harold, 39–40
Ireland, famine in, 19, 33
Ireland, John, 38–39, 50–51, 73–74, 177n57
Irish, John P., 65, 183n42
Irish-American, 18–19, 34–35, 69
Irish American editors. *See specific editors and newspapers*
Irish American newspapers, early history of, 17–19
Irish Americans: affinity and resentment toward African Americans by, 9–10, 44; black press attitudes toward, 96; immigration trends, 19–20; paradox of asserting difference, 84–85; social trajectory of, 9. *See also* Catholicism; Ford, Patrick; Yorke, Peter C.
Irish Catholicism. *See* Catholicism
Irish Citizen (New York), 18
Irish language, 36–38
Irish Republican Brotherhood, 32
Irish World and American Industrial Liberator, 4, 10; anti-imperialism and racial egalitarianism of, 20; on Boer War, 46–49; Fortune in, 95; funding of, 5, 33–34; Gaelic column in, 36–38; and Hoag-Ford ownership dispute, 24; on immigrant nationalism and the American fabric, 54–55; on imperialism, 45–46; investigated under Espionage Act, 169; Irish American nationalism and, 31–33; Irish caricatures and, 25–31; masthead of, 31, 32–33; mission statement of, 21–22; "News from Ireland" section in, 40–42; versus *Pilot* as leading Irish American

Irish World and American Industrial Liberator (continued)
newspaper, 24; race, racial egalitarianism, and, 9, 43–46, 49; Republican Party patronage, 35; space-biased versus time-biased media and, 39–40; Thompson on Reconstruction in, 52–54; Yorke and, 60, 68–69. *See also* Ford, Patrick
Italian immigrants, 192n44

Jacobson, Matthew Frye, 6, 181n126
Jacoby, Isodore, 188n133
James, William, 162
Japanese Americans, 99–100, 104, 183n42, 192n37
Jenks, Jeremiah W., 103, 193n56
"Jim Crow colonialism," 7, 165, 173n26
job printing, 140–141
Johnson, James Weldon, 162
Johnson, Sol C., 110–111, 152
Johnston, Archibald, 144
Jordan, William G., 91
Joyce, William Leonard, 17
Judge, 25–26, 108
Jun, Helen H., 205n7

Ka Makaainana, 194n60
Kaplan, Amy, 116
Kazal, Russell A., 180n119
Kazin, Michael, 183n36
Ke Aloha Aina, 104, 129
Kentucky Irish American, 47
Kenyatta, Jomo, 168
Know-Nothing Party, 19
Knox, George, 111–112, 113, 120, 196n95
Kramer, Paul, 166, 173n24, 193–194n57
Kreiling, Albert Lee, 90–92
Kruger, Paul, 46–47
Kurashige, Lon, 193–194n57

labor in Hawaii, 99–105
labor movement: anti-Asian racism and, 83; Chinese exclusion and, 82; coal strike (Pennsylvania, 1902), 100–101; Ford and, 34, 35–36; German Americans and, 35; Leo XIII's *Rerum Novarum*, Yorke, and, 61–67; racial imagery and, 30; Teamster waterfront strike (San Francisco, 1901), 62–65
La Democracia, 118
Lamar, William H., 169
Land League, 9–10, 33

language: Gaelic, 36–38; German, 38–39
Lasch, Christopher, 173n24, 206n32
The Leader: Catholic Church and, 74–76; on Chinese exclusion, 83; on Philippine war, 70–71; place of, 56; World War I and, 169. *See also* Yorke, Peter C.
Le Caron, Henri (Thomas Beach), 21
Leo XIII, Pope: *Longinqua* encyclical, 42–43; *Rerum Novarum* encyclical, 36, 58, 61–67, 182n21; Taft meeting with, 73; *Testem Benevolentiae Nostrae* encyclical, 42, 43, 67–68; Yorke's private audience with, 68
Levins, Thomas C., 17
Lewis, David Levering, 202–203n67
Lewis, Henry J., 148
Liang Qichao, 115, 196–197n112
The Liberator, 2
Liberty Hall, 10
Lincoln, Abraham, 53, 77, 109
Linton, W. J., 124
Longinqua encyclical, 42–43
Lott, Eric, 149
Loughran, Trish, 13
Love, Eric T. L., 173n24
Loyal National Repeal Association (LNRA), 17–18
Lynch, Patrick, 18
lynching: Ford's condemnation of, 44–45, 51; imperialism linked to, 51–52; Thompson on, 53; Wells on, 138

MacPhilpin (McPhilpin), John, 41
Maguire, James G., 66
Manila American, 114, 117, 127, 196n102
Marks, James, 77
Marshall, T. H., 172n13
Matthews, Victoria Earle, 89–90
McCabe, Edward P., 98
McClatchy, Charles K., 64, 65–66, 86, 167
McGee, Thomas D'Arcy, 18
McGerr, Michael, 183n34
McGreevy, John T., 181n4
McKinley, William, 49–50, 52, 72, 73, 115
McLuhan, Marshall, 40, 171n2
McMahon, Cian, 20, 46, 175n8 (chap. 1)
McMaster, James A., 46
Meagher, Thomas Francis, 46
Meagher, Timothy J., 175n7 (chap. 1)
Meehan, Patrick, 18–19, 34, 184n59
Mehta, Uday, 172n13
The Menace, 60

Miller, Bonnie M., 196n95
Miller, Kerby A., 177n47
Miller, Monica, 150
Miller, Sally M., 5
Mindich, David T. Z., 178n70
minstrelsy, 148–150, *149*, 161
Missionary Review of the World, 115
Mitchel, John, 18, 46
Mitchell, Michele, 189–190n2
Mizruchi, Susan L., 29, 151
Molly Maguires, 32
The Monitor: anti-Asian sentiments of, 83–84; on church looting in Philippines, 69; on Church opinion and the *Leader*, 74–75; origins of, 77–78; on Philippines and Catholic civilizing, 184–185n65; Schurman Commission and, 72; Yorke as editor of, 56, 59, 185n73
Monroe Doctrine, 106
Montgomery, George, 75
The Moon, 136, 157
Moore, Fred R., 135
Morgan, John Tyler, 97–98, 114, 191nn24–26
Mott, Frank Luther, 12, 135, 174n40
Mount, Guy Emerson, 190n7
Muhammad, Khalil Gibran, 145–146, 203n68
Murphy, Angela F., 178n79
Murphy, Gretchen, 190n2
Myrdal, Gunnar, 90

NAACP, 136
Nast, Thomas, 25, 71
The Nation (Dublin), 18
The Nation (U.S.), 18
National Afro-American League, 96
nationalism: Irish, 17–20, 169; Irish American, 31–33, 34, 54–55; racio-religious versus civic, 13
nationhood as contested, 4
Native Americans: African Americans to help "civilize," 129; Catholic missionaries and, 51; as "dying race," 110; Filipinos and stereotypes of, 108; Ford on, 9, 25; Fortune on, 129; in leather postcard, 29–30, *30*; uplift programs and, 7
Native Hawaiians, 104
nativism, 19–20, 85
Nawahi, Joseph Kahooluhi, 104
Negro Problem, 9; Fortune on, 127; Hoffman's *Race Traits and Tendencies of the American Negro* on, 202n62; Root on, 106; Stemons and, 12, 91, 130, 142–144, 154; use of the phrase, 142
Negro World, 168
New Departure, 33, 34
New Negro art, 162
New Thought, 155–156
New World, 76
New York Age, 95; Associated Press and, 159, 205n3; on Filipino immigrants, 129; letters to, 111; on migration schemes, 98; Washington and, 136, 158, 167; Wells at, 138. See also *The Freeman* (Indianapolis)
New Yorker Staats-Zeitung, 35
New Yorker Volkszeitung, 35
New York Globe, 95, 97. See also *The Freeman* (New York)
New York Sun, 98
Nicholson, A. J., 69–70, 184n60, 184n62
Nordstrom, Justin, 60, 64
North Star, 2, 89
Nye, David E., 55

Oak, Vishnu V., 90
Oakland Enquirer, 65
objectivity in early journalism, 41–42
O'Brien, William, 21
O'Connell, Daniel, 10, 17–18, 19, 30, 44, 96, 178n79
O'Day, Alan, 176–177n37
Ogden, Robert Curtis, 135
Okihiro, Gary, 109
Oliver, Bartley P., 187n112
O'Reilly, G. A., 74
O'Reilly, John Boyle, 1, 46, 56
orientalist discourses, 119, 128–129, 205n7
Orvell, Miles, 198n142, 199n148
O'Shea, Michael, 34

Pacific Commercial Advertiser, 109
Paddison, Joshua, 6, 188n145
Paris Exposition (1900), 124, 199n149
Park, Robert E., 2, 5, 94, 163
Parnell, Charles Stewart, 30, 32, 33, 96
Pasulka, Diana Walsh, 187n119
"patent back" material, 111–112
Peiss, Kathy, 152
Penn, Garland, 90
Pentecost, George F., 72
personal journalism: age of, 135; moral hazards of, 4, 14, 167, 206n32
Peterson, John, 44–45

Phelan, James D., 83
Philadelphia Public Ledger, 144
Philippine-American War: anti-imperialists and, 173n24; black press and, 110–111; Catholicism and, 50, 69–71; empire, race, and nation intersecting in, 6–7; Ford's *Irish World* and, 46; human-rights abuses in, 69–71; Yorke on, 69–71
Philippine Commission (Taft Commission), 116
Philippines during U.S. occupation: American newspapers and racism in, 114–118, 166; "benevolent assimilation" policy, 49–50; in black press, 110–114, *112*; and Catholic civilizing, 184–185n65; Denby's "What Shall We Do with the Philippines?," 165; establishment of legislature in, 197n115; Fortune's Luzon travel and *Voice of the Negro* articles, 118–120, 127; Fortune's poll of Filipinos on black emigration, 118; Fortune's recommendations for, 127; political groups in, 127–128, 196n102; public education debate, 71–74, 108; transpacific cable and, 159. *See also* Filipinos
Phillips, Wendell, 54
photography: Douglass on, 124; Fortune self-portrait, 93, *94*, 120; in Fortune's *Voice of the Negro* articles, 120; halftone technology and portraiture, 120–127, *121*, *122*, *123*; optimism toward, 205n18
physical force nationalism, 31–32, 34
The Pilot: anti-imperialism and racial egalitarianism of, 20; on Boer War, 49; closure of, 168; on Cuba, 50; economics of, 137, 139–141; versus *Irish World* as leading Irish American newspaper, 24; job printing and, 140–141; launching of, 138–139; Mary Stemons's writings in, 156; O'Reilly and, 1; on Philippine education, 73; recognition from, 156–157
Pingree, Geoffrey, 125
Pledger, William A., 98
Poe, Marshall T., 171n2
Popkin, Jeremy, 3
portraiture. *See* photography
postcards, 25, 29–30, *30*
Powderly, Terence, 80
print capitalism, 4, 78
printed word, era of, 1–2
printing presses, 140
private property, Leo XIII on, 62

Progress and Poverty (George), 35
Progressivism: attacks on Irish political machines, 86, 164; Catholicism and, 64; facts-based rhetoric and, 63–64, 178n70, 183nn34–35; "Jim Crow colonialism" and, 165; segregation and, 54
Protestantism: American Protective Association (APA), 20, 58, 59–60, 65, 85; Anglo-Saxonism and, 45; Catholicism and, 42, 181n4; Irish immigration patterns and, 19; liberty and, 184n54; and missionaries in Philippines, 51, 72; Philippine public education debate, 71–74; reform movement and, 11, 54, 58, 64; in San Francisco, 60; Yorke and, 60, 64, 85, 167, 188–189n148
Puck, 25–26
Puerto Ricans, 100
Puerto Rico, 108

Quimby, Phineas, 155
Quinn, Peter H., 53, 180n123

race and racism: American press in Philippines and, 114–118; Anglo-Saxonism, 45–46, 54, 111, 179n91; Filipinos and, 8, 107, 108; imperial remaking of, 166; Irish language and, 37–38; race/labor typologies, 99–100; racial discord, 105–110; religion, citizenship, and, 6. *See also* Chinese exclusion; whiteness and white supremacy
Rafael, Vicente, 179–180n106
Reconstruction: constitutional amendments during, 4; end of, 164; perceived failure of, 52–53, 106, 143; race, religion, and citizenship during, 6, 13
religion: American civil religion, 187n119; as belonging fault line, 13; black churches, 134; Ford on the Irish and, 22; imperialism, race, and, 45; Irish American difference and, 84; Philippine public education debate, 71–74, 108; race, citizenship, and, 6, 206n22; Yorke and, 57, 80. *See also* Catholicism; Protestantism
Repealers, 18, 19
Republican Party, 35, 96–97, 104
Rerum Novarum encyclical, 36, 58, 61–67, 182n21
Richardson, Heather Cox, 154
Richmond Planet, 110, 116, 159, 195–196n89

Riis, Jacob, 163
Riordan, Patrick W., 59, 74–75
Roche, James Jeffrey, 20, 50, 51
Rodechko, James, 6, 35, 52, 175n8 (chap. 1), 176n28
Roediger, David R., 6
Rogers, William Allen, 179–180n106
Roosevelt, Theodore: American press in Manila and, 116; black political appointments of, 105, 106, 194n66; Brownsville black troops dismissed by, 142; coal strike (1902) and, 100–101; Ford and, 52; Fortune and, 97; Morgan and, 191n25; Philippine-American War and, 50
Root, Elihu, 74, 97–98, 105–106, 142, 164, 191n25
Rossa, Jeremiah O'Donovan, 31–32
Rourk, W. W., 140–141
Ruskin, John, 124, 162
Russwurm, John Brown, 89

Sacramento Bee, 64, 65, 86
Salt Lake City *Broad Ax*, 110
Sandage, Scott A., 204n98
San Francisco Call, 59–60, 67–68, 182n13
San Francisco Chronicle, 59, 182n13
San Francisco Daily Evening Post, 2
San Francisco Examiner, 59–60, 63, 182n13; "On the Mind of the Pope" (Yorke), 64–65
San Francisco *Vindicator*, 96
Satolli, Francesco, 43
Savannah Tribune, 110–111, 113, 116, 152
Saxton, Alexander, 188n136
Schaefer, F. A., 102
Schiff, Jacob, 136
Schmidt, Peter, 173n26
Schudson, Michael, 178n70, 183n35
Schurman, Jacob, 72
Schurman Commission, 72–73
Schwab, Charles M., 144
segregation, 7, 14, 30, 54, 111, 145, 165–166
separatism, African American, 130, 143, 162
Shahan, Thomas J., 37–38
Shakespeare, William, 163
Shamrock (*Hibernian Chronicle*), 17
Sinclair, William A., 156–157
Skirmishing Fund, 18–19, 34
Skirmishing Sons of Liberty, 34
slavery, Yorke on, 70
Smith, James "Jim," 184–185n65

Smith, Shawn Michelle, 124, 199n149
sociology, birth of, 163
South African (Boer) War, 46–49
space-biased versus time-biased media, 39–40
Spanish-American War, 49, 50, 110–111
Spencer, Herbert, 53
Spreckels family, 182n13
State Capital Reporter, 84
Stead, W. T., 118
Steinway, William, 35
Stemons, James Samuel, 130–134, *133*; adoption of white stereotypes by, 150; and concern with legacy, 91; *Courant* and, 134–137; *A Cry from the Oppressed*, 132, *133*; development of black doll by, 147–148, 154; Du Bois and, 142, 154, 157; economics of the black press and, 135–137; Fortune and, 12; individualism and, 154–155; as inventor, 154, 155; *Jay Ess*, 168; *The Key*, 141, 144–145, 202n58; labor movement and, 30; later years of, 168; on Negro Problem and African American advancement, 130, 142–144, 154; New Thought and, 155–156; *Pilot* and financial issues of, 137, 138–141; protest-accommodation divide and, 91; recognition received by, 156–157; respectability politics and, 144–148; *As Victim to Victims*, 146–147; Washington and, 142–143, 154, 157, 168
Stemons, Mary, 154, 156
Steward, T. G., 128
Stewart, T. McCants, 103
Stillman, Amy Ku'uleialoha, 110
Sumida, Stephen H., 197n113
Summers, Mark Wahlgren, 205n3
Sumner, Charles, 164
Synge, John, 162

Taft, William Howard, 52, 73, 74, 97–98, 117
Taft Commission (Philippine Commission), 116
Teamster waterfront strike (San Francisco, 1901), 62–65
The Tempest (Shakespeare), 163
Tennyson, Alfred, Lord, 119
Testa, F. J., 103–104, 194n60, 195n86
Testem Benevolentiae Nostrae encyclical, 42, 43, 67–68
Texas Siftings, 26

Thomas, Patrick J., 77
Thomasites, 72
Thompson, Robert Ellis, 52–54, 69, 142, 164, 180n119
Thornbrough, Emma Lou, 93–94
"Thought News," 2
Tillman, Benjamin, 44–45
time-biased vs. space-biased media, 39–40
Tindley, Charles Albert, 141, 156, 202n49
Tobin family, 182n13
Torrey, R. A., 157
Towne, Elizabeth, 155–156
trading cards, 25–31
Trans-Atlantic Club, 34
transpacific cable, 159
Trotter, William Monroe, 167
True American, 89
Truth Teller, 17
Tuam News, 41
Tucker, Moses L., *102*, 148–149, *149*, 161
Turner, Henry McNeal, 98, 111
Tuskegee Institute: advertisement of, 125; editorial independence from, 136, 201n24; Fortune and, 95, 97; Harlem Renaissance and, 124, 162; Moore and, 135; Park and, 163; Philippines and, 107, 108; provincial internationalism and, 94; Stemons and, 144, 168. *See also* Washington, Booker T.
Twain, Mark, 2, 163
Tweed, William W., 71

Union News Co., 141
United Irishman, 32, 96
The Universe, 77
uplift ideology, 134
"uprooted" immigrant groups, 6

visual culture. *See* cartoons, caricatures, and visual culture
Voice of the Negro, 113, 119–120, 127, 129, 200n163, 203n84

Walker, C. J., 152
Walsh, James, 57–58
Walsh, Terrence, 41
Ward, Samuel Ringgold, 89
Washington, Booker T.: Afro-American Council and, 167; artistic philosophies of, 124; "Atlanta Compromise" speech by, 154–155; on bodily examination of the Filipino, 8; Du Bois-Washington dichotomy, 91; "The Educational and Industrial Emancipation of the Negro" (Bronx address), 93, 106–107; embrace of African art and culture by, 162; and financing of periodicals, 135–136; Fortune and, 93, 94, 95, 97, 105, 107, 115, 136; German cotton planters in West Africa and, 125; influence of, 90; Knox and, 120; *New York Age* and, 158; Park and, 163; separatism and, 130, 143, 162; Stemons and, 142–143, 154, 157, 168; *Up from Slavery*, 154; at White House, 104
Washington Post, 97–98, 193n52
Weekly Star, 83
Welke, Barbara Young, 206n22
Wells-Barnett, Ida B., 89–90, 137–138
Wendte, Charles W., 60
Wesley A.M.E. Zion Church, Philadelphia, 134
West, Nancy Martha, 123–124
Wheeler, Benjamin, 167
Whelehan, Niall, 176n36
whiteness and white supremacy: African American adoption of discourses of, 150; American press in Philippines and, 114–118; anti-interventionism and, 165; ethnic multiplicity and, 83; Irish American difference and, 84; scholarship on, 6
Whitman, Walt, 2
Wilcox, Robert William Kalanihiapo, 104
Wild Goose, 1
Williams, Daniel R., 116–117
Williams, Frederick Wells, 103
Williams, Samuel Wells, 193n57
Williams, Thomas, 63
Woods, Robert Gordon, 93, 119–120, 127, 128
World War I, 169
Wormsley, Capt., 93, 119
Wright, Carroll D., 99–100, 192n45
Wright, Luke E., 116

Yorke, Peter C., 56–58, *57*; "Americanism" controversy and, 67–68; background of, 58–59; blessing troops, 185n67; campaign of, against APA, 58, 59–60, 65; on Catholic editors, 76; at Chinese Exclusion Convention (1901), 80–84; Church opinion distanced from, 74–76; "The Dragon's Teeth" lecture by, 70; on education and religion in Philippines, 71–74; and feud with McClatchy, 64, 65–66; Ford compared to, 43, 57; Ford on, 60; Gaelic League speech by, 68–69; *The Ghosts of Bigotry*, 56, 61; later years of, 166–167; as *Monitor* editor-in-chief, 56, 59, 185n73; negative and positive aspects of, 84–85; "On the Mind of the Pope" (*Examiner*), 64–65; "On the Real Question at Issue," 63; on Philippine-American War, 69–71; pope and, 68; on *Rerum Novarum* and labor movement, 58, 61–67; as University of California regent, 56, 66, 85, 188–189n148. See also *The Leader*

Young Ireland movement, 17–18, 46

Brian Shott is a writer, editor, and independent scholar. He earned his Ph.D. in American history from the University of California, Santa Cruz, and has taught history at San Quentin Prison in a college-accredited program run through Patten University.

www.ingramcontent.com/pod-product-compliance
Lightning Source LLC
Chambersburg PA
CBHW061254230426
43665CB00027B/2942